The Complete Guide
to a
Successful Leveraged Buyout

The Complete Guide
to a
Successful Leveraged Buyout

Allen Michel

Israel Shaked

Dow Jones-Irwin
Homewood, Illinois 60430

The analyses and facts included in the cases are for
illustration purposes only and are not intended to present
effective or ineffective handling of administrative situations.

This book was set in Century Schoolbook by Western Interface, Inc.
The editors were Richard A. Luecke, Joan A. Hopkins.
The production manager was Carma W. Fazio.
The designer was Sam Concialdi.
The drawings were done by Rolin Graphics Incorporated.
R. R. Donnelley & Sons Company was the printer and binder.

ISBN 0-87094-891-1

Library of Congress Catalog Card No. 87–71442

Printed in the United States of America

3 4 5 6 7 8 9 0 DO 5 4 3 2 1 0 9

To Our Families

PREFACE

The growth in the number of leveraged buyouts during the past decade has been staggering. LBOs have become an integral part of the restructuring of corporate America. The surge in the number of buyouts has been fueled by management's willingness to commit funds and energy to a debt-laden venture where the upside potential is enormous, but the downside risk awesome. Leveraged buyouts have become symptomatic of the boundless and ever present American entrepreneurial spirit. Yet LBOs have not been limited to the United States. The same reasons which have caused them to flourish in the United States are now causing them to appear in Europe, Asia, and other parts of the world, anywhere free enterprise and capitalism thrive.

Leveraged buyouts are reported constantly in the media. Whether the LBO is of a division, subsidiary or an entire company, months of planning and hard work have gone into the deal. For most investor/managers, this is a first time experience. While management is no doubt comfortable and confident of their ability to manage the business, an LBO brings with it new jargon, complex issues and a shocking leap into the financial world. This book is designed for the manager and investor contemplating an LBO. It provides an easy-to-read assessment of issues to which the manager and investor must become aware. We cover the spectrum, from valuing the business and understanding the numbers to learning who the key players are likely to be. It also includes a managerial perspective of the tax, legal, and structural issues faced by the investor/manager group.

The task of putting together a comprehensive and readable guide for managers and investors is a major undertaking. We owe a debt of gratitude to many people who have contributed to our knowledge of the subject. They include: Joe Achenbaum, Ubiyathalla Ismath Bacha, William Barry, Eric Berke, Brad Bloom, Pat Brady, Mike Brennan, Adrienne Catanese, Roseann Colot, Seth Cunningham, Tim Durning, Fred Eckert, Fred Escherich, Robert Fish, Joseph Flynn, Ted Forstmann, Yu Kun Hahm, Philip Horowitz, Warren Idsal, Chris Johnson, Wes Jones, Kishore Khaitan, Diane Kaplowitz, Louis Kelso, Henry Kravis, Tom Lee, Mark Leff, Leslee Luedke, Neil Mackinnon, Helen Mazareas, Mike McAuliffe, David Michel, Lisa Michel, Bruce Miller, Fred Morse, Frank Nickell, Yu Oen, Eduardo Perez, Tuan Phamdo, Joe Rice, Ian Ried, Bruce Rink, Hanson Robbins, Dean Schaeffer, Keith Schwartz, Sharon Seidman, David Simon, Margaret Tobin, Richard White, and Jack Whittier.

In particular, we wish to thank the following people for their research, analysis and writing: Guillermo Anaya, Raj Chandaria, Harpal Chawla, Mary Ellen Eagan, Mary Feddersen, Bill Garrett, Brian Gorman, Kimberly Haynes, Laurie Hearne, Dan Herbert, Dianne Kelly, Judy Kirshner, Janet Kracke, Anne Lauer, Jay Liska, Chet Lyons, Paul McManus, Tom Murphy, Larry Richardson, Miguel Ringvald, Max Sherman, Tom Sidley, Lisa Stavro, Eric Sullivan, Tim Van Dam, Pankaj Wadhwa, and Jack Weis. Without their very significant contribution, this book would still be unfinished. Their effort is also acknowledged in the relevant sections of the book.

We also very much appreciate the guidance and encouragement of our editor at Dow Jones, Dick Luecke. His wisdom and gentle prodding assured the timely completion of the book.

Without the prompt word processing help of Marie Jeanne Curtenaz and Vince Mahler, this project would have taken many months longer than it did.

In gathering data for this book we have relied on many interviews and publicly available information. However, the descriptions and analyses presented in the book are strictly our own and do not represent the opinions of the individuals or corporations involved. We have striven to ensure accuracy in our depiction of the LBO arena and any misinterpretation or misstatement is greatly regretted.

For the manager/investor contemplating an LBO, reading this book is a first step. To avoid serious errors, it is incumbent upon him/her to obtain sound professional counsel early in the process of doing the buyout.

Above all, we thank our families, who undoubtedly have suffered through many boring discussions of LBOs.

CONTENTS

CHAPTER 1   Lessons from Classic LBO Successes
and Failures   1

CHAPTER 2   Valuing a Company: How Is It Done?   41

CHAPTER 3   The Players in the Leveraged Buyout
Arena   170

CHAPTER 4   The LBO Number Jungle: Finding
Your Way   198

CHAPTER 5   The LBO and the Law: Protecting
Management from Litigation   225

CHAPTER 6   Structuring the Deal: Making It Work   244

CHAPTER 7   The LBO and the Tax Man   278

CHAPTER 8   ESOPs: Employees Buy Corporate
America   297

Index   361

CHAPTER 1

LESSONS FROM CLASSIC LBO SUCCESSES AND FAILURES

Takeover-weary investors often joke that they foresee the day when every company in the United States will finally be merged into one huge enterprise called the All-American Industries and Services Corporation. However the punch line is that people won't even be able to invest in the new super-conglomerate because it will be a privately held company formed by a gigantic leveraged buyout and loaded with enough borrowing power to make the national debt look like a down payment. The leveraged buyout phenomenon has been described as "the endlessly ingenious creativity of American capitalism," and occurs when a group of investors, often the top management, acquires a company in a transaction financed largely by a borrowing, using the acquired company's assets and future cash flows as collateral. Ultimately the debt is paid with funds generated by the acquired company's operations or sale of assets. Going against all established rules of economic prudence, the companies bought in these transactions typically wind up with long-term debt accounting for 90 percent or more of their total capital—about three times what most corporations would think reasonable.

The notion of leveraged buyouts (LBOs) goes back 50

We appreciate the research, analysis, and writing done by Guillermo Anaya, Harpal Chawla, Anne Lauer, Miquel Ringvald, and Pankaj Wadhwa. Without their very significant contribution, the completion of this chapter would not have been possible.

years or more. The deals were then called "bootstrap financing" indicating the inherent risk involved. Lenders provided lines of credit on the bought-out companies' assets. The modern LBO emerged about a decade ago when owners of privately held companies who were near retirement used them to "cash out" their investment. The stock market was too anemic for them to get their money by going public. The founder's children or an outside group would put together an LBO and buy Dad out. The trend accelerated in the late 1970s as diversified companies began selling off subsidiaries that either were poor growth prospects or didn't fit into their long-term strategy. Often the only buyers for these operations were their managers who put up minimal sums and borrowed or "leveraged" the rest. Then a strange thing happened—firms seemed to prosper under the new arrangement. In many cases, the new owner-managers, "mature entrepreneurs," as they liked to be called, seemed to run the companies much more efficiently than they had when they were on salary. Inflation was another bonus. The companies could pay off their LBO loans with depreciated dollars and often pared down their debt by selling off some of their own assets.

The recent craze in leveraged buyouts can be explained in three words: Gibson Greeting Cards. In January 1982, Wesray Corporation acquired Gibson Greeting Cards from RCA Corporation for $81 million. Wesray put up $1 million in cash, raising the rest through bank borrowings and real estate leasebacks. In May, Gibson went public and the 50 percent interest held by Wesray's two top partners (one of them the former Secretary of the Treasury William Simon) had a total market value of $140 million.

With enormous debt-to-equity ratios ranging from 4:1 up to 10:1 one might wonder how these companies succeeded? "It's a classic case of statistics lying," claims Brian Young, a leveraged buyout specialist at First Boston Corporation. "There have been a few hundred deals in the last two years and they worked." Work they did, and the failure rate has been minuscule. Lenders and investors are pouring into the LBO market because of success stories such as Gibson Greetings, Metromedia, Wometco, and others. Banks are offering loans for up to 10 years, unusually long for them, and mezzanine financiers like insurance companies and pension funds, lured by rates of return that have often exceeded 50 percent, are also jumping in. The leveraged buyout phenomenon is no longer the exclusive enclave of Wall Street specialty houses like Kohlberg Kravis Roberts (KKR) and investments banks like Merrill Lynch and First Boston Corporation. Today, many firms on Wall Street boast of a leveraged buyout department and *The Wall Street Journal* is full of advertisements of smaller private firms who claim to be experts in the field.

There are a lot of winners in a leveraged buyout transaction. The managers get the opportunity to become owners, their entrepreneurial juices flow, and they are freed from quarterly profit imperatives mandated by the market. Shareholders on the whole gain by receiving premiums over the market price. For example, shareholders of Metromedia received a 67 percent premium over the market value of their shares. Banks earn handsome returns and are secured, so that even if the company goes bankrupt the loan is typically met by the sale of the assets. Mezzanine financiers enjoy high rates of return and have done very well. The investment bankers and lawyers reap large fees and have made an industry out of this phenomenon. The only loser seems to be Uncle Sam, as most companies pay little or no income taxes during the early years following the buyout. The tax reduction is a result of tax advantages on both depreciation and interest payments. Though the Tax Reform Act of 1986 reduced the value of the tax benefits, Uncle Sam still subsidizes a significant part of the deal. So it seems that until there is a large failure, and as long as there are financial rewards, people will continue to create leveraged buyout deals.

The purpose of this chapter is to briefly review the leveraged buyout phenomenon by studying and analyzing seven deals. Five successes—Metromedia, ARA Services, Scoa, Levi Strauss, and Gibson Greetings—and two failures that ended up filing for Chapter XI—Thatcher Glass and Brentano's. A common thread section will be used to integrate the findings and discuss the rewards and risks associated with such deals.

Metromedia—King Kluge's Golden Touch

At the age of 65, when most chief executives focus on golf, travel, and other sundry pleasures of retirement, John W. Kluge (pronounced kloo-gy), chief executive officer, president, and chairman of Metromedia Inc., proposed the largest single financial transaction in broadcasting history—a management-led leveraged buyout valued at $1.45 billion, the largest leveraged buyout of its time.

Kluge, who was born in Chemnitz, Germany, and moved to Detroit when he was eight, got into the television business in 1959. In that year, he and some friends bought control of Metropolitan Broadcasting. Metromedia (as he renamed it) owned two radio stations and television networks in New York and Washington, D.C. Over the next 25 years, Kluge built a nationwide empire of seven TV stations and 14 radio stations, the maximum permitted by regulation. It became the nation's largest independent broadcasting company as well as the largest owner of television stations. The corporation also owned Metromedia Producers Corporation, a producer of entertainment programs, the Ice Capades, the Harlem Globetrotters, ICS Communications, which was a radio paging firm, and also advertising and mail marketing firms. Its assets as of October 1983 were $1.3 billion, and it had sales of $550 million.

Kluge himself remains something of an enigma. A one-time Washington, D.C., food broker, his door has generally remained closed to reporters and security analysts. An avid reader of weekly profit and loss statements, he has a healthy aversion to taxes. Metromedia's headquarters are located in Secaucus, New Jersey, to avoid the high taxes of New York City, barely three miles away. He bought the depreciation rights to $100 million of New York City's buses and subways and acquired billboard companies and road shows like the Globetrotters because of the fast depreciation they provided. Kluge's name often appears in gossip columns and in May 1981 he married an Englishwoman, aged 36, in one of the most dramatic weddings New York has ever seen. A fiercely independent man, who by his own admission does not like to be handcuffed by quarterly earnings, he waited for the right moment to make his next move. Indeed, in November 1983, the time seemed to be right. With Metromedia trading at $20, down from its high of $57 earlier that year, Kluge contacted Boston Ventures Management, a Boston "hot money" investment banking concern. The biggest financial decision of his life had been made. He decided to take the company private.

His team consisted of three Metromedia executives—Robert Bennett, George Duncan, and Stuart Subotnick, as well as noted luminaries like publishing magnate Rupert Murdoch; 20th Century Fox co-owner, Marvin Davis; Washington Redskins owner, Jack Kent Cooke; TV and film producer, Jerry Perenchio; San Diego Charger owner, Gene Klein; a Denver oilman and a movie theater chain owner. All became limited partners in the Boston Ventures Limited Partnership. By formally aligning itself with some of the biggest names in entertainment, business, and sports, the company was well positioned to take advantage of almost every conceivable avenue open to it in the field of entertainment and communications. To accomplish the buyout, Kluge formed a new corporation—JWK Acquisition Corporation—which he partially capitalized by contributing 4.5 million of his own shares of Metromedia. At the time of consummation, JWK Acquisition Corporation planned to merge with Metromedia which would then emerge as the surviving corporation. The transaction was really a pro forma matter since Kluge, owning 25 percent of Metromedia's stock, had de facto control. After the transaction, he was expected to have de jure control.

A total of $1.45 billion had to be raised. This was to be used to: (*a*) purchase the 28.6 million outstanding shares; (*b*) refinance the existing debt; (*c*) purchase the stock options held by the employees; (*d*) pay for the fees and costs incurred in the transaction, and (*e*) provide adequate working capital for the coming months. A group of 10 banks led by Manufacturers Hanover Trust provided $1.3 billion in loans using

Metromedia's assets as collateral. An equity investment of
$125 million came from Prudential Insurance and $10 million was contributed by Boston Ventures Limited Partnership.
The management group provided $12 million, though Kluge
did not ante up cash, but instead paid with 4.5 million of the
7.2 million Metromedia shares he owned. In addition, he
cashed in his remaining shares, coming out $115 million
richer. The terms of the bank loan were stringent. Metromedia had only eight years to pay it back. The company had to
reduce the principal in stages beginning with $200 million
by June 1985. The rate of interest was pegged to the prime,
starting at 1.5 points above prime and declining rapidly
thereafter. Associated with the loan was a covenant requiring the company to maintain a minimum net worth of $100
million. The consortium of banks didn't do badly, receiving
up-front fees of $13 million. Lehman Bros., Kuhn Loeb, and
Bear Stearns were retained as investment bankers for Metromedia, while Boston Ventures Management represented
JWK Acquisition Corp. Adding to the troops of professionals,
both Metromedia and JWK were represented by leading
merger and acquisition law firms.

On December 6, 1983, Kluge finally announced his plan
and the terms of the offer. It included $30 in cash per share
and $22.50 worth of a new issue of Metromedia's subordi-
nated discount debentures due July 1, 1998. Since the debentures would not pay interest until the sixth year, it was
expected that their market price would be substantially less
than their face value. Analysts estimated their market value
between $9.50 to $10 apiece, giving the entire package a
value of $40. Kluge used his inventive mind and financial
savvy to create what was then a new kind of bond—a zero
coupon on which holders need not report any imputed
interest. This was the first use of a zero coupon in such deals.
Metromedia stood to gain from the bond's structure as it did
not have to pay interest in the earlier years when the financial pressures of the new company were expected to be most
severe. The bondholders also gained, as they were expected to
pay capital gains tax only when they sold the bonds. Unlike

radio stations and a Texas radio network from Metromedia for $285 million. Brazell obviously learned from the master. Like Kluge, he used a leveraged buyout.

At the end of the buyout Kluge said, "It is difficult to leave the radio after more than 30 years, but we have decided to concentrate on Metromedia's substantial telecommunications business." Yet only four months later, Kluge stunned the industry by selling its cellular telephone and paging operations for $1.65 billion to Southwestern Bell. Naturally, it was a record price for cellular telephone properties.

The scorecard on Kluge's buyout is clear. It may well be American business's major all-time LBO success story. Kluge put no cash into the deal and to date has converted more than $4.6 billion of Metromedia's assets to cash. Even after paying off his $580 million in long-term debt, he didn't do badly for a few years' work.

ARA Services—A Defensive LBO?

In July 1984, William M. Siegel, who left ARA in 1982 after 11 years of service, was having lunch with Joseph Neubauer, the present chief executive officer of ARA. While at lunch, he served Neubauer a surprise dish. He offered to buy ARA for $722 million or $60 cash per share. Siegel had been enlisted by his business partners in Texas to present the bid. Although Neubauer said he wanted to think it over, it didn't take him long to reach a conclusion. The following day he turned the deal down flat.

Siegel, a 54-year-old entrepreneur who lives in Bel Air, California, is a man of many hats. He was the chairman of Bedford National Corporation; a major shareholder and director of First Texas Financial Corporation, a Dallas-based savings association holding company; and similarly served Encino-based AVG Group Ltd., a maker of educational films. To round out his holdings he also owned two Texas oil companies bearing his name. His partners were the well-known sports personalities—B. J. McCombs, owner of the Denver

Nuggets professional basketball franchise and Charles Thomas, owner of the Houston Rockets basketball team. The investor group was eager to tackle a "big deal" and ARA cropped up in their search. Having been inside ARA, Siegel obviously saw some untapped potential in the company. Trying to win over the ARA executives, Siegel initially offered them a 10 percent stake in the company. In addition, he promised them that the investor group would be involved in formulating the company's policy, but would leave the day-to-day operations to the existing management. "I don't intend to move back to Philadelphia where ARA is located," he said.

After deciding that the Siegel group's proposal was inadequate and not in the best interest of the company and its shareholders, Neubauer and a group of other ARA top executives initiated a bid themselves to acquire the company in a leveraged buyout.

Joseph Neubauer graduated from Tufts University and received his M.B.A. from the bastion of free market thinking, the University of Chicago. He was assistant treasurer and vice president of commercial lending at The Chase Manhattan Bank from 1955–71 after which he became vice president and treasurer of PepsiCo, Inc. Like Kluge of Metromedia, Neubauer is a workaholic, working a "half day" from 7 A.M. to 7 P.M., and is an avid supporter of the local art establishment. In addition to serving on the board of the Philadelphia Chamber of Commerce and the University of Chicago's Business Council, he sits on the boards of the Philadelphia Orchestra and the College of Art. He is also chairman of the board of Inroads—Philadelphia, an organization that sponsors minority development programs. He is a builder of companies and, although his background is in finance, he has been "accused" of "creative management" along the way. It was the growth opportunities at ARA that attracted him there, and he joined in 1979.

Although offers like his are always subject to allegations of conflict of interest, Neubauer refused to state whether the leveraged buyout offer was motivated by a desire to prevent Siegel or others from launching hostile takeover bids. But it is possible, that in addition to mounting a defense, he also saw strong prospects for earnings growth. ARA's businesses were expected to benefit from the demographic changes in the U.S. population. Its child care centers were likely to benefit from increasing numbers of women entering the work force, while its nursing-home operations were poised to benefit from the aging of the American population.

When ARA was started 25 years ago, it placed candy and coffee machines in industrial plants and went by the name of Automatic Retailers of America. Today, it is simply known as ARA Services and with its 116,000 employees it can take on unusual and gargantuan tasks. For example, when the Olympic Games in Los Angeles needed an organization to feed and transport the athletes, ARA was there.

In fiscal year 1983, its five business segments combined to produce revenue of $3 billion and a net of $4.51 per share. For the first six months of 1984, revenues were up 13 percent over the previous period. More and more government units, institutions, and businesses were willing to contract with outside firms for services formerly provided by their own employees. Food and refreshment services made up a little more than half of ARA's business. In addition to companies and institutions, other customers included airports, stadiums, arenas, convention centers, parks, ski resorts, and race tracks. It also targeted and managed upscale restaurants located in large office building complexes. And prior to ARA's April 1984 divestiture of its Air La Carte subsidiary, it also offered in-flight meals and refreshments to air passengers.

Distributive services was the smallest of ARA's business segments accounting for 10 percent of its 1983 revenues. It provided magazines and other published materials to 25,000 retail locations in 30 states.

A fast-growing Health and Family Care segment managed more than 260 nursing homes and special care facilities. It also operated 135 day-care centers and provided emergency room staffing for 300 hospitals and medical centers across the country. ARA even entered the prison business, supplying medical and dental care to inmates in 19 institutions.

ARA's broadest business segment was made of textile

rentals, including uniforms, linens, building cleaning, maintenance and laundry equipment services for apartment houses, colleges, and military bases. This segment accounted for 72 percent of corporate revenues in 1983 and contributed 23 percent toward operating income.

On September 12, 1984, at an ARA board meeting Neubauer submitted a proposal on behalf of his management group and other potential investors. In exchange for each share of ARA common stock, shareholders would receive $62 in cash and $8.50 of debentures. Retaining Goldman Sachs & Co. as its investment banker, the management group submitted commitment letters to the board from Chemical Bank and Morgan Guaranty Trust Co. These banks agreed to form and lead a syndicate that would provide a $950 million revolving credit in order to finance the transaction. Sixty to 85 executives would be offered a chance to participate in the LBO.

In order to evaluate the proposal, a special committee of independent directors was formed. Surprisingly, even though the bid was made by colleagues and friends, the board rejected the offer arguing that it was too low. So, in October 1984, the offer was sweetened. At $62.50 a share, the cash portion of the new proposal was 50 cents a share higher than the earlier offer. Shareholders would also receive debentures with a face amount of $9.25, 75 cents higher than before. The 15-year debentures would pay a hefty 16.5 percent interest annually.

It was amazing how ARA's stock fluctuated over a short period of time. In August 1984, before the LBO proposal, the stock sold at 40¼. In September it went up to 64¼, and after the proposal was approved by the board, the price climbed to 67⅜.

More than a billion dollars had to be raised. The money was used primarily to make cash payments to the holders of outstanding shares. But it was also used to pay the holders of options under the company's option plans, to retire certain debts, to provide for working capital and to cover the fees and expenses incurred in connection with the LBO.

On August 31, 1984, the deal was completed. The management believed that there were significant opportunities in ARA's constituent businesses and that it was important to preserve the existing key executives who ran those businesses.

EPILOGUE

In August 1985, one year after the LBO was consummated, ARA began a public offering of $150 million 10-year subordinated notes bearing an interest rate of 13.75 percent. The proceeds were used to prepay a portion of the outstanding debt. Then in October 1985, ARA completed the purchase of Cory Food Services, which provides coffee services to businesses in the United States and Canada. The management felt that this addition would be an excellent complement to ARA's already existing lines of business.

In June 1986, Neubauer made a bid to buy Saga Corp. While Marriott later topped his offer, the bid itself reflects how far the company has come in the 18 months since the buyout. In addition, ARA at the time was more than $50 million ahead of schedule on debt repayments.

Unlike many others who led an LBO, Neubauer is proud of the fact that ARA hasn't had to sell major operations or slash capital expenditures. He emphasizes that "we have demonstrated to the financial institutions that we know what we're doing. It's against every norm that people have set for going private."

Neubauer attributes the better than forecasted results to signing up more businesses, better management of working capital and inventories, the sale of small noncritical vending operations that were marginally profitable, and the acquisition of other small businesses. Other important reasons are the declining interest rate environment following the LBO and the fact that owning a piece of the company has been a strong motivating factor for the nearly 70 executives who participated in the buyout and the 275 managers who have received stock options.

For now, Neubauer is scouring the horizon for future acquisitions.

Shoe Corporation of America (SCOA)— An LBO Close to the Heart

For Thomas H. Lee, a leveraged buyout specialist, the announcement that an investment group he heads planned to purchase Scoa Industries for $637 million represented more than a sound business decision. In a sense, the deal sent Lee back to his roots. He reminisced that "My grandfather Robert Schiff founded Scoa in 1905, and it feels wonderful to be able to do this." Lee, president of Thomas H. Lee & Co. (THL) and a graduate of Harvard learned the ropes at the First National Bank of Boston. He spent 10 years there as a lending officer to high-tech companies before founding his own company in 1974. "Lending to high-tech companies gave me a keen appreciation of fast-moving profit and loss statements and balance sheets," he explained. In the last 10 years, Lee participated in over 30 leveraged buyouts, many of them high-tech companies, but he has slowly been getting involved in retailing deals. In addition to Scoa, Lee was involved in a leveraged buyout of National Shoes and the purchase of Guilford Industries, a textile manufacturer.

On December 10, 1985, Scoa's stockholders approved the previously announced proposal under which Scoa would be acquired by THL in a leveraged transaction. Under the proposal, THL would be merged with Scoa and the name of the company would be changed to Scoa Industries, Inc. Each shareholder would receive $30 in cash and .20 shares of cumulative preferred stock series B (liquidation value of $25 per share). The proposal was made in conjunction with Drexel Burnham Lambert and involved 44 members of Scoa's management team. The leading members of the management group were George R. Friese, president; Herbert H. Goldberger, a director; Stephen A. Goldberger, president of Hills (a subsidiary); and Larry Vockar, a vice president of finance and treasurer. Following the buyout, all members of the management team were expected to retain their respective jobs. Thomas H. Lee's 68-year-old uncle, Herbert H. Schiff, Scoa's chairman and chief executive officer, was not a member of the buyout group. However, he fared well, receiving a $2.5 million "golden parachute" for going along with the transaction.

Scoa Industries is a diversified retailer which operates 131 department stores, 127 units in department stores and over 600 retail shoe stores and shoe departments. During fiscal year 1984, Scoa derived approximately 84 percent of its revenues and 96 percent of its profits from general merchandising, principally through its Hills chain of discount stores. Hills is one of the 10 largest discount department store chains in the United States. According to one retailer, Hills is a "gem" and Scoa has been quite successful with Hills in small cities where there is little competition for discount department stores. The remainder of Scoa's revenues and operating profits are derived from footwear operations. The shoe business is highly seasonal with a substantial proportion of the earnings generated in the last two months of the year. Fiscal 1984 reported annual sales of approximately $1.4 billion. Of this, net income was a somewhat paltry $41 million and debt service was kept to a meager $17 million.

THL is a private investment firm organized in 1974 which makes deals and takes positions in leveraged buyouts. It is known as one of the premier boutique LBO firms in the country and has substantial interests in a number of companies in diverse industries. It has extensive operating, strategic planning, acquisition, banking and financial experience. From August 1984 through spring 1985, Stephen and Herbert Goldberger met with Lee to discuss the possibility of a leveraged buyout of Scoa involving certain members of management (the Lee group). The group requested that the debt wizards of Beverly Hills, Drexel Burnham Lambert, assist them in arranging the financing for the acquisition, and retained Shearson Lehman Brothers as its adviser. On June 25, 1985, the proposal was formalized. The Thomas H. Lee Company, on behalf of the Lee group, submitted a proposal to purchase 85.7 percent of the outstanding shares for $35 cash per share and the remaining 14.3 percent shares for preferred stock having a liquidation value of $25 per share. At that time, Scoa had about 17 million shares outstanding. The new preferred would be junior cumulative preferred stock and would pay dividends at a rate of 12 percent per year. At the issuer's option, this dividend could be paid in the form of additional shares of preferred stock for the first four years. The preferred stock would be redeemed at its liquidation value plus accrued dividends at a rate of 20 percent per year, beginning at the end of the 11th year after the closing of the deal.

On the last trading day prior to the buyout proposal, Scoa's stock closed at 31¼. By November, it had risen to $32.50 per share. On the last trading day prior to the announcement, the closing price of the $100 principal amount convertible debentures was $129. By November, it had risen to $133.

In order to finance the merger, substantial debt had to be incurred. It amounted to $607 million and was required to: (1) finance the cash portion of the merger, (2) pay certain fees and expenses expected to be incurred in the transaction, and (3) pay the taxes associated with the merger. THL Holdings and THL Acquisitions, both subsidiaries of Thomas H. Lee Company, secured approximately $250 million. Under credit facilities of various banks, Bankers Trust and Manufacturers Hanover were the major participants in this credit line and in turn received fees of $1 million. The remainder of the cash portion of financing, approximately $318 million, was provided by the sale of senior notes, senior subordinated debentures and series C preferred stock to certain investors. Another source was the cash held by Scoa which amounted to $39 million. In all, $547 million of the $607 million raised was used to pay for the common stock. The remaining components were for taxes and fees which amounted to $28 million and $32 million, respectively.

The fees were sizable. Drexel Burnham Lambert received fees of $15.1 million, and First Boston Corporation received a fee of $1 million. Shearson Lehman was paid a retainer of $15,000 per month in connection with its financial advisory services. In addition, it received a fee of $4.3 million upon consummation of the initial merger. The whole street seemed to be in on the deal. Bear Stearns also received a fee of $250,000 for its services to Scoa.

Substantial debt was undertaken which significantly increased Scoa's debt-equity ratio. But Lee, familiar with the principle of leverage, argued that in the post-LBO period, the high leverage would allow the value of common equity to increase more rapidly on a percentage basis compared to an identical corporation with a larger equity base. "Besides," Lee pointed out that, "going private will allow Scoa to tap the immense potential Hills Company has." The debt service charge over the next year was expected to be $54 million. Although later denied by Lee, some analysts and shoe manufacturers speculated that because of this sizable debt obligation, Scoa would have to sell its 600 shoe stores.

At the same time, Lincoln Capital Management Company, representing shareholders having about a 6.7 percent stake in Scoa, filed a class action suit challenging the offer as being inadequate. They argued that because the primary sponsor of the proposal was the chairman's nephew it deserved a major airing. The court discarded the claim calling it "baseless."

On December 10, 1985, the buyout was approved and completed. THL held 74.5 percent of Scoa's common stock while Drexel Burnham accounted for 10 percent. The rest was divided among the key management investors. Herbert H. Goldberger, director of Scoa since 1968, was appointed the chairman and chief executive officer. As the transaction concluded, analysts were skeptical that the shoe division would be retained. Lee, however, once again denied this and called the buyout "smooth, a friendly offer and all in the family."

EPILOGUE

Unfortunately, nobody is perfect, and Lee could not keep all 600 shoe stores. In January 1986, Scoa sold 274 stores to Volume Shoe Corp. of Kansas and in March of that year, Scoa sold the division's footwear distribution center. It planned to use the proceeds to repay part of its debt. Besides this, Morse Shoe reached a preliminary agreement to acquire certain footwear departments that were operated by Scoa. As the last part of its divestiture program, Scoa sold the $100 million Dry Goods Co. subsidiary to a group including Oppenheimer & Co. and several executives of the Cohoen Specialty Stores Ltd. These asset sales were necessary to enable Scoa to meet the very significant debt payments assumed during the course of the buyout.

Nevertheless Scoa still would be classified as a success if its plan continues to succeed. The plan called for the Hills department store subsidiary to open 10 new stores in 1987 and each year thereafter. It is not unlikely that Lee, having reduced Scoa's debt obligations, will be in a position to successfully operate and expand both the department store chain and other parts of the organization as well.

Levi Strauss—"Thank You Bruce Springsteen"

Robert H. Haas, the great great grandnephew of Levi Strauss, the Bavarian immigrant who traveled to California in 1850 to make his fortune during the gold rush, is part of the same breed of ambitious managers who make dreams come true, such as Kluge of Metromedia, Neubauer of ARA, or Lee of Scoa. While his predecessor turned canvas into a pair of pants tough enough to survive the rigors of the mining camps, Robert Haas made uniforms for the American athletes at the 1984 Olympic Games.

Haas lived a privileged childhood in San Francisco's fashionable Pacific Heights. He followed his father and uncle in attending the University of California at Berkeley. His four years there, he recalled, opened his eyes to a world of injustice and poverty. After graduating in 1964, he joined the Peace Corps becoming the only English-speaking person in a town of 10,000 in the Ivory Coast. Once again, he followed in the footsteps of his father and uncle by attending Harvard Business School. Following a year as a White House fellow he began his business career in the San Francisco office of

McKinsey & Co. But he was too ambitious to stay there. As a result, he decided to look for opportunities in marketing-oriented companies which met an unusual set of characteristics. They could not pollute, cared about people, and had a social conscience, not just a concern for the bottom line. He realized that the only company around with those kind of characteristics was Levi's, saying "I am lucky because my personal values and the traditions of the company tend to be very tight." Robert Haas came relatively late to Levi's and until he asked permission to "apply for a job" one day over lunch in 1972, he and his father never discussed the idea of a Levi's career even though a family member has always run the business and Robert Haas was the oldest of Walter Haas's three children.

The Haas family is as closely associated with philanthropy and social responsibility as Levi Strauss & Co. is linked with the denim blue jeans that its founder created more than a century ago. To encourage literacy, the Haas-owned Oakland A's baseball team gives out free tickets to kids who sign "reading contracts" and fulfill them by reading 10 books. During the 1950s, long before civil rights laws were enacted, the Haas family insisted that new plants built by Levi Strauss in the South be integrated. Indeed, today, Levi's refuses to do business with South Africa.

Moreover, its liberal principles produced a donation to the producers of "The Life and Times of Harvey Milk," the Oscar winning documentary that celebrated the life of San Francisco's first openly homosexual supervisor who was slain in 1978. The company also pioneered safe working conditions in an industry where sweatshops were the norm. So it is little wonder that Levi's won the Lawrence A. Wein Prize for social responsibility from Columbia University in 1984, or that the Haas family won 1985's Alexis de Tocqueville award for volunteerism from the United Way.

Strauss, a bachelor and the founder of Levi's, was something of a philanthropist himself supporting orphanages and educational institutions. Strauss died in 1902 and left the business to his nephews. One nephew, Jacob Stern, ran the company until 1927. Stern's daughter, Elise, married Walter

Haas, Sr., in 1914. Rhoda Goldman, his daughter, said she was weaned on social responsibility. Once while on a trip to New York that featured outings to theaters and fine hotels and restaurants, her father took the three children to see New York's poorest ghettos. "He wanted to underscore that we had a responsibility to those less fortunate than ourselves."

The family dream of taking Levi's private again was the brainchild of Robert D. Haas. He became the leader of a new generation of Haas's—an extremely intelligent person with a strong sense of family.

Levi Strauss, founded in 1850, is the world's largest brand name apparel manufacturer. It designs, manufactures, and markets a diversified line of apparel for men, women, and children including jeans, slacks, shirts, jackets, skirts, and hats. Most of the company's products are marketed under the Levi's trademark and are sold in the United States and numerous foreign countries throughout South America, Europe, Asia, and Australia. The company's revenues are derived largely from the sale of basic styles of denim and corduroy jeans. Levi's went public in 1971 after more than a century of family ownership. In 1983, the company rebounded from the recession after two years of big profit declines, registering a 54 percent rise in earnings to $194.5 million or $4.61 per share on sales of $2.7 billion. Most of the rise, however, was a result of retailers restocking inventories and Levi's filling the pipelines for Sears Roebuck & Co. and J. C. Penney Company, Inc.—two new customers. Some retailers, angry at Levi's for turning to mass merchandisers, dropped the Levi's line entirely. Customers suddenly decided that they wanted more fashionable sportswear and began to turn away from such old-time favorites as blue jeans. As a result of this trend Levi's had to restructure its organization, shutting down several factories, incurring in huge compensation expenses paid to laid-off employees. Levi's sales for the first nine months of 1984 slipped 6 percent and, earnings plummeted 72 percent. In 1984, the company recorded a significant drop in earnings to just $81 million on sales of $2.5 billion. Although the company dominated the denim jeans market and accounted for more than 125 million of the 500 million pairs sold in the United States, it faced a flattening demand for jeans and a strong dollar which kept foreign sales depressed.

With two thirds of its worldwide sales derived from denim and corduroy products—mostly jeans—analysts doubted whether Levi's could recapture the glory of the late 70s when profits jumped at an annual rate of 37 percent. According to Robert Haas, "Innovation is what's going to be required to be successful down the road." Since succeeding Robert Grohman—the only nonfamily member who ran the company from 1982 to 1984—Haas has reorganized Levi's into two divisions: Battery Street Enterprises which handles fashion apparel, and The Jeans Co. which handles traditional jeans. But his key moves have been to reduce overhead. He closed 23 plants worldwide and cut 6,500 people from a work force of 44,000. The first six months of 1985 were promising with an earnings increase of a stunning 165 percent. The big question was: Could Levi's successfully pursue both the basic jeans and higher fashion market, something it has failed to achieve in the past?

The buyout would allow management to focus on the "long term" and would be the most appropriate way to ensure that the company continued to respect and implement the important values and traditions of the family. Under the proposed transaction, family ownership in the company would jump to 92 percent from its pre-buyout level of 40 percent. The rest would be owned by nonfamily management and Hellman and Friedman, a San Francisco investment bank, with close ties to the Haas family. A group of banks led by San Francisco-based Wells Fargo would lend $1.45 billion for the acquisition and an additional $250 million in working capital. Another $300 million would come from buyers of subordinated debt which was to be underwritten by Salomon Brothers. According to Robert Haas, in the future the company would no longer be subject to shareholder pressure when presenting its quarterly earnings performance, and would not have to apologize and endlessly explain its financial results. Does the fact that the deal looked like a good one for the Haas family mean that it was a bad deal for the nonfamily shareholders? Not at all. In short, the deal was a bonanza for all shareholders. Levi's stock was trading in the mid-30s prior to the announcement of the deal in July 1985 and $23 a year earlier. On July 26, 1985, it closed on the New York Stock Exchange at $48.

Robert Haas, Levi's president and CEO presented the $50 a share leveraged buyout offer at a special board meeting held on July 15, 1985. The all cash offer was submitted by HHF Corp., a newly formed company designed for the purpose of the buyout. The board appointed a special committee of four independent directors to evaluate the offer and engaged Goldman Sachs & Co. as its financial adviser. The buyout proposal was supported by family members controlling about 40 percent of the company's 37.1 million outstanding shares. On July 29, 1985, the special committee met with Goldman Sachs who declared that the $50 cash offer was fair.

The $1.7 billion financing required by HHF was needed to purchase all outstanding shares. It was also used to pay related fees and expenses, make payments associated with the cancellation of employee stock options, replace existing debt, and provide working capital. Wells Fargo organized and led a syndicate of banks who provided the $1.7 billion financing. Another $300 million in subordinated debt underwritten by Salomon Brothers was needed to repay a like amount of borrowing under the revolving credit facility. The interest rate paid on this debt was structured to be approximately 14 to 14.5 percent. While the interest expense of more than $150 million a year for five years was likely to consume at least 40 percent of Levi's operating profit, the buyout was completed and Robert Haas's dream of bringing the company back into the family finally came true.

ENTER BRUCE SPRINGSTEEN

The most prominent item in the rock superstar's working-class wardrobe was a pair of faded Levi no-frills 501 jeans. Even though Springsteen did not make product endorsements, the "true blue" fans would never mistake the pair of jeans on the cover of his album "Born in the USA." The popularity of the 501 came as a welcome boost for Levi Strauss which suffered through the designer jean craze and the general slump in denim sales. With a little help from Springsteen, the 501 has been riding a fashion U-turn back to the all-American look and therefore is helping the Haas family pay the sizable debt outstanding.

Gibson Greetings—The Granddaddy of LBOs

In 1952, William E. Simon, the son of an insurance agent from Patterson, New Jersey, graduated from Lafayette College in Easton, Pennsylvania, and headed for Wall Street as a $75-a-week stockbroker. By 1972, at 45, when he went into government, he was earning $2 million a year as head of the government bond department at Salomon Brothers. He started his brief governmental career as deputy secretary of the treasury. Then he became an "energy czar" while serving as the first administrator of the Federal Energy Office between 1973 and 1974. Finally, he was appointed secretary of the treasury.

While in government, he faced the Watergate scandal, the oil crisis, and the rising inflation with such strong resolve that White House aides nicknamed him the "Mississippi riverboat gambler." He also gained a reputation as "Bad Bill" for demanding that subordinates match his workaholic habits.

Since his transition back to private life, he has benefited from the enhanced status that a businessperson can acquire from a few years of Washington, D.C., prominence. He has kept himself extremely busy. During his four-year Washington stint, his holdings were sequestered in a blind trust managed by Citibank. His net worth dwindled from $5 million to $2.5 million. But, when he regained control of his funds in

1977 he was soon able to increase his net worth to over $25 million.

At the time of the Gibson Greeting Cards' deal, he was a consultant to Allstate Insurance and to Tamco Enterprises Inc., the investment arm of the Gouletas family. He was also chairman of Crescent Diversified, Ltd., a company that manages the U.S. investment portfolio of Saudi businessman, Suliman S. Olayana. However, the always busy Simon had a large portfolio of his own to manage: interests in oil and gas properties in Louisiana, Oklahoma, and Texas; a large farm in Brazil; Brazilinvest, a holding and development company in São Paulo; 11,000 acres of prize undeveloped land in Colorado; interest in a string of racehorses; and more. He also held directorships in several large firms: Citicorp and Citibank, Dart & Kraft, Halliburton, Power Corporation of Canada, United Technologies, and Xerox. All these activities and investments brought him an annual income of well over $2 million by the time he entered the Gibson deal.

What seemed leisurely to Simon was a breakneck pace to others. He also was involved in several projects including Lafayette College, where he watched over a $100 million endowment, and the John M. Olin Foundation, which funded conservative scholars. He also headed an independent group of conservative scholars and business leaders which voiced strong support for American capitalism in response to the critical stance of the Roman Catholic Church in the United States. An avid tennis player, he was president of the U.S.A. Olympic Committee during the 1984 Olympic Games at Los Angeles. He also started a private fund to support Nicaragua's contras.

In addition to Simon's involvement in eleemosynary causes, he is also chairman and cofounder of Wesray Corporation, a company specializing in leveraged buyouts. He used his connections to help make deals. Frank Bailey, for instance, a college classmate, guided him in making lucrative oil investments. Wesray's purchase of Wear-Ever Aluminum grew out of a casual conversation with a fellow Lafayette College trustee.

Simon's cofounder of Wesray, Ray Chambers, was the numbers man. In 1968, he helped found Metrocare, a health care company listed on the American Stock Exchange. He later left to start his own investment banking firm and in 1981 joined forces with Simon. Wesray—Wes from Simon's initials and ray from Chambers' first name—was the acquisition vehicle for at least 19 companies. They were mostly subsidiaries of huge conglomerates ranging from greeting cards to crude oil.

The most publicized of Wesray's purchases was Gibson Greeting Cards. Although its other acquisitions have received less media attention, they include an impressive and varied list of companies: Anchor Hocking's glass container division; Allis-Chalmers' Simplicity Manufacturing, a maker of lawn equipment; Occidental Petroleum's Permian Corporation; Atlas Van Lines; Heekin Can Company, a producer of metal containers; Wear-Ever Aluminum, a manufacturer of pots and pans; Mobile Music Man, a music instruments rentals company; Long Island Oyster Farm; Tactec Systems; and in 1985 the acquisition of Wilson Sporting Good Company from PepsiCo. Wesray did not conform its purchases to companies of a particular size or industry. It simply looked for good deals.

According to Simon, Wesray looks for companies with high-quality and high earning assets. In structuring an LBO for the target, Simon and Chambers usually put up only a small percentage of the purchase price. They then pledge the company's assets as collateral. Usually they retain anywhere from 50 to 70 percent ownership, almost always keeping existing management and giving them equity participation. At one point Simon stated, "We have never been involved in a hostile takeover and never will be."

One of the most well-known acquisitions ever made was the Wesray purchase of Gibson Greeting Cards. According to Simon, he felt he was "just darn lucky" about Gibson. But more than lucky, Simon and Chambers clearly set the standard and wrote the textbook for doing a leveraged buyout.

Gibson was founded in 1850 by Robert H. Gibson as a small manufacturer of greeting cards. In 1895, the business was incorporated in Ohio under the name of Gibson Art Company. The common stock was listed on the New York Stock Exchange from 1962 to 1964. Then in 1964, CIT Financial Corporation acquired all of Gibson's assets and formed a wholly owned subsidiary, Gibson Greeting Cards, Inc. Changing hands again in 1980, RCA acquired CIT and Gibson became a subsidiary of RCA.

Gibson's major products were greeting cards and gift wrapping paper. With 1984 sales of $304 million, Gibson was the third largest producer of greeting cards, following Hallmark Cards and American Greetings Corporation. Many of Gibson's products used well-known proprietary characters such as Popeye and certain Walt Disney characters. The company also owned the fat cat cartoon character, Garfield, which was syndicated in over a thousand newspapers, and had been featured in many best-selling books and network TV specials.

Financially, Gibson performed well. Thomas M. Cooney became Gibson's chief executive in 1978. As a salaried manager for RCA, he was making approximately $200,000 annually when Simon and Chambers asked him to be part of Gibson's buyout team. For a mere $51,000, Cooney was able to buy 5 percent of the company. That works out to about 10 cents a share. Since Cooney took charge, he doubled Gibson's share of the greeting card products market to 10 percent. He was successful in doing so by improving distribution, quality, and snaring licenses to popular characters such as Garfield. Total revenues went up from almost $132.5 million in 1978 to $197 million in 1982. Net income also tripled from $5.5 million to $14 million. In 1984 Gibson's sales were $302 million with earnings jumping 27 percent over 1983 to $28.3 million.

Back in 1979, following a long period of diversified acquisitions, RCA, the former owner of Gibson, announced long-range strategic plans to concentrate on what seemed to be its four core businesses: Hertz, NBC, financial and consumer products and services, and electronics and communications. These strategic plans led RCA to several divestitures and acquisitions. In 1979, the company sold Alascom Telephone Company, Banquet Foods, and Random House. In 1980, following a number of management changes, RCA bought CIT Financial Corporation and intended to strengthen its financial services division. In 1981, RCA sold Avionca Systems, Oriel Foods Ltd., Picker Corporation, and Raco Inc. Finally in 1982 as part of this whole strategic divestiture program and despite the healthy earnings of the company, RCA decided to seek a buyer for Gibson. Simon and Chambers stumbled upon the deal while negotiating the purchase of Tactec Systems, RCA's mobile communication unit. The lucky dealers ended up buying both companies. Eighteen months later Gibson turned out to be the real fat cat.

In January 1982, Wesray closed the deal and received an investment banking fee of $580,000 in connection with the purchase of Gibson Greeting Cards. As a result of the transaction, Simon and Chambers assumed control of 70 percent of Gibson's outstanding common stock. Management and certain employees of Gibson were given 20 percent of the stock. The deal was structured such that although the buyers paid $80.6 million for the company, RCA received only $58 million, and the remaining $22.6 million was used to repay the debt owed to CIT by RCA.

The $58 million paid to RCA, the $22.6 million paid to CIT, and the $4 million required to cover related acquisition expenses were obtained from a variety of sources:

1. New Gibson stockholders invested $1 million in equity.
2. General Electric Credit Corporation (GECC) loaned $39.8 million as part of a revolving credit line. In return, Gibson pledged its receivables, inventories, and other assets. GECC also took a subordinated security interest in Gibson's machinery and equipment.
3. Barclays American Business Credit, Inc., loaned $13 million. Gibson pledged its machinery and equipment. Barclays also took a subordinated interest in its receivables, inventories, and other assets.
4. Gibson also raised $30.8 million by selling and leasing back its three principal manufacturing and distribution facilities.

Gibson gave GECC warrants to purchase 2.3 million shares of stock at $0.143 per share. The warrants could be exercised at any time and could not expire earlier than 1992. The agreement also provided that GECC would receive additional interest amounting to the before-tax equivalent of one third of any dividends declared as long as the warrants are held by GECC. It's worth noticing that in January 1983, Gibson declared a dividend of $2.8 million or 39 cents per share, resulting in an additional interest cost to the company of $1.88 million.

Gibson also entered into a 10-year agreement for a $13 million loan, the principal amount of which was to be paid in monthly installments. The interest rate on this loan varied depending on the prime. This loan was collateralized by a first security interest in Gibson's machinery and equipment (including all future acquisitions) and a subordinated security interest in all trade receivables, inventories, and other assets. In 1982, the annual weighted average interest rate was a staggering 19.04 percent.

Lenders like to play it safe. Barclays, for example, placed several restrictions on Gibson. According to the agreement, prior to 1985, annual cash distributions including cash dividends and any additional interest payable to GECC, could not exceed 25 percent of Gibson's adjusted net income. Thereafter it could not exceed 50 percent of its adjusted net income and it could not reduce Gibson's adjusted tangible net worth below $5 million.

Gibson sold its principal executive, manufacturing and distribution facilities, located in Cincinnati, Memphis, and Berea, Kentucky, to Realty, a firm controlled by Ray Chambers. In exchange for the properties, Realty issued a promissory note for $30.95 million. Realty immediately resold these properties for $35.4 million to two unaffiliated publicly held limited partnerships which thereupon leased these properties to Gibson. Chambers' Realty collected fees and expenses amounting to $4.196 million. Realty also loaned Gibson $30.78 million in exchange for its promissory note. Such lease arrangements, in addition to their function as source of financing, defer reporting a gain on the sale of the properties for income tax purposes.

EPILOGUE

No doubt, the Wesray partners were lucky in buying Gibson's fat cat for less than $1 million in cash. Eighteen months later they decided to sell it. It was May 1983 when Simon and Chambers cashed in. They took Gibson public at $27.50 per share. The total offering of more than 10 million shares was valued at $290 million. Certainly, for Bill Simon and Ray Chambers, greeting cards were good business. Considering a purchase price of $80.6 million only 18 months earlier, the Wesray bonanza set the stage for the mammoth LBO wave which was to follow. Indeed, Simon's own bonanza probably did more to spur LBOs than any other single deal. Through the deal, his $330,000 investment turned into an unbelievable $66 million.

Even after the deal, Gibson kept making headlines. Its stock slumped to $18 per share but then, following takeover rumors, climbed to $28. In August 1984, the company was caught in a lively takeover drama featuring Walt Disney Productions and corporate raiders Saul Steinberg and Irwin Jacobs. Gibson was approached by Walt Disney Productions with an offer of more than $300 million.

The drama started in June 1984, when Disney offered to acquire Gibson via a stock swap. Disney did so in the midst of its looming proxy battle with financier Saul Steinberg. Steinberg, only a few days later, won his way when Disney agreed to buy his stock position. Not unexpectedly, Steinberg accepted the "greenmail" offer. Shortly thereafter, Irwin L. Jacobs, 43, a Minneapolis takeover shark, surfaced and announced he was accumulating Disney shares, and was growing increasingly hostile to the Gibson deal. Jacobs was heading a group which purchased around 6 percent of Disney's shares. Those shares, purchased for more than $90 million, enabled him to call a special stockholder meeting to vote on the Gibson purchase. In fact, he threatened that if Disney directors persisted in trying to buy Gibson, he would ask the shareholders to vote them out. Belief that Jacobs had support from some major stockholders like the Bass family in Texas, or Roy E. Disney, pushed Disney's directors to terminate the intended merger. As a result, for exercising its right to terminate the merger, Disney agreed to pay to Gibson $7.5 million plus related expenses.

In addition, Walt Disney Productions granted Gibson exclusive rights to use Disney characters on greeting cards, gift wraps, and related products for the following three years. The licensing agreement was needed to end Gibson's veiled threat of legal action.

Gibson's chief executive officer, Thomas Cooney, insists that greeting cards are the best business to be in. The product is used just once and there is no foreign competition. "If I could be reincarnated, I'd come back as a greeting card salesman." Cooney, in his current incarnation as CEO, achieved solid 1985 results. Sales reached $329.9 million and earnings hit $31.4 million. Since then, the founding partners of Wesray, Simon and Chambers, have split. It's now run by Chambers, while Simon went off to Australia on his 125-foot sailboat to work on his most recent project—creating a transpacific banking network.

But while the partners have cashed in, Chambers got out at the right time. In October 1986, Gibson announced that a sluggish retailing environment and pricing pressures from competition were hurting the company. Third- and fourth-quarter results were expected to be disappointing. For Bill Simon and Ray Chambers timing was everything.

Thatcher Glass—The Price of Failure

"We don't expect that the glass container industry has too many new horizons; the cyclical energy intensive business uses cash heavily and will encounter increasing competition from the plastic container industry. Thus the unit, despite its profitability, won't help the parent meet its long-term financial goals." With these words, Dart & Kraft, a leading food and consumer products manufacturer sold its subsidiary Thatcher Glass Manufacturing Company in December 1981 to Dominick International Corporation, a closely held concern based in New York. This leveraged buyout would ultimately set a milestone in leveraged buyout history. The first significant buyout to fail.

The spinoff was a nice way for Dart & Kraft to unload its ailing container business. The unit was a victim of competition from plastic bottles and aluminum cans, and even though it took a loss of $70.5 million or $1.30 per share on the sale, Dart & Kraft had realized that the glass industry was mature with limited growth potential. The industry did not fit the parent company's strategic objectives, so it decided to sell the unit and use the proceeds to trim its short-term debt.

Thatcher Glass was the third largest manufacturer of glass containers in the United States. It produced 3 billion bottles annually from six plants coast to coast for customers such as Seagram, Anheuser-Busch, and H. J. Heinz. Its 1980 sales of $347.7 million, which accounted for nearly 4 percent of Dart & Kraft's total sales, and its net income of $30.4 million made it one of the most profitable glassmakers in America. For the first nine months of 1981, prior to the sale, its sales rose by 12 percent from the previous year to $287.1 million and pretax profit also rose 12 percent to $23.7 million.

In order to accomplish the buyout, Dominick & Dominick formed a new corporation, Dominick International Corporation. This new company was partially owned by a group of Thatcher's senior officers led by its president, William H. Greenberg. Following the sale, Greenberg would become president, chief executive officer, and chairman, with the same management team continuing to operate the company. Dominick & Dominick served as investment bankers for the new company, and Morgan Stanley represented Dart & Kraft. Interestingly, several investment bankers refused to handle the deal because of the difficult state of the glass industry. Furnaces had to be rebuilt every five to seven years at a cost of approximately $12 million each. Cash was likely to be tight; as a result, reinvestment was likely to be ignored.

Thatcher was offered $120 million in cash and $17.9 million in specially issued subordinate debentures and preferred stock of Dominick International. To raise the money, Dominick International borrowed $110 million from a group of banks which included Manufacturers Hanover, Chase Manhattan, Bankers Trust, and NCNB (National Bank of North Carolina). The interest rate was floating and was set above the prime which was hovering at the atmospheric level of 20 percent in 1981. A $20 million note from Dart & Kraft at 16.75 percent interest and a $6 million note from Dominick International provided the remainder of the funds. In early 1982, the $140 million management buyout was completed and Thatcher Glass Manufacturing Company went private.

Overnight, Thatcher's lean capital structure ballooned to 95 percent debt consisting of bank loans and notes at precariously high interest rates. The watery thin equity consisted of the $4 million Dominick paid for Thatcher's stock, plus Dominick preferred valued at $3 million. Nevertheless, until early 1984, the new Thatcher Glass faced few problems and didn't seem to require additional equity. Until then, sales had been strong. Extra cash was squeezed out by slashing inventories and the firm managed to meet its debt obligations.

However, by the end of 1984 the glass container market took a downturn. Sales began to deteriorate rapidly because of increasing competition from plastic containers. In addition, due to falling aluminum prices, the beer and soda industries shifted to aluminum containers. Other glassmakers reacted by shutting down facilities. Thatcher tried to survive by taking on marginal businesses simply to keep furnaces burning—a strategy often required to feed cash hungry LBOs. Soon after, Thatcher hired a consultant (a sure sign of panic) who, instead of advocating selective shutdowns accompanied by commensurate layoffs which would have helped weed out the unprofitable plants, advocated massive firings. Following this recommendation, 80 percent of Thatcher's 4,000 employees were given the pink slip. As expected, the inevitable had to happen to a company saddled with uneconomic production and a depleted work force. On December 29, 1985, four minutes before noon, lawyers representing Thatcher walked into the Bridgeport, Connecticut, Federal Courthouse and filed for Chapter XI protection, listing assets of $160 million compared with liabilities of $166 million. Thatcher had hoped to reschedule its debt payments and avoid filing for bankruptcy. Unfortunately, at the last minute, one of the banks backed out. On the positive side, the four major banks agreed to provide enough financing to last four weeks, allowing Thatcher to plan its reorganization. Charles Whiteman, an outsider, replaced Greenberg as CEO to preside over the company's dismantling.

Thatcher owed the consortium of banks a total of $77 million. The largest unsecured creditor was Dart & Kraft who was owed $32.2 million, representing principal and interest on the note advanced to Thatcher at the time of the sale. The second largest unsecured creditor was Thatcher's main supplier, Stauffer Chemical Company, who was owed $1.7 million.

In an effort to gain capital to pay off Thatcher's debt, things began to move rapidly. Dominick International decided to liquidate three of Thatcher's six manufacturing plants in Elmira, New York, Saugus, California, and Tampa, Florida, as well as two office buildings located in New York state. Diamond-Bathurst Inc., a subsidiary of a Canadian packaging company bought most of Thatcher's assets at fire sale prices. The initial offering price was $63 million. However, the offer was reduced after land and buildings at the three plants were excluded from the transaction. In the second round, the buyers offered $50.5 million which was again reduced following a review of Thatcher's inventories and receivables. The final price was $40 million compared with the $140 million that Dominick paid Dart & Kraft. Ironically this acquisition resulted in making Diamond-Bathurst one of the largest and healthiest glass container manufacturers in the United States.

Who takes the beating when a leveraged buyout turns down? Four parties were involved in this morass—Thatcher's owner, Dominick & Dominick, the four major banks, the company's employees, and its unsecured creditors. The group of banks did not lose a substantial amount of money from the experience. Sale of Thatcher's assets to Diamond-Bathurst covered the bank's loans down to $17 million. At the same time, the loans had been earning interest at 2.5 percent over prime. When Forbes Magazine called the banks to learn the advisability of setting up such a lightly anchored leveraged buyout, all the four major banks ducked the question. Dominick & Dominick, the captain and owner, didn't go down with the ship as expected. As of June 1985, it only had $6 million remaining in Thatcher—$4 million in equity and $2 million in loans. But the kicker is that while Thatcher was sinking, owner Dominick accrued tax benefits from operating losses and investment tax credits worth more than $17 million. It remains to be seen how much of these credits the Internal Revenue Service will allow Dominick to keep, but it walked away relatively unscathed.

The unsecured creditors seem to have a remote chance of recovering their money in Thatcher. However, Dart & Kraft announced that it carried the amount on its books at substantially less than face value, and therefore, it was expected that the sum would not have any material effect on its earnings. Also Stauffer Chemical stands to lose a great deal, as Thatcher was its principal buyer. Competitors expressing their opinions, alleged that over the years, repairs and modernization of Thatcher's plants were ignored while lavish management bonuses, based upon debt repayment, were given. This in turn translated into many of Thatcher's problems and led to its unfortunate demise, including having three fourths of its employees fired and its eventual bankruptcy. While these employees were looking for new jobs, most of them had no benefits such as severance pay, accrued vacation wages, and health insurance. Even though Thatcher's union was contesting the loss of these benefits, its chances of recovery seemed shaky at best. Obviously, these employees were the real losers, paying the price for management's mistakes and owners' greed.

Thatcher Glass is an example of the fact that leveraged buyouts require much more than a management team and a lot of debt. The company ignored the maxim that cost cutting is the path to viability of leveraged buyouts. It was so bundled with debt that it was unable to make the capital investment needed to survive in an era of intense competition. Even though the failure rate of LBOs has been minuscule, Thatcher is a reminder that things can go wrong and that great care must be taken in the process of identifying viable companies and structuring the deal.

Brentano's—Trimming Dead Wood

The Brentano's Inc., bookstore chain started in 1853 as a newsstand in front of the old New York Hotel. It was founded by August Brentano, who immigrated from Austria. Over the years, its operations expanded. By 1962, Brentano's was comprised of 16 stores and was sold to Macmillan Inc., a diversified publisher. Under the Macmillan umbrella, the number of stores rose to 31, the flagship being the Brentano store at 586 Fifth Avenue in New York City.

In the following years, Brentano's faced increasingly vigorous competition from newer but aggressively run stores such as Walden Books and B. Dalton. The Walden and Dalton empires, comprised 1,240 stores, spread all over the United States and controlled over 20 percent of the retail business. Brentano's, meanwhile, was lying dormant with a minuscule market share of only 2 percent. The 31-store chain lost money in most years during 1970–80, and in 1980 it lost more than $1 million on its $30 million sales. Unfortunately, a similar pattern was expected in the coming years.

Macmillan, itself, wasn't doing well either. With total revenues of $568 million and a reported loss of approximately $9 million in 1980, it was involved in corporate restructuring. This included "changes in management and organization" as well as several changes in "accounting principles and practices." Over this time, Macmillan had sold its 12 other subsidiary companies. In the first six months of 1981, Macmillan reported a loss of $2.4 million which forced its chief executive officer Edward Evan to put Brentano's up for sale. He argued that "Brentano's does not fit into the company plan," and decided to focus on education and publishing, while trying to phase out other areas. The prospective sale of Brentano's won praise on Wall Street. A senior executive at Smith Barney said: "Good riddance; Macmillan should have done this years ago. They did not know how to manage the chain." A senior executive at E. F. Hutton praised the move and stated that this was a further step by the management to clean up the company.

On August 2, 1981, Macmillan announced that it had sold the stock of Brentano's, its 31-unit bookstore chain, to Hillibore Inc., a newly formed organization that was owned by Brentano's top employees and a number of institutional investors. The new owners included Paul Ohran, Brentano's general manager who became chief executive officer; Peter Slater, merchandise manager for books who became vice president of purchasing and systems; Monica Hollander, merchandise manager who became vice president of marketing; and Ken Ferguson, controller, who became a vice president. Carl Hollander, a lawyer, was appointed as the chairman. The deal was for cash plus secured notes payable in three years. The proceeds were to be used by Macmillan to reduce its outstanding short-term debt. The Bank of New York and a group of private investors put up the acquisition money, with the key figure being Francis Oaker Hunnewell, a 43-year-old investment banker. His Paris-based Lansdowne Financial Service played a major role in financing the LBO. He was approached by Paul Ohran in January 1981. Soon after, a cash and preferred stock deal was struck. Hunnewell himself is based in Paris, but maintains business offices in New York and Wellesley, Massachusetts, where his family lives. Following the completion of the buyout, Carl Hollander was replaced by Hunnewell as the chairman of the newly formed Brentano Consolidated Companies. He became responsible for financial and real estate matters while Ohran looked after the daily operations.

When the new management took over, they maintained that Brentano's problems were neither due to flagging book sales nor discounting by competitors such as Barnes and Noble. They were simply due to the lack of planning and inadequate control of expenses, margins, and inventories. Ohran stated: "The company has never been planned properly." Unlike the larger stores which packed their shelves with a broad spectrum of titles, Brentano's emphasized quality. Under the new management, Brentano's decided to strike out in two directions. First, it tried to develop a mail-order business so that it could maintain supremacy in the specialty mail-order/catalog field. Second, the company added to its merchandise mix gift selections geared to the home library business. To achieve this, Brentano's planned to open new sections in its stores that would carry merchandise reflecting traditional and contemporary collectible items for libraries. Plans were also made to add book galleries to their stores. At the time, Brentano's had sales of $30 million. As a result of management's changes, they expected sales to increase substantially in the coming years.

But there seems to be a lot of wisdom in the words, "It is easier said than done." In May 1982, Brentano Consolidated

Companies unexpectedly announced that its Brentano Inc. unit would file Chapter XI in order to reorganize its ailing 28-bookstore chain. Hunnewell, the chairman, declared that "We have taken a very positive step in the rehabilitation of a name that has been in the business for 150 years. The filing [will] help the company drop unprofitable stores, revamp the others and we expect to retain half the currently operating stores." The papers were filed in a federal court in New York on April 27, 1982. Brentano's reported assets of $9.7 million against liabilities of $13.4 million. Brentano's had been posting losses of approximately $1 million per year for the prior three years and in 1981, the year of the buyout, it had revenues of $22 million with a net loss of $4 million. Management claimed that the company was thwarted in its attempts to improve conditions because it was unable to resolve lease arrangements with the owners of the stores. The period was also marked with high interest rates which made financing difficult. All this, coupled with increasingly aggressive competition, forced Brentano's into bankruptcy. In 1982, the company had sales of $572,000, only 1.9 percent of the revenue prior to the buyout phase.

In October 1983, unsecured creditors were expected to recover 40 cents for each dollar, but this was later revised to half that amount, or 20 cents. The company held a hearing where it received offers for the purchase of its stores. All but three of its stores and the flagship store on Fifth Avenue were sold. In April 1984, Waldenbooks bought all of Brentano's stock for $950,000 and acquired each of the three stores except the flagship. With that minor transaction, LBO history was made. The travails of one of the major names in American bookselling came to a grinding halt.

THE BOTTOM LINE

Captain of the Ship

The presence of a "strong" leader backed by an efficient and experienced team is necessary for an LBO to be a success as these examples have repeatedly shown. Kluge of Metromedia had 24 years of experience in the broadcasting industry and was backed by a team of top executives and some of the biggest names in entertainment, business, and sports. Haas of Levi's had very strong family support and was helped by his father's extensive experience in the apparel business and the expertise of Hellman and Friedman, the investment banker which had close ties with the Haas family. Thomas Lee of Scoa was a veteran of 30 LBOs in hi-tech and retailing. Neubauer of ARA had the support of a strong management team and key figures in the sports and entertainment arena. These executive bandwagons consisted of highly motivated, strong willed and experienced personalities. Greenberg of Thatcher Glass and Ohran of Brentano's, on the other hand, went in alone backed only by a handful of senior officers from the company. Obviously, a ship without an experienced captain and an efficient crew has little chance of making it to the port. An LBO team without a savvy leader and determined players has little, if any, chance of success.

Sweet Timers

Metromedia, Levi's, Scoa, and ARA Services can be branded as "sweet timers." They went through LBOs during or after 1983 when corporate culture as a whole was undergoing a radical change in the United States. They stepped into the era of "takeover madness" at the right time. The timing was appropriate—the economy was stable, the industries they operated in were booming, interest rates were relatively low, and future projections were optimistic. Metromedia's new line of cellular phones was enjoying explosive growth, Levi's main product, blue jeans, was experiencing resurgence, ARA was entering into new businesses, and Scoa's Hills subsidiary was expanding rapidly. These existing conditions were tailor made for an LBO transaction and the companies exploited the conditions.

On the other hand, in 1981, not only was the economy facing a recession, but interest rates were also high. The glass industry was mature and faced increasing competition from plastic bottles and aluminum cans. Brentano's had been losing money for almost a decade and was facing stiff competition from newer and more aggressive bookstores like Walden and Dalton. The cyclical downturn in the economy hurt both Brentano's and Thatcher as well as other companies. For example, back in 1981, Kohlberg Kravis Roberts paid $425 million for Bendix Forest Products. Shortly thereafter, business plummeted because of the housing construction slowdown. KKR had to return part of the forestland to Bendix in exchange for canceling $65 million of debts. In total, KKR and its partners lost $5 million of their $95 million equity position. Thus, Brentano's, Thatcher, and several other buyout deals were unfortunate in that the trends in the industry and economy were against them, but a little foresight would have prevented these deals, or at least led in altering their structure to include less debt and new product lines. This would most definitely have prevented the bankruptcies that followed later.

Debt Load Caused "Short Circuits"

It is evident from Thatcher Glass that it was leveraged to the hilt compared to the other companies described. The year Thatcher and Brentano's underwent an LBO was a year marked by record high interest rates. An upward surge in interest rates made borrowing more expensive, consequently increasing the financial distress of the companies. The table below summarizes the debt-equity ratio undertaken in the LBO and interest rates at the time of the announcement of the deal for all the companies discussed.

Company	Debt-Equity Ratio	Date of Announcement	Prime Rate (percent)
Levi's	8:1	July 10, 1985	9.5%
Scoa	9:1	June 28, 1985	9.5
ARA	9:1	July 12, 1984	13
Metromedia	9:1	Dec 6, 1983	11
Thatcher	19:1	Nov 17, 1981	17
Brentano's	NA	May 22, 1981	20

It is clear from the table that the Metromedia, Levi's, Scoa, and ARA deals were struck when the prevailing conditions were favorable. In contrast, in 1981, the prime rate ranged from 17 to 20 percent. Typically, interest rates in LBO deals are set at 2 to 3 percent above prime. This, coupled with high debt-equity ratios, led to the enormous debt payments which both Thatcher and Brentano's had to service, and it ultimately caused them to go down the tubes.

The Investment Banker Reputation and Skill

The credibility and expertise of the investment banker plays a key role for an LBO to be a success. Enough evidence is presented in the situations described to show that all the LBO successes involved well-respected investment bankers. Metromedia had Boston Ventures Management, a "hot money" acquisition specialist, Scoa had Shearson Lehman and Drexel Burnham Lambert, ARA had Goldman, Sachs while Levi's enjoyed the services of Hellman & Friedman, a top San Francisco investment banker. These companies also had the services of the best and brightest bankers, like Salomon Brothers, Morgan Stanley, and First Boston.

On the other hand, Thatcher Glass and Brentano's retained the services of less well-known players such as Dominick & Dominick and Lansdowne Financial Services, respectively. These bankers had less extensive experience in leverage buyout transactions. The fact that other well-respected investment bankers refused to represent Thatcher should have been a warning to Dominick, but they persisted and went through with the deal, with calamitous results.

CHAPTER 2

VALUING A COMPANY: HOW IS IT DONE?

"Everything is worth what the purchaser is willing to pay for it."

Publius Syrus (circa 100 B.C.)

Value is in the eyes of the beholder. The perception of how much an asset is really worth is often not the same for each party. There are a host of factors, which, acting in concert, produce a perception of value for each side. These factors range from projections about the future performance of the economy and future competition in the industry to performance of the existing management. Also relevant is the extent to which accurate information about the company is available to the respective parties. It is precisely the differences in the perception of value which bring together the buyer and the seller in the first place. Negotiation takes place to reach a price at which the completion of the transaction is feasible.

In a leveraged buyout, the sellers are the existing shareholders of the company, and the buyers are usually members of the existing management group of the target backed by a small group of investors. The buyer could also be another corporation. A number of Wall Street investment firms such as Kohlberg Kravis Roberts & Co., Forstmann Little and Co.,

---

We appreciate the research, analysis, and writing done by Raj Chandaria. Without his very significant contribution, the completion of this valuation section would not have been possible.

41

and Clayton Dubilier have emerged as specialists in buying out publicly traded companies and taking them private. The purchase of the shares is financed by taking on large amounts of debt. The heavy debt burden results in the firm being funded by minuscule amounts of equity. This has several effects. On the plus side, it magnifies the return on equity to the new owners. It also increases the interest burden which has the beneficial side effect of reducing the firm's tax burden. Even with the Tax Reform Act of 1986, the tax burden can, in some cases, be reduced by revaluing the company's assets and taking increased depreciation charges. On the minus side, it increases the risk to the new owners. There is little margin of error if the forecasted cash flows do not become realized.

VALUE—GOLD IS IN THE EYE OF THE BEHOLDER

We will examine the various issues which affect the different perceptions of value arrived at by the parties involved in a leveraged buyout (LBO). In addition to investigating the different methods used by Wall Street pros to value a company, we will look at financing constraints imposed on an LBO, nonfinancial motivating factors such as the need for autonomy and power, and the conflict of interest issue. Each of these considerations affects the value that a party places on a company.

The most basic method of valuing a company is to add up the book value of all the assets, subtract the current and long-term liabilities against those assets and divide the remainder by the number of shares outstanding. This gives a benchmark figure for value. It is, however, highly misleading since those assets were recorded at their original cost. The value of plant, property, and equipment is most likely to be understated since the replacement cost of the property may be far in excess of its value on the company's books. In some cases, however, such as in industries where there is excess capacity, the actual selling price of assets may well be below book value. Hunt International, for example, sold its beet processing plants for $34.5 million compared to its book value of $105 million. The use of accelerated depreciation methods has increased the distortion of the value of fixed assets on numerous balance sheets. The book value of inventory and marketable securities, valued at the lower of cost or market value, may also provide a misleading picture of the true worth of these assets.

THE GOING PRICE

A favorite method used by analysts to value a company is to estimate the market or replacement cost of its assets. This is best illustrated by considering the Holly Sugar case. Some analysts thought that the chief executive officer, Michael Buchsbaum, was playing games with reported earnings by stockpiling valuable inventories of refined sugar. Since the inventory is carried on the books at historical cost, it could be a ready source of profit when the company is taken private. The profits would be sheltered by the high debt that the company would presumably take on in an LBO. In the meantime, Holly has been selling repurchased sugar at a slim margin of only one or two cents a pound.

Another situation was described in a *Barron's* article entitled "BUYOUT OR SELLOUT? Are Shareholders Getting a Raw Deal?" Lauren R. Rublin reported on a management LBO offer by Stanwood Corporation, an apparel maker traded on the American Stock Exchange. The management bid of $9 per share was evaluated by Rublin and others as being totally inadequate. The argument, fairly typical of the method used by many analysts to arrive at a minimum price, was as follows:

> The company boasted current assets of $68 million, including $1.4 million in cash, $24 million in receivables, and $41.4 million in inventory. Liabilities, including $14.7 million in long-term debt add up to $55.2 million. The difference between the two is $12.8 million or almost $8.50 a share, in

net working capital. Stanwood also has a LIFO reserve of $4.4 million, which works out to another $2.85 or so a share and a pension plan overfunded by $3 million, or a little more than $2 a share. Finally, the company owns a pile of property in Knoxville....It's not prime Manhattan property, to be sure.... Still the buildings are worth something, and in any case, are valued on the company's books at $10.4 million or about $6.75 a share.

The total amounts to $20.10 a share, more than double management's bid of $9.00.

"BREAKING UP IS HARD TO DO"— OR IS IT?

Another method which is frequently used in valuing an LBO is by determining what its component divisions or business segments would be worth if spun off and sold. An example of this is Revlon, where the management opted for an LBO after getting commitments to purchase the cosmetics line for $900 million and the Reheis Chemical and Norcliff Thayer divisions for $350 million. Revlon management had its own estimate of the value of the health care business, a segment that it wished to retain after the LBO. Lazard Frères & Co. Revlon's investment bankers had valued the Vision-Care and NHL divisions at $600 to $700 million. The Technicon, Medical Diagnostics, and Ethical Pharmaceuticals segments were valued by analysts at approximately $1.1 billion, bringing the breakup value to approximately $3 billion. Obviously, if the value placed by prospective purchasers on the different segments of the company exceeds the current market value of the company as a whole, there is an incentive for a potential investor to buy out the shares of the company and either sell or operate the businesses.

Interestingly, between 1981 and 1987, 260 public companies have gone private. Of these, about 30 have been taken public again or have been broken up through asset sales. The average increase for these 30 has been about 150 percent.

Not bad for the incumbent management. Indeed, the following table indicates the miraculous change in market values resulting from breaking up the firm's assets.

Company	LBO Price on Acquisition Date	Estimated Value on Sale Date
Beatrice	$6.2 billion	$10 billion
Blue Bell	$470 million	$792 million
Metromedia	$1.1 billion	$6.5 billion
Fred Meyer	$420 million	$900 million
SFN	$450 million	$1.1 billion
Uniroyal	$900 million	$1.4 billion

Management certainly did well. They pocket the difference between the breakup value and the amount paid for the LBO. The minimum return in the above examples is 55 percent. No wonder many investors are asking, "Is something fishy going on here?"

"WALL STREET ZEROES IN ON CASH FLOW"

A Dun's *Business Month* article in July 1985 reviewing the increasing popularity of LBOs and takeovers stated "Cash flow is the new gospel, and financial analysts, investors and takeover specialists praise its power....Wall Street began to grasp this distinction largely in the wake of numerous LBOs—the feasibility of which are a function of cash flow projections as well as of the collateral value of assets." The 1985 LBO offer from Macy's management prompted comment in *The Wall Street Journal's* "Heard on the Street" column.

> Already some retailing analysts and investors have discarded their old valuation methods because of Macy's proposal. New York-based Oppenheimer & Co had previously estimated the value of a retailing stock at six times free cash flow, or cash flow remaining after required expenditures such as interest. Following the Macy's proposal, which the securities firm believes is worth slightly more than nine times Macy's cash

flow, Oppenheimer now is advising its clients to use a multiple of eight times free cash flow to estimate the theoretical value of retailing buyouts. Cash flow is considered as a better measure of a firm's true value because earnings figures are distorted by accounting conventions concerning depreciation and change in working capital.

It is from the level and predictability of cash flow that the large amount of debt typically taken on in LBOs, can be serviced. The maximum price that should be paid is therefore dependent on today's forecasted future cash flows.

Cash flow is one of the most misunderstood concepts in finance. It represents the funds which are available to the firm to meet both debt and equity payments. In other words, cash flow can be used to meet interest and principal payments to debt holders as well as equity contributions of dividends, share repurchases, and reinvestment in the firm.

If one begins the cash flow calculation with net income, it is necessary to make a number of adjustments to obtain cash flow. For example, one must add back all noncash expenses such as depreciation, which were originally subtracted from revenues to arrive at net income. Since interest payments were also subtracted out to arrive at net income, they must also be added back. But an adjustment must be made for the tax benefit of the interest payments. As a result, not the full interest payment but [(1 − tax rate) × interest payment] is added back to net income to obtain cash flow.

Two further adjustments must be made to net income. The first is a working capital adjustment. If inventory, for example, is projected to increase over time, the firm will have fewer funds available to distribute to debt and equity holders. In other words, increases in working capital items such as inventory decrease cash flow. Similarly, decreases in working capital items increase cash flow.

The second adjustment deals with capital expenditures. As capital expenditures increase, fewer funds are distributable to shareholders and debt holders. These relationships can be seen in the Holly Sugar cash flow calculations.

In order to determine the value of equity, several steps must be taken. First, using cash flow the value of assets is determined.

CASH FLOW—THE KEY TO MEASURING VALUE

The value of assets is equivalent to the present value of the firm's cash flow. In other words, if next year's cash flow is expected to grow at a steady rate g, and is discounted at a cost of capital r, the present value of all future cash flow is the value of the firm's assets. For example, if next year's cash flow is expected to be $10 million, with an anticipated growth rate of 8 percent and a cost of capital of 12 percent, the value of the firm's assets can be calculated as

$$\text{Asset value} = PV(\text{cash flow})$$

$$= \frac{10(1.08)}{1.12} + \frac{10(1.08)^2}{(1.12)^2} + \frac{10(1.08)^3}{(1.12)^3} + \dots \quad (1)$$

$$\text{Asset value} = \frac{.10}{.12 - .08} = \frac{10}{.04} = \$250 \text{ million} \quad (2)$$

As can be seen, this results in an asset value of $250 million. The shortcut in (2), where the cash flow is divided by $(r - g)$, is a standard simplification of the cash flow growth formulation seen in (1). It is applicable in situations where the cash flows are expected to continue growing at the steady rate g.

To determine g, we assess the firm's anticipated growth rate. For example, if the firm's cash flows are expected to grow 50 percent in year 1 and decline 50 percent in year 2, the arithmetic average growth rate is 0 percent. But let's look at a simple example. If we start with a cash flow of $100 and increase it 50 percent, the following year's flow is $150. If the next year's flow is then reduced by 50 percent, the corresponding cash flow is $75. In other words, the arithmetic average produces a 0 percent change from $100, an obviously incorrect result. To obtain the correct cash flow we use the fact that $100 invested for one period results in a value of $100 × (1 + rate of return), or in our case $100 × (1.50) = $150. Then $150 invested for one period results in $150 × (1 + rate of return) or $150 × (.50) = $75. In other words, $75 equals $100 multiplied by the average rate of return compounded for two periods. Thus,

$$\$100 \times (1 + \text{Average rate of return})^2 = \$75$$

or

$$\text{Average rate of return} = -.134$$

If one starts out with $100 and loses 13.4 percent each period for two periods, the final principal amount is $75. The name given to the calculated value of −13.4 percent is the geometric average return. In general, it can be determined using the following relationship:

$$\text{Initial cash flow } (1 + \text{Geometric average return})^N$$
$$= \text{Initial cash flow} \times (1 + \text{Rate of return}_1)$$
$$\times (1 + \text{Rate of return}_2)$$

While the calculation of g may have seemed complex to many students of finance, the cost of capital is a more difficult concept. Though the cost of debt is straightforward enough, the cost of equity poses the problems. First, the cost of capital is a weighted average of debt and equity, weighted by the percentages of debt and equity in the firm's capital structure. The costs are on an after-tax basis, so for example, if the firm's cost of debt is 8 percent and the tax rate is 34 percent, the after-tax cost is .08 × 66 or 5.28 percent.

Let's now turn to the cost of equity. A basic premise in determining the cost of equity is that the greater the risk, the greater the expected return. The cost of equity is indeed defined as the rate of return required by investors to reward them sufficiently for the risk they are accepting in making an equity investment. An investor who invests in a stock expects to receive a return at least as great as the risk free rate found in T-bills. If not, the investor would always be better off getting a higher yield with less risk by investing in T-bills. Many on Wall Street therefore calculate the required rate of return as the risk free rate plus a factor related to risk. This factor is often called the *beta (β) factor*. In particular, the greater the risk, the greater the beta and the greater the required return. If the market goes up, those stocks with high betas will typically go up more than those with low betas. A similar pattern emerges when the market goes down. Those stocks with high betas will likely fall more than those with low betas. A beta of 1 reflects the beta of the market. A high beta stock might have a beta of 2, while a low beta stock might find its beta as .6. The betas are regularly calculated by many of the major brokerage firms such as Merrill Lynch. Typically, the required return on equity is found using a relationship analysts on Wall Street and academics around the world call the capital asset pricing model (CAPM), or simply modern portfolio theory:

Required return on equity = Risk free rate

+ Beta (Expected return on market − Risk free rate)

Thus, if the risk free rate is 6 percent, the expected return on the market is 12 percent and a firm's beta is 1.5, the required return is calculated to be 15 percent.

If the company has 20 percent debt and 80 percent equity in its capital structure, the weighted average cost of capital can now be simply calculated:

$$.20 \times 5.28 + .8 \times 15 = 13.06$$

The cost of capital is now determined, except for one thing. An LBO plays havoc with the firm's capital structure. Increasing the debt levels significantly, an LBO usually increases the risk in owning the stock. As a result, the required rate of return commensurately increases.

When adjusting for the leverage taken on in an LBO, two steps are necessary. First, the beta is "unlevered" and then it is "relevered" for the new debt absorbed in the LBO. This process is predicated on beta increasing as additional amounts of debt are incorporated into the capital structure. The process of "unlevering" and "relevering" is calculated as follows:

Unlevering

$$\text{Beta}_{\text{unlevered}} = \frac{\text{Beta}_{\text{old debt}}}{1 + (1 - \text{Tax rate}) \times \dfrac{\text{Old debt}}{\text{Old equity}}}$$

Relevering

$$\text{Beta}_{\text{new debt}} = \text{Beta}_{\text{unlevered}} \left[1 + (1 - \text{Tax rate}) \times \frac{\text{New debt}}{\text{New equity}} \right]$$

In the Mary Kay LBO, for example, the beta obtained from Value Line (based upon Mary Kay's old debt) was 1.3. Unlevering reduced the beta to 1.08 and relevering increased it to 4.05. Obviously, with a beta of 4.05, the required return on equity skyrocketed from 16.9 percent based on Mary Kay's old debt to 36.3 percent based on the post-LBO leverage. This increase resulted in the cost of capital increasing from 9.48 percent to 14.05 percent.

Ironically, the vast increase in required return on equity does not always have a market impact on the weighted cost of capital. Sometimes, because of the small percentage of equity in the new capital structure, even a sizable required return will only have a marginal effect on the cost of capital. While it is more accurate to adjust for leverage, as in the Mary Kay, Dr Pepper, or Macy's examples, analysts frequently determine the weighted average cost of capital using figures unadjusted of a changing capital structure. For example, see the case of Holly Sugar.

Now, since we know what is the relevant cash flow and how to determine both the cost of capital, r, and the growth rate in cash flow, g, it is a simple calculation to determine asset value. From this figure, as in the case of Dr Pepper and Macy's, we simply subtract the firm's debt burden to obtain the value of its equity. Then, dividing by the number of shares, we obtain the price per share which the company is worth based on the assumed values of r, g, and the initial cash flow figure used.

It is interesting to note that it is possible to calculate the price per share using the present values of expected dividends instead of the present value of cash flows. For example, in the case of steady growth in dividends, one can use the relationship

$$\text{Price/share} = \frac{\text{Expected dividends per share}}{\text{Cost of equity} - \text{Dividend growth rate}}$$

In other words, in the numerator one uses the expected dividends instead of expected cash flow. And in the denominator, we substitute the cost of equity for the cost of capital and the expected growth rate in dividends for the expected growth rate in cash flows. With these changes, we can estimate the value of a firm.

NONFINANCIAL FACTORS

The Necessity of Timely Information

Since the future prospects of the company, both short and long term, are best known to those people who are responsible for day-to-day operations, the information advantage that the management has cannot be overstated. Although managements are generally expected to provide adequate information to alternative bidders for the company, several cases can be cited where information has been withheld or delayed so as to alter a bidder's perception of value. In the Dr Pepper leveraged buyout, timely access to information played a major role. In fact DPCC Acquisition Corp., a Castle & Cooke Inc. subsidiary, withdrew its $24 a share bid against management's bid of only $22 due to insufficient information upon which to "verify the financial assumptions on which the $24 offer was based." The DPCC team physically had the door shut in its face when it went to Dr Pepper's offices to inspect the books. In the KKR–led Beatrice LBO, 100 potential bidders were identified at the last minute and on Monday, November 11, 1985, a 4-inch thick package of financial information was distributed. But interestingly, KKR had had access to this information one month earlier, since mid-October. By Wednesday, November 13, Beatrice's board had accepted KKR's bid of $50 a share against Hutton's bid of $48. This is despite the fact that Hutton hinted that they might have bid higher given more time to examine the data. Forty-eight hours was just not long enough to plow through 4 inches worth of financial data.

Management Interests: Me First, Stockholders Second

The basis of the separation of ownership and management is that management is obliged to serve the best interests of the owners. Management is supposed to maximize shareholder wealth. In a leveraged buyout, where management wishes to buy out the existing shareholders, it has a conflicting interest; it wishes to minimize the price paid to shareholders. Shareholders obviously can refuse to sell their shares to management and would like, possibly through the process of competitive bidding, to get a higher price. Nevertheless, one can find instances of the conflict of interest affecting value. Stephen Fraiden, a merger law specialist at Fried, Frank, Harris, Shriver and Jacobson, speaking about management LBOs, states "I think there will be some that won't pass the smell test." William Klein II, a class action lawyer who has brought class action suits against many managements involved in LBOs argues that "the LBO is a parasitic device, where the tender offer is not. I'll go one step further: The LBO is...a scam." In the Dr Pepper case, W. W. Clement's initial reaction, when asked if he regarded a $24 bid as acceptable, had been to tell them "to get lost." Subsequently, Clements announced a management/Forstmann Little LBO at $22, which was ultimately carried out. In the Revlon case, Michel C. Bergerac had stated at the start of hostilities that he would not consider any offer below $65. Yet, when Revlon put forward the management/Forstmann Little LBO, the bid price was only $56. If management had put its money where its mouth was, and bid $65, who knows what the final price would have been. Management usually has a great deal of credibility among shareholders and it is apparent that this conflict of interest, while not having an excessive impact on perceptions of value, does influence the final price paid in an LBO.

The Ego Factor

The desire to escape from the constant scrutiny of Wall Street analysts and speculators with their emphasis on short-term results serves as a powerful motivating force for taking the company private. The more powerful this force, the higher the price that management is willing to pay. The $70 per share LBO bid by Macy's management took most analysts by surprise. Kidder Peabody's retailing analyst, Bob Simonson, commented on the thinking of management in an LBO. "Now I can do what I wanted to do all along. I was afraid that if I did it, every analyst on the Street would go into a catatonic fit." Simonson also hinted that the price that Macy's management had offered was higher than really necessary. The company was thus valued higher than it might have been in the absence of nonfinancial motivating factors. Going private eliminates the amount of time the executives must spend with investors and regulators. Congoleum's Byron Radaker said that he once spent 80 percent of his time with the two groups. "When I reported for work the first day after the company went private, I got the greatest surprise of my life. I had nothing to do." However, this relief can be short lived. The interests of the debt holders replace those of the stockholders. Also, some time in the future the company may well go public again in order for the management and shareholders to cash in. Radaker states that "a lot of people miss the point: you have the obligation to sell it out."

The style and personality traits of key executives may also influence the perceived value of the company. The Value Line report on Holly Sugar states "Clearly the market is not valuing Holly Sugar on the basis of its reported earnings, but rather on the distinct possibility that the company may be taken private at $75 to $100 per share by Chairman Michael Buchsbaum if the needed financing can be lined up." Some analysts, at the end of 1985, claimed that Buchsbaum was already running Holly like a private company. He had surrounded himself with a very cooperative board. Buchsbaum, who is reported to sometimes answer his phone "Genghis Khan," has been accused of being egotistical and arrogant. While it may be true, it is also clear that the market was betting on his intent to take the company private.

Steamrollers

The pressure applied by the various players in the LBO process does exert an important factor in determining the value of a company. For example, consider the $50 paid for Beatrice. When faced by a rival bidder, KKR threatened to withdraw its bid unless it was accepted by the Beatrice board during the next couple of days. The KKR offer was accepted by the Beatrice board. This gave no time for E. F. Hutton to raise a counterbid, a bid which may well have increased the returns to Beatrice shareholders. Indeed, a Beatrice source acknowledged that the Dart-Hutton group wasn't given enough time to assemble its corporate-bidder combination and get financing.

FINANCING CONSTRAINTS

LBOs are by definition financed by taking on a large amount of debt. The price that the buyers in an LBO offer to the sellers must be acceptable to the lenders. A price in excess of what the company is really worth would mean that the buyers would have to take on more debt than the assets of the company are capable of servicing. The value perceived by lenders is therefore just as important as that perceived by the buyers. Not long after *The Wall Street Journal* announced Macy's buyout bid at $70 per share, there was speculation that it may be reduced by $1 to $4 because Goldman, Sachs & Co. was having difficulty in arranging financing at that price. One investment banker commented "Everyone thinks $70 is way overpriced. I assume there will have to be a reduction in the offering price." Michael Buchsbaum's attempt to take Holly Sugar private in an LBO at $65 per share was abandoned when the General Electric Credit Corporation (GECC) declined financing. This occurred because Holly's earnings were erratic, cash flow volatile, and its fixed assets did not provide adequate collateral for the debt.

THE BOTTOM LINE

The importance of valuing the company correctly cannot be stressed enough in the case of LBOs. The "winners curse," where the winning bidder pays too much, is of particular relevance here because interest is being paid on an amount often greater than the firm could have presumably financed prudently. If the cash flows predicted is not realized, the company will not be able to cover its large interest expense. The firm may have to sell off assets if it can, or may eventually have to file for Chapter XI. As Robert Davis, head of Dean Witter Reynolds' LBO group said of KKR's plan to take Wometco private, "Wometco's is a very high price—$842 million for a company with $31 million in earnings. I know the only way they can pull it off is by selling assets." Although not widely publicized, some firms involved in LBOs other than Brentano's and Thatcher Glass have indeed gone through Chapter XI. Two of these were Eli Witt and Bristol Brass. In at least two other cases, Cobblers and AMC Corp, the equity investors lost their money.

The difficulty in valuing a company is due to the number of estimates used in the calculation. In the cash flow method, depending on how optimistic or pessimistic one is about the future, a large range of cash flows need to be estimated. Even in the case where a firm liquidates some of its assets, unless the firm already has a signed contract for the sale, the firm may be overoptimistic as to what the selling price might be. And in some cases even book value may be greater than what the market is willing to pay.

In valuing a company, one cannot forget the importance of the nonfinancial factors. In many cases, a lack of information can lead to overvaluation. Management egos may also help raise the price, especially if there is an outside bidder who threatens the safety of the executives' employment. Top dollars are being paid for companies which are not considered industry leaders. The question is whether future cash flows justify this.

The price being paid, not infrequently, exceeds a reasonable estimate of the company's value. What will happen if business conditions worsen and/or interest rates rise? Speculation is that due to overvaluation, more LBOs will fail in the future. Therefore, bidders are caught in a catch-22. A low and perhaps accurate bid may not be high enough to win the company. Yet, too high a bid may eventually lead to cash flow problems.

Macy's: Shopping for an LBO

On October 21, 1985, the senior management of R. H. Macy & Co., Inc., announced a plan to take the retailer private in a $3.58 billion leveraged buyout. The proposal, the first leveraged buyout proposal for a major retailer, offered shareholders $70 a share, an amount that represented about 19 times 1985 earnings and 2.7 times book value. Following the announcement, the stock, which had closed at 47⅛ the previous day, surged 16⅛ a share to close at 63¼.

In making the buyout announcement, Edward S. Finkelstein, Macy's chairman and chief executive officer, and Mark S. Handler, the president and chief operating officer, indicated that their new management group would include "an unusually large number" of Macy's executives. In fact, the desire to retain top-management talent was one of the major reasons for the buyout proposal. Equally important, was the

---

We appreciate the research, analysis, and writing done by Jack Weis. Without his very significant contribution, the completion of the Macy's case would not have been possible.

desire of management to free itself from the pressures of short-term performance required in a public company.

At the time of the announcement details of the financing structure were not yet finalized. Nevertheless, the announcement was made because takeover rumors on Wall Street during the prior week had caused heavy trading of the company's stock with a corresponding jump in price of more than $4.00 a share. Despite the lack of firm financing commitments, Finkelstein stated that $70 a share was offered because it was "the maximum price that anyone would pay." He also felt "fully confident" that at that price Goldman, Sachs & Co., the management group's investment bankers, would be able to arrange the necessary financing. Finkelstein further indicated that the proposal would be formally presented to Macy's board once financing was in place. However, he stated that during the six months management was considering the buyout, the board had been consulted and the directors were generally supportive of the $70 a share price.

The initial reaction by industry analysts was that, at best, the price was high enough to discourage other potential bidders. In fact, many analysts openly speculated that Macy's would have trouble raising the needed financing. As the weeks passed following the initial announcement, skepticism mounted. Finally, on December 19, 1985, two months after the initial buyout news, financing difficulties forced the management group to lower its offer to $68 a share. This proposal was approved by the company's board the following month, on January 16. The board also announced that a shareholder meeting to vote on the proposal would be held in the spring.

During the period between the announcement and approval by the board, a total of four class action lawsuits were filed by shareholders against management and the board of directors. These suits argued that management and the board violated their fiduciary responsibilities by accepting an unfair and inadequate price which was not based on any appraisal of the company's value. They went on to conjecture that management's sole reason for the LBO was to obtain ownership and control for themselves at the most favorable price.

FROM SMALL SHOP TO THE WORLD'S LARGEST STORE

R. H. Macy & Co., Inc., commonly known as Macy's, is the nation's ninth largest general merchandise retailer, measured in terms of both sales and assets. The company is recognized nationwide because of its sponsorship of the popular annual Thanksgiving Day parade in New York City and because of its association with the popular Christmas movie, "Miracle on 34th Street."

The company was founded on October 27, 1858, when Rowland Hussey Macy, a 36-year-old former Nantucket whaler, opened a small, fancy dry goods store on Sixth Avenue in New York City after four unsuccessful attempts at retailing in Massachusetts and California. His first day's sales were $11.06.

Beginning in 1866, and continuing throughout the 1870s, R. H. Macy began expanding by acquiring adjacent stores. By the time of his death in 1877, the dry goods store had become a department store carrying a full range of products.

Then four years before the turn of the century, Isidor and Nathan Straus, who first opened a china and glassware concession in 1874, obtained complete control of the company. Throughout the next three generations, until the retirement of Jack Straus in 1969, a member of the Straus family ran Macy's. Jack Straus continued to serve as honorary chairman until his death in 1985.

In 1902, Macy's opened its new Herald Square store. Through a series of additions during the 1920s and early 1930s, the store grew to encompass the entire block between Broadway and Seventh Avenue and between 34th and 35th Streets. The store remains the chain's flagship store and, with approximately 2,151,000 square feet, is considered the world's largest store, containing more space than most large regional shopping malls.

In 1919, the firm incorporated as R. H. Macy & Company, Inc., and in 1922, it issued its first public stock. During the 1920s and 1940s, Macy's undertook an aggressive expansion program, acquiring retailers in New Jersey, California, Georgia, Ohio, and Missouri. These acquisitions formed the foundation for the five operating divisions of Macy's which existed up through 1985—Macy's New York, Bamberger's, Macy's California, Davison's (since renamed Macy's Atlanta), and Macy's Midwest.

Beginning in 1983, Macy's, through its New York division, began a program of store expansion in the Sunbelt. Since 1983, it opened five new stores totaling almost 1.2 million square feet in Miami, Houston, and Dallas. Within a year of the planned LBO, they intended to open new stores in Houston, New Orleans, and Birmingham, Alabama.

Simultaneously, Macy's was in the process of selling off the Midwest division stores. From 1982 through 1985, the company closed five stores in Ohio and Missouri and on August 5, 1985, it sold its four remaining Ohio stores. Subsequent to the buyout proposal, it also sold the 12 remaining Midwest division stores in Missouri and Kansas. With these sales, Macy's operated 83 stores in 12 states containing approximately 22.3 million square feet of store space and employing over 54,000 workers.

A BLIP AFTER FIVE YEARS OF VIRTUOSO PERFORMANCE

For the fiscal year ended August 3, 1985, Macy's sales were $4.2 billion. With only a 7 percent increase in sales, fiscal 1985 represented the smallest growth in over a decade. Particularly disturbing was the fact that its gross operating margin declined 4.8 percent and net earnings dropped 13.7 percent. During this period the company also experienced the departure of seven key executives. While Macy's itself did not offer any explanation for the slump, several were provided by industry analysts. They included an overall slump in the retail industry, the high cost of Macy's expansion into the

Sunbelt, and an expensive program to upgrade customer service and introduce more high-margin, private-label goods.

Macy's 1985 performance, however, was in clear contrast to its performance during the previous five years. As indicated by the Peer Group Comparison table, during the period of 1980 to 1984, Macy's sales growth of 14.6 percent was slightly above industry standards. But its net operating margins and profit margins were significantly better than its peer group's, averaging 11.2 versus 7.2 percent and 4.9 versus 3.4 percent, respectively.

Furthermore, Macy's sales per square foot, a rough measure of productivity, averaged $137 during this five-year period compared to an average of $108 for the peer group.

Macy's management attributed their historical growth and profitability to strategies of store expansion and modernization, innovative merchandising, productivity and cost control, and management development. Macy's self-assessment is generally supported by knowledgeable industry observers. Under the stewardship of Edward Finkelstein, Macy's emerged to become one of the nation's most successful department store chains. Its management is considered one of the best in the industry and its expansion program has been considered highly successful.

THE DEAL

In order to feel the sense of the uncertainty faced by the investment group, both the proposed LBO and the valuation analysis will be discussed using only information that was available prior to the actual completion of the deal. Indeed, the following analysis uses management's assumptions contained in its preliminary prospectus filed with the Securities and Exchange Commission (SEC) on February 19, 1985.

The proposed leveraged buyout would offer existing common shareholders $68 a share for their stock and would redeem preferred shares at $107.50 a share. The buyout would require approximately $3.687 billion worth of financing. Of that amount, $3.322 billion would be financed

MACY'S
Peer Group Comparisons (1980–1984)

	Allied	Associated Dry Goods	Carter, Hawley, Hale	Dillard's	Federated	May	Mercantile	Average	Macy's
1984 Sales (millions)	$3.971	$4.107	$3.724	$1.277	$9.672	$4.744	$1.707	—	$4.065
Sales Growth									
1980	2.6%	9.5%	9.4%	20.3%	8.5%	6.5%	3.8%	8.7%	15.3%
1981	20.5	40.9	9.0	26.0	12.2	8.0	14.6	18.7	11.9
1982	17.7	15.9	6.4	20.0	8.9	7.4	12.5	12.7	12.1
1983	14.3	16.6	18.9	19.1	12.9	15.3	13.8	15.8	16.4
1984	8.0	10.5	2.5	50.7	11.3	12.6	5.0	14.4	17.2
Average	12.6%	18.7%	9.2%	27.2%	10.8%	10.0%	9.9%	14.1%	14.6%
Net Operating Margins									
1980	6.7%	6.0%	6.4%	3.7%	7.3%	7.3%	7.9%	6.5%	9.9%
1981	6.9	6.9	5.4	5.9	7.6	7.8	9.2	7.1	10.4
1982	6.6	6.8	5.5	5.5	6.7	7.8	9.8	7.0	11.0
1983	8.1	7.6	5.2	6.3	7.9	8.7	10.6	7.8	12.4
1984	8.0	7.0	4.3	6.6	6.7	9.2	10.3	7.4	12.4
Average	7.3%	6.9%	5.4%	5.6%	7.2%	8.2%	9.6%	7.2%	11.2%

MACY'S
Peer Group Comparisons (1980–1984) (concluded)

	Allied	Associated Dry Goods	Carter, Hawley, Hale	Dillard's	Federated	May	Mercantile	Average	Macy's
				Return on Sales					
1980	3.7%	2.7%	2.2%	1.8%	4.4%	3.7%	3.8%	3.2%	4.3%
1981	3.2	2.5	1.6	2.7	3.7	3.7	4.6	3.1	4.5
1982	2.8	2.5	1.6	3.1	3.0	3.9	4.9	3.1	4.6
1983	3.5	3.1	1.9	4.0	3.9	4.4	5.1	3.7	5.4
1984	3.5	2.9	2.4	3.9	3.4	4.5	5.0	3.7	5.5
Average	3.3%	2.7%	1.9%	3.1%	3.7%	4.0%	4.7%	3.4%	4.9%
				Sales per Square Foot					
1980	$ 76	$ 71	$ 98	$ 74	$120	$ 83	$110	$ 90	$113
1981	75	79	103	83	131	87	124	97	121
1982	88	93	108	85	132	91	139	105	132
1983	99	109	124	100	148	103	163	121	151
1984	107	116	139	102	160	114	168	129	170
Average	$ 89	$ 94	$114	$ 89	$138	$ 96	$141	$108	$137

through additional debt, $300 million would be financed through equity, and the remaining $65 million through Macy's excess cash.

In order to illustrate the complexity of the deal, each of the financing components will be described:

Bank Debt

Macy's bank debt is projected to consist of a $795 million seven-year loan, a $225 million one-year loan, and a revolving working capital loan. Interest will initially be set at 1.5 percent above Citibank's prime rate, with the seven-year loan gradually declining to .5 percent above prime.

At the time the buyout was approved by Macy's directors, Citibank and Manufacturers Hanover Trust Company were each committed to provide 10 percent of the total bank debt and to use their best efforts to form a syndicate of banks to finance the remainder.

Senior Real Estate Debt

Macy's management anticipates obtaining at least $800 million in nonrecourse 11 percent loans secured by first or second mortgages. These mortgages are on the 75 stores not sold or financed to pay off the one-year bank note, with Prudential Insurance acting as the lead lender. Should the amount that Macy's receives under this real estate loan exceed $800 million, the excess will be used to retire the seven-year bank loan.

Senior Notes

Macy's expects to obtain $200 million of senior notes with three insurance companies, Equitable Life Assurance Society, Teachers Insurance and Annuity, and New England Mutual Life Insurance Company, committing a total of $121.5 million. The notes will be for a term of 10 years at an interest rate of 13.5 percent.

Senior Subordinated Debt

General Electric Credit Corporation has committed itself to purchase $400 million worth of senior subordinated debentures. These debentures will have a 12-year term and bear interest at a rate of 14.5 percent.

Subordinated Debt
Macy's anticipates raising $450 million through the sale of subordinated debentures to the public. Macy's management assumed that the debentures would be for a term of 15 years at an interest rate of 15.5 percent. Beginning in 1997, Macy's will pay a 20 percent annual sinking fund which will retire 80 percent of the issue prior to maturity.

Subordinated Discount Debt
Macy's also expects to raise $250 million through the public issuance of 20-year subordinated discount debentures. These debentures have a principal value of $770 million. They will not bear any interest during the first 7 years and are then assumed to carry a coupon of 16.5 percent in years 8 through 20. Coupled with the original discount, the annual yield to maturity has been estimated at 17 percent. Macy's will be required to make sinking fund principal payments of 20 percent of the face amount beginning in the 16th year.

Common Stock
The Macy management group, which is anticipated to include at least 300 of Macy's managers, will purchase 100 percent of the shares of common stock at the time of the buyout for $17.5 million. However, this stock will represent only 20 percent of the total common stock once the preferred shares have been converted.

Preferred Stock
Macy's plans to raise $282.5 million through the sale of convertible preferred stock to several of its creditors such as GECC and the senior note holders, as well as to Goldman, Sachs, other institutional investors, and certain sophisticated individual investors.

While the above components represented the management group's best estimate of what the final financial structure would be, a number of issues remained to be settled. The private financing must still be arranged, the SEC must approve the public debt, and the buyout plan must still be approved by two thirds of the shareholders before it can be certain that the buyout would go through and before the final financial structure would be known. Until all the financing is committed, it is likely that there would be changes in the amounts, terms, and interest rates of the various components. Nevertheless, as mentioned earlier, the valuation analysis will use management's estimates and other information available at the time of the buyout proposal.

VALUING THE DEAL: IS IT FAIR?

In analyzing the appropriateness of the proposed buyout, it is obviously critical to determine a reasonable value for the company. Having done that, it is then necessary to look at the risk inherent in the proposed financial structure.

In determining value, there are three widely used approaches. The first approach is the asset valuation method, which looks at the current value of a company's underlying assets by adjusting the book value. The other two approaches, the earnings valuation method and the discounted cash flow method, value the company based on its expected future earnings and cash flow potential. Because most companies, except those experiencing a steady decline in sales and earnings, can expect to create incremental value through the productive use of their corporate assets, the two earnings valuation approaches will generally give a more accurate assessment of a company's value. Nevertheless, it is helpful to analyze a company using all three approaches.

The Adjusted Book Value Approach

The asset valuation method begins with the company's stated book value and adjusts it for differences between the historic cost and the market value of various assets. In the case of Macy's, as of August 3, 1985, the company had a book value of $1.332 billion, or $25.87 per share. As indicated by the Adjusted Book Value Methodology table, making adjustments for the market value of inventories, property, plant and equipment, and factoring in the surplus assets in the company's pension plan, raises this value to $2.197 billion, or $42.67 per share.

However, it is clear that the public market was looking beyond the asset value to the ongoing earnings potential of the company. It is best evidenced by the fact that on the day of the buyout announcement, Macy's stock was trading at 47⅛ per share.

Earnings Valuation

The earnings valuation method is an improvement over the asset valuation method in that it considers the company's ability to generate earnings. The valuation of the company is based on capitalizing earnings per share at some price-earnings ratio.

The proposed buyout at $68 per share represents an

MACY'S
The Adjusted Book Value Methodology

Adjusted book value: (in millions)	
Total current assets	$ 979.0
− Total current liabilities	686.9
= Working capital	$ 292.1
+ Increased value of inventories	51.9
+ Replacement value of property, plant and equipment	1,823.3
+ Surplus assets in pension plan	93.3
+ Other assets	283.8
= Replacement value of assets	$2,544.4
− Long-term debt	134.2
− Capitalized leases	50.5
− Other liabilities	162.9
= Adjusted book value*	$2,196.8
Stated Book Value ($ million)	1,332.0
Per Share Analysis†	
Adjusted book value per share	$42.67
Stated book value per share	$25.87

*As of August 3, 1985.
†Based on 51,485,357 shares.

amount equal to approximately 18.4 times 1985 earnings per share. At the time of the announcement, Macy's stock was trading at a P/E ratio of about 12.8, which was more in line with the company's average P/E ratio over the past three years of 11.8 and significantly above the average P/E ratio of 8.4 found among its peer group. Thus, by the earnings measure, the proposed buyout offer is well above what one would expect the company to be worth.

Unfortunately, while the earnings method is an improvement over the asset method, it is a very crude measure which looks only at current or historic earnings at one point in time. Thus, a discounted cash flow analysis, which looks at a range of projected cash flows over time and discounts them at the firm's cost of capital, is a more accurate method of valuing a company.

Discounted Cash Flow Valuation

This methodology determines value by taking a projected stream of cash flows and discounting them at the appropriate discount rate. Though it sounds simple and straightforward, the process, if done correctly, requires both an in-depth understanding of the principles and tedious number crunching. With respect to the principles, the valuation consists of three steps:

1. Developing a set of base case scenario cash flows. Though it varies from case to case, it is usually done for a period of 7 to 10 years.
2. Deriving the appropriate discount rate, often referred to as the cost of capital.
3. Discounting the cash flows from step 1 at the cost of capital derived in step 2. After accounting for the value of existing debt, the value of the target's equity is obtained.

Step 1. The Base Case Scenario Cash Flows. The base case cash flows are based on the company's projections included in the February 19, 1986 prospectus. The assumptions underlying the projections include:

- Annual sales growth in existing stores—7.8 percent in 1987 and 1988, and 8.0 percent thereafter.
- New store openings of three or four per year through 1990, and two per year thereafter.
- A gross operating margin of 15.1 percent in 1987 and 14.9 percent thereafter.
- Capital expenditures in excess of $200 million in 1987 and 1988, and $156 million per year thereafter.
- Obtaining additional mortgage financing on its new stores in the amount of $100 million in 1987 and $75 million in 1988 and 1989.
- A corporate tax rate of 50 percent.

Based on these projections and several other assumptions regarding working capital (i.e., inventory, cash, accounts receivable, accounts payable, and other short-term financing), pro forma balance sheets and income statements for the 10-year period 1987–96 are derived. Equipped with these financial reports, we are ready to develop the cash flow needed for the valuation framework.

As illustrated in the Projected Cash Flow table, both the pro forma income statements and balance sheets are used in deriving these cash flows: We started with the income statement; first by adding the depreciation expense to the net income. In addition, any other noncash expenses are added back to the net income. Second, given that our initial objective is to assess the total after-tax cash flow available to both debt and equity holders, we add the term $(1 - t) \times$ interest expense. By doing so, we account for the fact that the interest expense reduces the tax bill, but it is also an amount available to creditors. The total after-tax cash flow is then obtained by further subtracting the increase in working capital and the amounts allocated to capital expenditures. Interestingly, as indicated by the table, although the cash flow from operations exhibits a significant increase over the period 1987–96, after accounting for the expected increase in working capital and capital expenditures, the net after-tax cash flow available to creditors and equity holders levels off around the $400 million level. The last two rows of the Pro-

MACY'S
Projected Cash Flow (in millions)

	1987	1988	1989	1990	1991	1992	1993	1994	1995	1996
Net income	($ 66)	($ 40)	($ 5)	$ 34	$ 78	$122	$169	$227	$295	$379
+ Depreciation	223	233	240	246	250	249	255	262	268	262
+ $(1-t)$ × Interest expense	245	246	252	256	254	261	276	317	310	306
+ Other noncash expenses	87	93	97	105	113	122	104	21	22	21
– Increase in working capital	133	129	42	69	214	266	338	208	328	437
– Capital expenditures	252	197	156	156	156	156	156	156	156	156
Total cash flow	$104	$206	$386	$416	$325	$332	$310	$463	$411	$375
Present value factor (10.5%)	.905	.818	.741	.670	.607	.549	.497	.449	.407	.368
Present value	94.1	168.5	286	278.7	197.3	182.3	154.1	207.9	167.2	138.0

jected Cash Flow table deal with the discounted value of these cash flows. We'll come back to discuss it once the appropriate discount rate is derived.

Step 2. Deriving the Appropriate Discount Rate. This step of the analysis is composed of three separate units. First, we have to assess the amount and cost of each of the debt financing instruments and calculate the weighted average of these costs. Second, we must adjust the rate of return required by stockholders (often referred to as the cost of equity) to reflect the fact that in the post-LBO period the firm's leverage is significantly higher than the one in the pre-LBO period. Third, given the proportions of the firm's financing obtained as debt and equity, and given the cost of each of these forms of financing, a simple weighted average cost of capital is calculated. The following briefly covers the three units of the cost of capital derivation.

Cost of Debt

Macy's sources of debt capital in the post-LBO period can be broken into seven general categories.

As illustrated by the Cost of Debt table, the largest debt component is a real estate mortgage ($800 million), followed by a bank loan ($795 million), subordinated debenture ($450 million), senior subordinated debentures ($400 million), subordinated discount debenture ($250 million), and senior notes ($200 million). In addition, Macy's indicated its intention to maintain $120 million of its existing (pre-LBO) long-term debt. The table provides the interest rate charged on each of these debt instruments and their respective weights as a percentage of the company's total debt. As indicated by the table, the cheapest source of debt is the existing long-term debt, bearing an 8 percent rate. However, this source amounted to only 4 percent of Macy's total debt. In contrast, about $1.3 billion of the debt is bearing interest rate more than a 13 percent. Once all these rates and weights are taken into account, Macy's before-tax weighted average cost of debt is determined to be 12.94 percent. However, given that interest payments can be deducted from Macy's income for

MACY'S
The Cost of Debt

Type of Debt	Interest Rate (percent)	Amount (millions)	Weight
Existing long-term debt	8.0%	$ 120	.04
Real estate mortgage	11.0	800	.27
Bank loan	12.0	795	.26
Senior notes	13.5	200	.07
Senior subordinated debentures	14.5	400	.13
Subordinated debentures	15.5	450	.15
Subordinated discount debentures	17.0	250	.08
Total		$3,015	1.00

Pretax cost of debt = .04 × 8 + .27 × 11 + ... + .08 × 17 = 12.94%
After-tax cost of debt = 12.94(1 − .50) = 6.47%

tax purposes, the relevant measure is the after-tax cost debt. Because Macy's management assumes a tax rate of 50 percent, the 12.94 percent pretax is effectively only 6.47 percent after tax.

Cost of Equity
We start with the basic relationship between risk and required rate of return. Our objective, given Macy's market risk, is to obtain an estimate for the minimum rate required by its stockholders. Some elaboration is needed. We are able to easily observe Macy's market risk prior to the LBO. Based on historical data we observe that Macy's beta is about 1.10. In other words, a 1 percent change in the market return was associated with a 1.1 percent change in Macy's stock. However, variability is closely related to leverage. Prior to the LBO, Macy's debt-to-equity ratio was .146. Using the relationship between market risk, tax rate and debt-equity ratio, we are able to estimate Macy's market risk (i.e., its beta) if it would have no debt. This is illustrated in Panel II of the Cost of Equity table.

MACY'S
The Cost of Equity

I. The Basic Relationship:

Cost of equity = Risk free rate + Market risk × Risk premium

II. Unleveraging Macy's Beta:

Beta with leverage = $\text{Beta}_{\text{no leverage}} \times [1 + (1 - t)\frac{D}{E}]$

$1.10 = \text{Beta}_{\text{no leverage}} \times [1 + (1 - .50).146]$

$\text{Beta}_{\text{no leverage}} = 1.02$

III. Macy's Post-LBO Beta:

Macy's post-LBO beta = $1.02 \times [1 + (1 - .50)10.05] = 6.15$

IV. Macy's Post-LBO Cost of Equity:

Macy's cost of equity = $7.6 + 6.15 \times 7.05 = 51\%$

This figure, often referred to as the unlevered beta, or operating beta, is 1.02 in the case of Macy's. Now, once we know the "no-debt" beta of Macy's, we are ready to incorporate the information on Macy's post-LBO capital structure. Given that it is expected to have $3.015 billion debt and $300 million in equity, the post-LBO debt-equity of 10.05 is used along with the firm's unlevered beta to obtain Macy's post-LBO beta of 6.15 (Panel III of the Cost of Equity table). Obviously, this is an extremely high figure for a market risk measure. However, a debt-equity ratio of 10 is similarly an exception in the world of corporate finance. As illustrated in Panel IV of the table, equipped with Macy's post-LBO beta, we plug it, along with the Treasury bill rate (7.6 percent) and the historically observed difference between the stock market return and the T-bill rate (7.05 percent), to obtain a cost of equity of 51 percent. Though 51 percent is a very high figure for the required rate of return on equity, one could learn by discussing LBOs with venture capitalists that it is well within their target range.

Weighted Average Cost of Capital
Once the costs and extent of financing have been worked out, the calculation of the weighted average cost of capital is straightforward.

MACY'S
Weighted Average Cost of Capital

Type of Capital	Cost (percent)	Amount (millions)	Weight
Debt	12.94%	$3,015	.91
Equity	51.00	300	.09
Total		$3,315	1.00

Weighted average cost of capital = .91 × 6.47 + .09 × 51 = 10.5%

As illustrated in the Weighted Average Cost of Capital table, Macy's debt constitutes about 91 percent of its total capital, with equity financing representing only 9 percent. After accounting for the cost of each of these components, Macy's cost of capital is estimated as 10.5 percent. This figure is then used in the valuation framework for discounting Macy's post-LBO projected cash flows.

Step 3. Valuation. By now we have all the input needed for valuing Macy's. In doing so, let us follow a systematic sequence of calculations.

a. We use the weighted average cost of capital of 10.5 percent as a discount rate. This is shown in the Projected Cash Flow table as the "present value factor." One dollar, expected to be received one year in the future, has a present value of 90.5 cents; for a two-year horizon, a dollar has a present value of 81.8 cents, and so on. First, we use these present value factors to discount Macy's projected cash flows for the period 1987–96. The discounted value of the cash flows are shown at the bottom of the table. For example, though Macy's investing group expects a $463 million net cash inflow in 1994, for the purpose of valuation, once discounted, it is worth (in terms of 1986 dollars) only $207.9 million. By adding up the discounted cash flows from the bottom of the Projected Cash Flow table we obtain an amount of $1,874 million. This represents the value to Macy's investing group of the projected cash flows for the period 1987–96.

b. Some assumptions should be made regarding the period following 1996. Following a review of the different assessments made by Macy's management, we use their projected compounded growth rate for the period 1989–96 (3.05 percent), as the best estimate for the post-1996 period. Under the assumption that Macy's cash flow following 1996 will grow at a rate of 3.05 percent per year and given a discount rate of 10.5 percent, the present value of the post-1996 cash flows (in terms of 1996 dollars) is derived as

$$PV = \frac{1}{r - g}$$

$$\frac{375 \, (1 + .0305)}{.105 - .0305} = \$5,187 \text{ million}$$

We just applied a relationship commonly used by finance professionals to derive the present value of a cash flow that grows at a constant rate. The term 375(1 + .0305) represents 1997's cash flow, which is assumed to be 3.05 percent higher than 1996's expected cash flow of $375. However, our objective is to obtain the value in terms of 1986 dollars. Therefore, the 5,187 million figure should be discounted back 10 years, which yields a value of $1,911 million.

c. Finally, in order to derive the value of Macy's equity, we add the present value of the cash flows for the period 1987–96 ($1,874 million), to the present value of the cash flows following 1996 ($1,911 million) and subtract Macy's existing debt ($120 million). This yields a value of $3.725 billion. Given that Macy's had 51.485 million shares of common stock, our valuation implies a value of $72.35 per share.

EPILOGUE

In March 1986, Chase Manhattan, Morgan Guaranty, and Bankers Trust refused to finance the deal. But it didn't stop Macy's from going private.

More than 78 percent of Macy's shares approved management's plan to take the company private. The deal had common shareholders receiving $68 a share and preferred holders receiving $107.50.

The buyout included a 347 member management group and was led by Finkelstein, the firm's chairman and chief executive officer. It included financing from a variety of sources, including $800 million from Prudential Insurance secured by mortgages on Macy's properties, $913 million in loans from banks and other institutions, $250 million in senior notes from more than two dozen insurance companies, and the placement of $282.5 million of preferred stock with investors.

Twenty percent of the new company's common stock went to the management group led by Finkelstein and 20 percent went to General Electric Credit Corporation.

Post-LBO financial results look good. Macy's sales outpaced projections in their first quarter as a private company, 16.4 percent versus 12.3 percent. Its huge debt burden is getting pared down. Macy's netted about $400 million from the sale of shopping center interests and used the funds to pay off some of their bank loans.

As long as the economy stays healthy, the largest LBO in retail history looks like it's going to payoff big to the 347 members of management who bought in.

Dr Pepper's Battleground: The Cola Wars and the Bidding Battles

THE FAT LADY SINGS

February 28, 1984 was Dr Pepper's last stockholder meeting. In an emotion-packed vote with many long-time shareholders crying, the proposal to take the company private through a

We appreciate the research, analysis, and writing done by Diane Kelly. Without her very significant contribution, the completion of the Dr Pepper case would not have been possible.

leveraged buyout was ratified. Stockholders would receive $22 per share. Dr Pepper would now be owned by 30 to 40 private holders, with senior management owning 11.5 percent of the company.

W. W. Clements, the down-to-earth chief executive officer, ended the meeting with a bit of a surprise. After announcing the ratification of the proposal, he exclaimed, "We all know the show's not over until the fat lady sings." With that, Melody Jones, a Dallas actress and singer dressed in a toga, entered singing "Auld Lang Syne." When it was over, Clements expressed relief by saying, "I thought it would be a unique way to end a stiff and formal meeting on a light note."

However, even when the show was over, there were still several unanswered questions. Did the $22 per share price represent the true value of the company? Had the shareholders been over- or underpaid for their equity in Dr Pepper? Did the $24 per share offer by DPCC Acquisition Corp., whose bid was rescinded, represent a more accurate valuation?

HOW SPICY IS THE PEPPER?

Dr Pepper Company manufactures, markets, sells, and distributes soft drink concentrates and fountain syrups through independent licensed bottlers. Although incorporated in Colorado, the company's main plant and headquarters are in Dallas, Texas. The company's products are sold in the United States and 80 foreign countries under the trademarks Dr Pepper, Sugar Free Dr Pepper, and Pepper Free. Principal competitors are the well-known thirst quenchers Coca-Cola, Pepsi-Cola, and 7UP. In this industry, competition is not only for consumers, but also for independent bottlers and shelf space in supermarkets. Although Dr Pepper was ranked number three in the soft drink industry, its main competitors had greater financial resources and were more diversified. Its largest followings were in the regional markets of the South and Southwest.

Dr Pepper's strategy had always been to promote its soft

drinks as unique, a different taste from Coke or Pepsi. In 1982, Dr Pepper broke from this strategy. An October 22, 1984 *Advertising Age* article characterized Dr Pepper's national marketing campaign introduced in 1982 more as a "me too" cola, than as an original taste.

Along with this marketing change, the company experienced the introduction of a new management style. Chuck Jarvie, a business school graduate who had previously worked for Procter & Gamble as a vice president of the food products division, was named president. It was hoped that he would be able to aid Dr Pepper in the acquisition of a food-related business. With him, he brought several other people trained in the P&G management style. This style was in direct contrast to that of the chairman, W. W. Clements, a down-home boss who started at Dr Pepper 48 years earlier as a route salesman.

GINGER ALE AND MIXERS

Around the same time, Dr Pepper went on a search for acquisition candidates. In 1981, the company bought the license for Welch's carbonated drinks. A major acquisition was made in 1982 when Canada Dry was bought for $155 million or five times its 1981 earnings.

The Canada Dry acquisition immediately increased Dr Pepper's market share from 7 to 11 percent. It added 26 brands to its existing four. Whereas Dr Pepper appealed to teenagers and was strongest in the South and Southwest, Canada Dry appealed to older customers and was strongest in the Northeast. In addition to the increased geographical diversification, the acquisition was expected to reduce the cyclicality of Dr Pepper's business. Dr Pepper sales were strongest in the second and third quarters of the year, whereas Canada Dry sales were strongest in the fourth quarter. In order to pay for the acquisition, Dr Pepper borrowed $105 million. This leverage took place in an environment of price cutting and increased marketing costs resulting from the "Cola Wars."

Financially, 1982 was not a good year. Faced with decreasing market share and a price war among the soft drink companies, Dr Pepper's earnings dropped to $0.58 per share, a 150 percent decline from 1981. (See Consolidated Income Statements, Consolidated Balance Sheets, and Selected Financial Information tables below.)

The return on average stockholder equity declined from 25.2 percent in 1981 to 9.2 percent in 1982. This was quite different from the heyday years 1968 to 1980 in which market share had increased from 3.5 percent to 6.8 percent and earnings per share increased from $0.22 to $1.31. Joseph J. Doyle of Smith Barney stated, "Maybe long-term Dr Pepper is a positive situation. But there's certainly no reason to be buying Dr Pepper now." Dr Pepper's share price was holding steady at $13.

THE ERROR OF DR PEPPER'S WAYS

In February 1983, Dr Pepper started realizing that several mistakes had been made in corporate strategy. The 1982 industry unit sales rose 2 percent, while Dr Pepper sales fell 3 percent. 7UP took over the number three position in the beverage industry. Dr Pepper found that it could not compete in the national market and therefore had to retrench to a regional strategy. Clements asserted that, "We lose the effectiveness of our marketing money when we try to paint with too broad a brush. This doesn't mean we'll abandon the Northeast, but we'll certainly try to strengthen our position where we're already strong. I didn't want to do the national campaign to begin with. We sure paid a consultant a lot of money for that one." Young & Rubicam, Dr Pepper's advertising agency, was quoted as saying, "We unfortunately tried to become a drink for the masses. That made our advertising a lot like Coke and Pepsi, except they had a much better accepted flavor and much more money to spend." The "Be a Pepper" ads just didn't click.

The press reported that Dr Pepper's concentration on national advertising was at the expense of cooperative pro-

DR PEPPER
Consolidated Income Statements
(in millions)

	1983	1982	1981
Net sales	$560.4	$516.1	$370.6
− Cost of sales	244.2	249.3	181.3
= Operating profit	316.2	266.8	189.3
− General, administrative and selling	268.9	227.8	137.5
− Other, income	0.2	1.5	1.9
= Income before interest and tax	47.5	40.5	53.7
− Interest	14.1	18.4	0.5
− Taxes	11.8	9.7	23.2
= Net income	$ 21.6	$ 12.4	$ 30.0
Earnings per share ($)	$ .93	$ .58	$ 1.45

motions with local bottlers. As bottlers became disgruntled, Dr Pepper was forced to buy up independent bottlers. This ensured the bottling of its concentrate, especially new brands, such as caffeine free Dr Pepper. As a result of these purchases, bottlers owned by Dr Pepper generated a sizable 60 percent of sales.

There was a clash in the management styles of Chuck Jarvie and Clements. Jarvie was not popular with the bottlers. He had a reputation for being tough and decisive. A picture of a school of sharks hung behind his desk. He told guests that when he jumps in the water, the sharks swim aside as a professional courtesy. Jarvie was replaced by Richard Armstrong, president of the Canada Dry Division. Armstrong was an experienced soft drink salesman. Unlike Jarvie, he was considered approachable. It was speculated that he would run the company in a "family style," similar to Clements.

In the first half of 1983, Dr Pepper sales increased 3 percent to $261.4 million. However, profits were down 54 percent to $6.5 million. This was due to increasing competition, causing price slashes and increased advertising ex-

DR PEPPER
Consolidated Balance Sheets
(in millions)

	1983	1982
Assets		
Current assets:		
Cash and marketable securities	$ 17.4	$ 14.5
Accounts receivable	70.4	63.4
Inventory	38.1	36.8
Other current assets	16.1	17.6
Total current assets	142.0	132.3
Long-term assets:		
Property, plant and equipment	135.3	132.3
Franchises and trademarks	63.1	64.2
Other assets	24.8	30.2
Total long-term assets	223.2	226.7
Total assets	$365.2	$359.0
Liabilities and Equity		
Current liabilities:		
Accounts payable	$ 48.3	$ 45.2
Other current liabilities	32.3	26.6
Total current liabilities	80.6	71.8
Long-term liabilities and equity:		
Long-term debt	115.2	125.1
Deferred credits and taxes	13.4	8.4
Equity	156.0	153.7
Total long-term liabilities and equity	284.6	287.2
Total liabilities and equity	$365.2	$359.0

penses, just to maintain market share. Dr Pepper also had to continue buying bottlers to ensure adequate support for its brands. All this required cash. Jesse Meyers, publisher of the industry newsletter, *Beverage Digest,* predicted that "Dr Pepper will have big financial demands developing in 1985." By that time, Dr Pepper was expected to begin repaying the $105 million bank debt from the Canada Dry acquisition. Thus, the increased financial squeeze resulting from reduced profitability and intensified competition, was clearly evidenced.

DR PEPPER
Selected Financial Information

	1983	1982	1981	1980	1979
Net sales ($000)	$560,415	$516,136	$370,613	$339,547	$297,131
Net earnings ($000)	21,590	12,474	29,944	26,933	23,964
Return on equity (%)	13.9%	9.2%	25.2%	25.5%	25.4%
Return on invested capital (%)	10.0	8.0	22.4	23.4	24.2
Per share of common stock ($):					
Net earnings	$0.93	$0.58	$1.45	$1.30	$1.16
Dividends	0.84	0.82	0.78	0.72	0.67
Book value	6.70	6.61	6.08	5.41	4.82

LOOKING FOR CASH

Under these pressures, Dr Pepper hired the investment banking firm, Lazard Frères & Co., to study options to raise the critically needed cash. One possibility was to sell the firm. Emanuel Goldman, a partner of San Francisco-based Montgomery Securities, said, "A merger or sale of Dr Pepper makes sense. They have a fine company with fine products, only they simply at the moment lack the financial horses to compete as they'd like." He estimated that the company could be sold for three times book value or approximately $20 per share.

When asked about a possible sale of Dr Pepper, Clements replied, "I don't have any enthusiasm for selling the company. But my objective after 48 years is to do whatever is necessary to support the brand." However, few potential buyers were believed to exist for Dr Pepper. Because of the firm's market share, a company then in the soft drink industry was thought likely to face an antitrust suit if it tried to acquire Dr Pepper. Companies not in the industry were likely scared away by the highly competitive nature of the industry.

A "SIGNIFICANT" ANNOUNCEMENT

On November 17, 1983, officials of Dr Pepper said the company would make a "significant" announcement following the special board meeting to be held the same day. Speculation over Dr Pepper's future plans had caused the company to ask the New York Stock Exchange to halt the trading on its stock on the 16th. By midday, 564,000 shares had been traded. At the time, the price was 17⅝. Wall Street analysts suggested that Dr Pepper could probably be bought for $20 a share. However, at about the same time, Clements stated that his reaction to a $24 a share bid would be to "tell them to get lost."

The "significant" announcement was made. Forstmann Little and Co., a New York private investment firm, would join Dr Pepper management in a $627 million leveraged buyout. This amount included $517 million to purchase the 23.5 million shares outstanding at $22 a share, in addition to $110 million to refinance Dr Pepper's long-term debt. Four New York banks and one Texas bank agreed to make the loans. Under the proposed LBO, management would own up to 20 percent of the new company and Forstmann Little would have the option to buy 4.15 million Dr Pepper shares at $22 per share. The investment firm also had the right under certain circumstances to require Dr Pepper to repurchase the option for $8 million. Ten major pension plans were expected to commit over $100 million of the financing in the form of equity and subordinated debt. For its part of the deal, Lazard Frères would receive $2.5 million if the buyout was completed.

Was the $22 a share offer by Forstmann Little a fair price for the company? Consider that Wall Street analysts said the company was worth $20 a share, and W. W. Clements said he would not accept less than $24 a share. Moreover, other interested parties got into the action. By Tuesday, November 22, a class action suit had been filed by a Dr Pepper shareholder, Josephine Garcia. Her suit alleged that the company, its officers, and its directors breached their fiduciary responsibilities, evidenced by the $9 million the firm's directors and management would gain on the options they held.

Another combatant, President Richard Armstrong, defended the leveraged buyout, stating that the deal "was a very good thing" for employees, stockholders, and management. "It was just what we wanted," he maintained. He defended the amount management stood to make on the deal by noting that the stockholders would be paid more than the 1978 high price of the stock of $20.66 (adjusted for inflation).

SURPRISE BID

On December 6, DPCC Acquisition Corp., a holding company formed to acquire Dr Pepper, announced it had offered $24 a share or $560 million for Dr Pepper.

This was 9 percent higher than the Forstmann Little bid

with which Dr Pepper had reached a definitive agreement on December 5. DPCC was partially owned by Castle & Cooke Inc., a Honolulu-based food products producer whose brands included Dole Pineapple. The identity of the other investors was not publicly revealed. Earlier in 1984, the company had acquired United Brand's A&W Root Beer for $55 million. This was then to be its second major beverage-related purchase within a year. By the time of DPCC's offer, Dr Pepper's stock had risen to 21¼.

Castle & Cooke looked upon the Dr Pepper acquisition as a calculated business move. Ian R. Wilson, president and chief executive officer, stated that the acquisition of Dr Pepper would help offset sharp swings in the profit of its fresh fruit and vegetable operations, Mr. Wilson saw similar benefits from Dr Pepper as those achieved from the acquisition of A&W Root Beer. He said, "The Dr Pepper soft drink is a market segment all by itself, and one that has remained relatively stable over the last several years. Dr Pepper also owns Canada Dry, which controls the ginger ale segment and is the largest factor in the mixer market. In all of these, we wouldn't be competing with Pepsi or Coke." Under an agreement with other investors in DPCC, Castle & Cooke would hold 40 percent of Dr Pepper, with an option to acquire 80 to 100 percent of the company over the following five years.

Castle & Cooke's plan for financing the leveraged buyout included $550 million of bank debt, $125 million of subordinated debt through an offering managed by the "junk bonds" specialists Drexel Burnham Lambert, and $50 million of equity capital from DPCC's investors. While this amount was $165 million more than the purchase price, the excess was expected to be used to retire some of Dr Pepper's debt and provide funds for working capital.

VALUING THE COMPANY

At this time, two bids were outstanding. One, by Forstmann Little for $22 per share, and the other, by DPCC for $24 per share. Which, if any, represented the value of the company?

As is often the case, the answer is "it depends." It depends on the analyst and on the methodology used. One approach, frequently referred to as the adjusted book value methodology, leads to a value per share higher than the book value, but still far short of the offered price. As illustrated in the Adjusted Book Value Methology exhibit, an analyst who has taken Dr Pepper's book value, adjusted it for the fact that the replacement costs of inventory plant and equipment are higher than their stated book value, and added the amount by which Dr Pepper's pension fund is overfunded, would obtain $417.9 million as the adjusted book value of Dr Pepper's assets.

Then by subtracting Dr Pepper's short- and long-term debt, the adjusted book value of equity is obtained. Finally, by dividing this value by the number of shares, the adjusted book value per share is obtained. Dr Pepper had 23.5 million shares outstanding. Based on that, the adjusted book value

---

DR PEPPER
The Adjusted Book Value Methodology

I. The adjusted value of equity (in millions):

Book value of assets	$365.2
+ Adjustment for replacement cost of inventory, plant and equipment	50.2
+ Overfunding of pension fund	2.5
= Adjusted book value of assets	417.9
− Current liabilities	80.6
− Long-term liabilities	128.5
= Adjusted book value of equity	$208.8

II. Adjusted value per share:

a. $$\frac{\text{Adjusted value per}}{\text{outstanding share}} = \frac{\text{Adjusted book value of equity}}{\text{Number of shares outstanding}}$$

$$= \frac{208.8}{23.5} = \underline{\$8.89} \text{ per share}$$

b. $$\frac{\text{Adjusted value per}}{\text{fully diluted share}} = \frac{\text{Adjusted book value of equity}}{\begin{array}{c}\text{Number of shares on a}\\\text{fully diluted basis}\end{array}}$$

$$= \frac{208.8}{24.2} = \underline{\$8.63} \text{ per share}$$

per share is $8.88. However, quite frequently analysts calculate the value per share on a fully diluted basis, which is the value per share derived under the assumption that all of the firm's convertible securities have been converted. Based on this approach, the value is derived by using in the calculation 24.2 million shares, and the adjusted book value per share is $8.63. Obviously, this is higher than the $6.64 reported book value per share. However, it is significantly lower than the $22 per share offered by Forstmann Little and the $24 per share offered by DPPC. The more comprehensive approach, the one based on the concept of discounting future cash flows, leads to values much closer to the bid prices. As illustrated in the Cash Flow Determination exhibit, in the first step, the cash flow is determined by adding the depreciation to the earnings before interest but after tax and adjusting for the change in working capital.

In the second step, we have to determine the cost of capital appropriate for discounting Dr Pepper's expected cash flows. In doing so, we first calculate Dr Pepper's cost of equity by initially unlevering its beta, and then adjusting it for the new (post-LBO) capital structure.

In other words, the Cost of Equity exhibit indicates that if Dr Pepper wouldn't have any debt its market risk as measured by the beta coefficient would be 0.89. However, after adjusting for its new 3.42 debt-equity ratio, the appropriate beta is 2.4, which yields 28.2 percent as the estimated

DR PEPPER
Cash Flow Determination (in millions)

Earnings before tax	$33.4
+ Interest	14.1
= Earnings before interest and tax	$47.5
− Tax	16.6
= Earnings before interest, after tax	$30.9
+ Depreciation and amortization	26.7
= Cash flow from operations	$57.6
+ Decrease in working capital	5.5
= Total cash flow	$63.1

DR PEPPER
Cost of Equity

---

*Data: Dr Pepper's Beta prior to the buyout = 1.22
          Debt-equity ratio prior to the buyout = 0.74
          Debt-equity ratio following the buyout = 3.42
          T-bill rate = 9%
          Risk premium = 8%

Step 1. Unlevering the beta:

$$\text{Beta} = \text{Beta}_{\text{unlevered}} \left[1 + (1-t)\frac{D}{E} \right]$$

$$1.22 = \text{Beta}_{\text{unlevered}} [1 + (1-.50).74]$$

$$\text{Beta}_{\text{unlevered}} = .89$$

Step 2. Adjusting for the new debt-equity ratio:

$$\text{Beta} = .74[1 + (1-.50)3.42] = 2.4$$

Step 3.   Cost of equity determination:

Cost of equity = Risk free rate + Risk × Risk premium

$$= 9 + (2.4 \times 8) = \underline{28.2\%}$$

---

rate of return required by Dr Pepper's stockholders. Given that following the buyout Dr Pepper would be 77 percent debt financed and 23 percent equity financed, its after-tax weighted average cost of capital is 10.95 percent. (See the Weighted Average Cost of Capital exhibit.)

Finally, we are ready to conduct a formal valuation. As illustrated in the Discounted Cash Flow Valuation exhibit,

DR PEPPER
Weighted Average Cost of Capital

Source of Capital	Weight	Cost (percent)
Debt	0.774	5.8%*
Equity	0.226	28.2
	1.00	

*The after-tax cost of debt = $11.67(1-.50) = 5.8\%$

Weighted average cost of capital = $.226 \times 28.2 + .774 \times 5.8 = 10.95\%$

the present value of Dr Pepper's future cash flow is about $674 million. Subtracting the existing long-term debt yields a value of $545 million for Dr Pepper's equity, which corresponds to $24.03 per share.

However, the valuation is crucially dependent on the assumed growth rate. In its proxy statement filed with the Securities and Exchange Commission (SEC), Dr Pepper's management projected an annual growth rate of 1.7 percent for 1984 and slightly higher thereafter. Given these projections, a 1.7 percent growth rate has been assumed in the base case scenario, yielding the $24.03 per share figure. As illustrated in the Sensitivity Analysis exhibit, any minor deviation from the 1.7 percent assumption immediately results in a significantly different bottom line.

For example, if a 0 percent growth is used in the discounted cash flow valuation, every Dr Pepper's share outstanding is worth $19.03, and on a fully diluted basis worth only $18.48 per share. Obviously, the sensitivity of the results works on both directions. If, for example, the investing group believes that it can promote Dr Pepper's brand name such that the company will enjoy a 6 percent growth rate rather than a 1.7 percent, a purchase at $24 per share is a bargain price given the $52.01 valuation.

No doubt, Forstmann Little and DPCC Acquisition Corp. added at least two other elements to their valuations. First, they accounted for the value of the tax shields from the hefty interest expense on the debt expected to be raised for the buyout. Second, they also added the value of the tax savings associated with the change in depreciation expense due to the step-up in value of Dr Pepper's assets. Castle & Cooke, a partner in DPCC, also assumed additional value created from the synergy with its own lines of business.

WAR OF WORDS

Though the buyout plan was well articulated, not everything was smooth. In a news release Dr Pepper claimed that DPCC

DR PEPPER
Discounted Cash Flow Valuation

Data: Most recent cash flow = $63.1 million
        Cost of capital = 10.95%
        Long-term growth rate = 1.7%
        Total debt = $129 million

The base case scenario:

$$\text{Value of assets} = \frac{\text{Cash flow}}{\text{Discounted rate} - \text{Growth rate}} = \frac{63.1(1 + .017)}{.1095 - .017} = \$674 \quad \text{million}$$

− Long-term debt	129 million
= Value of equity	$545 million
÷ Number of shares	23.5 million
= Value per share	$24.03

DR PEPPER
Sensitivity Analysis

Growth Rate	Value per Share*	Value for Fully Diluted Share†
0%	$19.03	$18.48
1	21.77	21.14
2	25.11	24.38
3	29.30	28.45
4	34.69	33.68
5	41.89	40.67
6	52.01	50.50

*Based on 23.5 million shares outstanding.
†Based on 24.2 million shares on a fully diluted basis.

Acquisition Corp. had raised only $300 million of the bank financing for the buyout. Ted J. Forstmann, general partner at Forstmann Little, said, "It is difficult to believe that any serious group or company could put forth a proposal of this sort given the uncertain nature of virtually every element in their financing scheme." DPCC counter claimed that the entire amount had been committed by six banks prior to the offer. These commitments were said to be subject to the same conditions as Forstmann Little's bank commitments. Dr Pepper stated that due to the DPCC offer, Forstmann Little could require Dr Pepper to repurchase Forstmann Little's option to buy 4.15 million of Dr Pepper shares for $8 million.

At the time of this exchange, Dr Pepper stock was trading at slightly more than $22 a share. Emanuel Goldman said, "The big moves are over. A price of about $24 a share adequately reflects the value of Dr Pepper's assets and cash flow from these assets. That doesn't mean there won't be a bid somewhat higher, but I would be surprised if it were significantly higher."

On December 10, Castle & Cooke met with Dr Pepper to discuss DPCC's offer. Ironically, at the time, heavy trading of Castle & Cooke shares suggested the company itself was the target of a takeover. Drexel Burnham Lambert was publicly confirmed to be an investor in DPCC. Rumors were that Citicorp Venture Capital was a third investor.

THE WAR HEATS UP

Dr Pepper's board rejected DPCC's offer based on a study of the bid by Lazard Frères. This study valued the bid by dividing the offer price by the number of shares that would be outstanding if all the Dr Pepper's convertible securities were actually to be converted. This number is often referred to as the "fully diluted basis." Based on this method, the number of shares would be 24.2 million and the bid value per share would be $23.12. This was in contrast to the $23.82 per share value quoted by DPCC, derived by dividing the offer price by the 23.5 million shares actually outstanding. Applying the 24.2 million shares to the Forstmann Little offer would lower its value to $21.36 per share, rather than the $22 figure quoted by them. The rejection was also based on the belief that the proposal was "highly conditional and incomplete," with the board contending the financing scheme was uncertain.

In justifying the decision to reject DPCC's offer, the board stated, "It would be unreasonable for us to abandon a $22 opportunity for our stockholders which could be realized by the end of February in favor of an uncertain DPCC proposal which is unlikely to occur for several months." Outsiders speculated the Forstmann Little offer was preferred because it allowed the board and management to maintain their current positions. Analysts speculated that Castle & Cooke, headed by a former top manager at Coca-Cola would not retain Dr Pepper's current officers. At the time of the rejected bid, Dr Pepper stock was selling at 22¼ per share.

Once DPCC's bid was turned down, events heated up. DPCC stated that although Dr Pepper's rejection of the proposal had been published, they had received no formal notice from Dr Pepper. A Dr Pepper adviser answered, "What's the matter, can't they read? I don't think they should wait for an engraved note from us." In this environment, DPCC planned to take its bid to Dr Pepper's outside directors. In addition, while DPCC was organized by Castle & Cooke for the acquisition effort, it was speculated that Castle & Cooke itself might make a tender offer for Dr Pepper.

RAISING THE BID

On December 14, DPCC increased its offer to $581 million, which translated to $24 per share on a fully diluted basis. DPCC argued that if the company was given immediate access to Dr Pepper's books, the deal would be closed by the end of February. "The reason we can't move faster is that they haven't opened the books."

Dr Pepper responded to the latest offer with W. W. Clements commenting, "There's nothing different in the latest offer except that DPCC's corrected its arithmetic." He also stated that Dr Pepper had been notified by DPCC's bankers that if their review of Dr Pepper's assets was not satisfactory, they might decline financing. Clements responded to outside speculation over which deal was best for management stating, "Management incentives in the Forstmann Little proposal are no more favorable than those offered in the DPCC proposal."

INFORMATION OR NO INFORMATION

The remainder of December and the beginning of January saw the two firms arguing over DPCC's access to Dr Pepper's financial data. DPCC argued that it was denied access to data necessary to secure financing for the deal. In contrast to DPCC's allegations, Dr Pepper claimed that DPCC would not agree to conditions concerning secrecy regarding further information. The company stated it could not open its books without this agreement.

The war of words continued. As reported by *The Wall Street Journal*, DPCC stated that Lazard Frères was interested in making sure Forstmann Little won. One DPCC investor alleged that Forstmann had already assured Lazard of more business, including the representation of Forstmann Little in the disposal of some of Dr Pepper's assets. Clements challenged DPCC to make a cash tender offer of over $22 a share for all outstanding Dr Pepper stock. Indeed, DPCC had not ruled out that possibility. However, two of its lenders indicated they would not finance a hostile tender offer. A Drexel Burnham spokesman stated, "There are all kinds of options. Nobody wants to do a hostile tender offer. But we're not ruling out that option."

At this time, another uncertainty arose for DPCC. A Houston investor, Charles Hurwitz, had accumulated a 7.9 percent holding in Castle & Cooke. Speculation was that banks would hesitate financing a deal with a company which was itself a potential takeover candidate. But Castle & Cooke did not seem worried about this new development. One of its attorneys pointed out that Hurwitz wrote Castle & Cooke's chief executive officer, Ian Wilson, a "nice" letter saying that he was "impressed with [their] fine company and its good and competent management."

ONE RETREAT AND A FINAL HURDLE

Finally, on January 27, 1984, the war was over. DPCC withdrew its bid for the Dr Pepper Company due to insufficient information required to "verify the financial assumptions on which the $24 offer was based." Without the information, it could not be sure that it had valued the company correctly in terms of its assets, future cash flows, and how it would enhance Castle & Cooke's present earnings. In contrast to DPCC's argument, Dr Pepper claimed DPCC was given more information than Forstmann Little had been given. Ted J. Forstmann, general partner at Forstmann Little, said, "When DPCC was finally left with no recourse other than to put up or shut up, they did what they should have done in the first place." Due to broad selling of Dr Pepper stock, it fell 87.5 cents to 21½.

In early February a new group entered the battlefield: the litigants. Six class action suits were filed against Dr Pepper, alleging management took steps to discourage third-party takeovers and caused delays for DPCC. In addition, the class action suits alleged that Forstmann Little had failed to disclose its strategy for disposing of some of Dr Pepper's assets, including Canada Dry and many corporate bottling companies. On February 23, these suits were settled out of court with the company agreeing to send a proxy statement supplement to all shareholders. Stockholders could change or withdraw their votes prior to the stockholder meeting to be held on February 28.

With this, the stage was set for the "fat lady to sing." On February 28, the leveraged buyout proposal was ratified and Dr Pepper went private for $22 a share.

SUCCESS OR FAILURE

At the time of the leveraged buyout of Dr Pepper, many analysts believed this buyout was the least likely candidate for success. Wall Street experts immediately criticized the price—which was more than 24 times reported earnings—as excessive. A *Forbes* article stated, "Dr Pepper's problem has been not having enough money to compete head to head with Pepsi and Coke. How will it solve its problems by hocking itself to the eyeballs?" Ted Forstmann's answer to the pessimists was, "The company in selling its Canada Dry subsidiary at a 'very, very nice price,' will sell many of its bottling operations at high prices, and we'll end up with Dr Pepper at eight or nine times earnings. . . . It will be the best deal we've ever done." He said Dr Pepper will have a bigger advertising and promotion budget than it had before the buyout. Clement's determination was expressed by saying, "All our energies and resources will now be devoted to Dr Pepper. We're going to get lean and mean." He quoted a figure of $5 million that would be saved each year just because the company no longer had to report to shareholders or the SEC.

How has Dr Pepper fared as a private company? On

March 7, 1984, Joe K. Hughes, executive vice president of Dr Pepper, was named to replace the resigning Armstrong as president. Hughes had been with Dr Pepper for 15 years. In the first eight months, sales increased, fueled by a heavier marketing budget. Forstmann Little sold Canada Dry to R. J. Reynolds for $177 million. The investment firm also proceeded to sell a number of their corporate bottlers. Following these sales, the Forstmann Little investment in Dr Pepper's remaining core business, the manufacture of soft drink concentrate, was about $200 million. Of that $200 million, $30 million was equity, and $170 million was borrowed money.

To meet their objective of becoming "lean and mean," the executive ranks were weeded out. While they cut salary expenses, they set their marketing budget for 1985 at a level 10 percent higher than 1984's estimate. They clearly planned on increasing the bottom line.

Their 1985 increase in sales has been suggested by some to be due to their change in advertising strategy, going back to the promotion of Dr Pepper as a "unique taste." A marketing survey showed the typical Dr Pepper drinker as "inner directed," not trying to live up to others' expectations. As a result, the 1985 jingle "hold out for the out of the ordinary," promoted Dr Pepper as a choice of independent thinkers. In addition to their advertising, some of Dr Pepper sales increase in the summer of 1985 may also have been due to the Coca-Cola old formula/new formula confusion.

In February 1986, Coca-Cola agreed to buy Dr Pepper for $470 million, including the $170 million of debt. That left $300 million for Forstmann Little and its partners, who included none other than the master arbitrageur and confessed insider trader, Ivan Boesky. But the deal with Coca-Cola that was to bring Forstmann Little 10 times its original investment did not come to pass. The Federal Trade Commission vetoed that merger plan in June due to antitrust objections.

Forstmann Little was not left in the cold for long. Two weeks after the plans were canceled, the company agreed to sell Dr Pepper to another investor group for $416 million, or more than eight times Forstmann Little's original investment.

Thomas O. Hicks and Robert B. Haas, the principals behind the acquiring investment firm of Hicks & Haas, are its new co-chairmen. Other members of the group include Shearson Lehman Brothers and members of Dr Pepper's top management.

Hicks & Haas moved to become a major force in the industry. In October 1986, Hicks & Haas became the third-largest soft drink concern in the United States following their purchase of Seven-Up's domestic operations from Phillip Morris for $240 million. This followed on the heels of their $75 million buyout of A&W Brands.

The Dr Pepper deal was a great success for Forstmann Little. Ted Forstmann, one of the firm's four general partners, said Dr Pepper was an ideal leveraged buyout candidate because the business had strong consumer loyalty and predictable cash flow. And importantly, certain assets on Dr Pepper's books could be sold without hurting the core business. But often forgotten is the role of Forstmann Little in creating its own success. Their aggressive management and marketing helped Dr Pepper's operating profit increase from $38.9 million in 1983 to $60.6 million in 1985. Jesse Meyers, publisher of *Beverage Digest*, stated, "The company's recent growth has proven you can get blood from stone and there is more growth yet to come." In the end, Forstmann Little proved their doubters wrong. They turned Pepper into gold.

How Sweet Is Holly Sugar?

WALL STREET "WUNDERKIND"

"Michael, my son, when can I expect to hear some good news about the Holly stock you talked me into buying?" asked Mrs. Buchsbaum. Michael Buchsbaum had heard this question so many times that the answer "any time now" would normally have rolled glibly off his tongue if this were not his mother posing the question. In June 1982, Michael Buchsbaum had been at the helm of Holly Sugar Corp. for about six months when he responded to his mother's concerns, saying something like "we've had some problems getting financing to take the company private, mom, but I'm still optimistic about being able to pull off the deal. I can't give you a date yet, but I'll keep you posted. I'm sure the company is undervalued and it's only a matter of time before we go private at a price that will put a smile on your face."

Buchsbaum, who spearheaded a bitter proxy fight against previous Holly management, took over as chairman of the board late in December 1981. On December 10, 1981 at a special shareholder meeting, his dissident group of shareholders won the battle conclusively (987,875 to 183,687) and replaced the existing board. Since then, Buchsbaum has been intent on taking the company private through a leveraged buyout. However, Holly, plagued with operating problems, was unable to attract the financing necessary for such a deal. The whole story of the major proxy fight and attempts to take the company private centered on one person: Michael Buchsbaum, the former Wall Street "wunderkind" trader and speculator.

Of his spectacular 16-year career on Wall Street as head of arbitrage trading with the New York investment banking

---

We appreciate the research, analysis, and writing done by Tim Van Dam. Without his very significant contribution, the completion of the Holly Sugar case would not have been possible.

firm, Ladenburg, Thalmann & Co., Buchsbaum said, "My goal was to make a 100 percent return on my money each year, and in the late 1970s there was never a year I didn't do it."

Like many other successful street fighters, Buchsbaum came to believe he could run a corporation better than existing management. After six months at the helm, Buchsbaum had perplexed the people in the sugar business with his swashbuckling Wall Street style of management, and had attracted a host of old Wall Street cronies who sold Holly stock short expecting Buchsbaum's attempts to turn the company around to fail. Not easily discouraged, Buchsbaum says of his critics "I know there are people trying to make money betting against me...but they usually lose because I always win."

What was it about Holly that so attracted Buchsbaum? Was the company so undervalued that he thought he could continue earning the kind of return on his money he'was making on Wall Street? Would the desire for power and control of a corporation cloud his judgment about the true value of the firm?

Buchsbaum's talent in commodity trading, including sugar, got him interested in Holly. He resigned from Ladenburg, Thalmann & Co. exchanging his equity in the company for 5,677 shares of Holly common worth in the neighborhood of $320,000 in December 1980. Having been known to bet $500,000 or more of his own and borrowed money on a single stock, Buchsbaum was not out of character in this move. In February 1981, he filed an amended schedule 13D with the Securities and Exchange Commission, disclosing his formation of a limited partnership with 67,489 Holly shares as part of its assets. These shares represented more than 4 percent of Holly's outstanding common. Three weeks later, the limited partnership, Arcanum 1 Partners increased its holdings of Holly shares to 79,189 or approximately 5 percent of Holly common.

In mid-April 1981, a state court judge ordered Holly to give Buchsbaum access to the list of shareholders after he made a sworn statement that he had no intention of liquidating the company. Some Wall Street traders estimated the liquidation value of Holly at $80 to $90. However, Holly's stock was traded at about half that amount at the time. Buchsbaum was not revealing what he thought Holly shares were worth, but his intentions of waging a proxy fight to gain control of the company were clear.

STOCKPILING AMMUNITION FOR THE HOLLY WAR

He and his dissident group charged Holly with not implementing the cumulative voting provision that had been overwhelmingly approved at the previous shareholder meeting in June 1980. Cumulative voting is a system that allows stockholders to concentrate their voting power by giving them one vote for each director for each share held and allowing them to distribute the votes as they wished among director nominees. This system would help Buchsbaum and his group have a better chance of winning a proxy fight. It was the middle of May 1981, and if the dissident group were going to sway other shareholders before the June 26th annual meeting, they would have to move fast. With the list of shareholders in hand, Buchsbaum began his assault.

Between May 12 and the annual meeting, Holly and Buchsbaum's group fired numerous salvos at each other in and out of court. Holly charged that the dissident group disseminated information to the stockholders that liquidation of the company's assets would yield over $100 per share. Realizing Buchsbaum's former relationship with the firm, Holly questioned the origin of these statements published by Ladenburg, Thalmann & Co. Holly alleged that Buchsbaum gave false testimony under oath in a New York court when he claimed that others were responsible for the statements. Ironically, Buchsbaum admitted in testimony before the SEC that he had provided most, if not all, the information and was responsible for the statements' contents. Holly also accused Buchsbaum of intentionally manipulating the price of the stock upward by means of an article published by his former

employer. Holly filed a complaint that Buchsbaum had violated SEC proxy rules by forming a limited partnership for
the sole purpose of illegally soliciting stockholders' proxies.

In several notices to stockholders Buchsbaum blasted
Holly management as being incompetent and negligent. As
evidence of his charges, he cited start-up problems in a California plant, poor earnings performance in 1980, and miserly
dividend payments. He also pointed out to the shareholders
that Holly would have reported a loss had it not been for
nonoperating gains in 1980. The group charged Holly with
failure to disclose 1980 losses on a sale of a subsidiary and
failure to report losses on sugar hedging attempts. Furthermore, he noted that Holly directors had sold around 90 percent of their personal holdings of Holly common over the past
five years. The dissident group informed stockholders that
they might sell some of the company's properties if elected.
They also proposed a slate of nominees for a new board,
including Buchsbaum and three former Holly executives.

MORE COURTROOM COMBAT

Holly counterattacked, claiming that the problems in the
California plant had been corrected, cash dividends had been
resumed, and earnings rose from $5.3 million in 1980 to
$14.2 million in 1981, which resulted in an increase in earn-
ings per share from $3.37 to $8.96. Fearful that Buchsbaum's
persistent attacks would sway stockholders his way, Holly
sought and won a preliminary injunction to bar the dissident
group from voting proxies at the annual meeting. The court
upheld Holly's claims that the dissident group's solicitations
for proxies "contained various misrepresentations." Judge
Zita Weinshienk ruled that Buchsbaum's proxy materials
were slanted to mislead the average shareholder. The judge
also ruled that there was reasonable inference that Buchsbaum tried to inflate the price of Holly stock to encourage
stockholders to consider the possible returns they might gain
if the company were liquidated. On several occasions Buchsbaum had denied these claims.

However, Holly tried unsuccessfully to permanently prevent the dissident group from voting the 60 percent block of proxies it had solicited. On June 26, the annual meeting in Colorado Springs, Colorado, was adjourned after the vote on directors was taken, though not yet tabulated. Holly refused to tabulate the votes until the pending litigation over the legality of the dissident group's activities was settled. Moreover, it adjourned the meeting without setting a date for a future annual meeting. John Bushnell, a member of Buchsbaum's group and future chief executive officer, said "Holly's refusal to recognize the lack of a quorum at the annual meeting. . . [and] the management's refusal to adjourn the meeting to a specific date permits Holly's incumbent directors to remain in control indefinitely and forces disenfranchisement of almost two thirds of Holly's shareholders."

Over the next four months, Buchsbaum and his Arcanum 1 Partners were involved in a fierce legal battle with Holly management for control of the company. Holly attempted to thwart Buchsbaum's efforts by postponing the continuation of the next annual meeting indefinitely. A New York court ordered Holly to explain the rationale of not setting a future date for an annual meeting. However, the New York State Supreme Court later denied Arcanum's request to set a date for a shareholder meeting. Buchsbaum and his troops brought in reinforcements by adding Skadden, Arps, Slate, Meagher, & Flom to their legal counsel, one of Wall Street's most prominent takeover law firms. Holly amended its bylaws to frustrate any attempts of Buchsbaum and his group to call for a special election of directors. Concerning this feeble attempt, Buchsbaum said to the press, "It's a sham. It's clear that management is deliberately seeking to frustrate the will of the majority of the company's stockholders."

On October 28, 1981 Arcanum 1 scored a major victory when a federal judge in a Denver court ruled that by December 10, Holly must hold a special shareholder meeting to elect a board of directors. On the same day, John Bunker, president and CEO of Holly submitted his resignation. One last halfhearted attempt by Holly to rid itself of Buchsbaum came in the form of an offer by MacAndrews and Forbes to buy Arcanum's 98,351 shares for $40 a share plus expenses.

The company, located on the upper east side of Manhattan, was a wholesaler of licorice, chocolate, and cocoa products as well as other consumer goods. Arcanum rejected the offer, which had been made with Holly's full knowledge and consent. The stockholders voted again and had to wait one week to hear the outcome.

BUCHSBAUM'S GROUP WINS THE BATTLE

When the votes were counted, it was clear that Buchsbaum and Arcanum 1 Partners scored an overwhelming victory. They controlled 987,875 shares, a 62 percent stake of the 1,583,140 shares outstanding. Only 183,687 votes (12 percent) were directly cast for the management slate with the remaining 411,578 votes (26 percent) going to the management slate by default. Management may have underestimated the tenacity and resourcefulness of a street fighter like Michael Buchsbaum. Speculators bidding up the price of Holly stock, believing in Buchsbaum's ability to improve the company's performance or in his ability to liquidate it at a higher price, also contributed to management's downfall.

Holly's new board elected Michael Buchsbaum as chairman and voted to reduce the headquarter's staff to 70 people from 111. The new board said it planned to reduce overall executive compensation and to impose stronger and more formal financial and operating control systems. In February 1982, the new board put partial blame for third-quarter losses of $548,000 on prior management's expenses of more than $1.5 million incurred during the proxy fight.

GREENMAILING THE WUNDERKIND

If Michael Buchsbaum thought his troubles were over once the proxy fight was won, he was sadly mistaken. Now he had to deal with 1,200 employees, 1,000 beet growers, numerous lenders, and about 1,000 stockholders. Only now Buchsbaum found his role reversed from an offensive dissident shareholder to that of a defensive manager. World sugar price fluctuations also plagued Buchsbaum in his new responsibilities.

The second week in March 1982, investor Jeffrey Picower and Decisions Inc., a company he controlled, disclosed ownership of 114,000 Holly shares or 7.2 percent of the company's outstanding common. Picower stated in the disclosure that he would favor liquidation of the company or any other proposal that would give the shareholders a fair rate of return on the true value of Holly's assets. It appeared that Buchsbaum was not the only investor to think that Holly stock was undervalued. On March 17, 1982, Buchsbaum announced that he was considering forming another group of investors to buy out shareholders at $65 per share. The group would consist of partners in Arcanum 1 and certain members of Holly management.

Perhaps the article published by Ladenburg, Thalmann & Co. concerning the $100 per share liquidation value of Holly stock prompted Picower to invest. Or he may have had some prior information about Buchsbaum's intentions to take the company private, rather than on a specific valuation of the company's assets. By November 4, 1982, Picower and his company controlled 129,000 shares or 9.3 percent of Holly's 1.4 million shares. Buchsbaum approached Picower hoping to buy all his shares on behalf of Holly's employee stock option plan. The two were not able to strike a deal. In June 1983, Holly agreed to give the dissident group (sound familiar?) five seats on its 12-member board, leaving Buchsbaum's control of the board in doubt. Picower agreed to not proceed with a proxy contest for a year, providing Holly would not dilute Picower's position by increasing the number of its shares outstanding by more than 20 percent.

Late in July 1983, Buchsbaum managed to strike a deal where Holly would pay Picower $7.4 million or an average of $57.36 per share for his stake in the company. While Picower did not reap any premium profits from the deal, he did give Buchsbaum a taste of his own medicine. At the same time, Holly dropped three of its outside directors from a proposed slate of board nominees. Two of the three had been strongly critical of Buchsbaum's preoccupation with taking the company private. Critics claimed that he surrounded himself with yes-men so he could have the authority to direct the company as he pleased and control its corporate funds. By eliminating both internal and external opponents, Buchsbaum better positioned himself to take the company private.

In May 1984, another investor, (speculator?) appeared in the arena threatening "Wunderkind" Buchsbaum. Charles Hurwitz, who had taken a major position in Amstar, another sugar company before it went private, purchased 4.9 percent of Holly's common for about $56.60 to $60 per share. In September, Holly bought out Hurwitz at nearly $71 per share netting him a tidy greenmail profit of around $800,000.

VALUE

Wall Street now focused on the question of how "sweet" is Holly Sugar? Were Picower and Hurwitz busy mustering a myriad of fundamental analytical techniques on their computers to determine Holly's intrinsic value? Or alternatively, were they betting on Buchsbaum's ego and desire to take the company private? What value did these men attribute to Holly that motivated them to invest in a sizable stake? How did Buchsbaum come up with his LBO proposal of $65 per share? Will the creditors buy into Buchsbaum's valuation and loan him the money to take it private? How would Wall Street analysts, investors, and speculators determine their positions concerning the market value of Holly stock? The answers may well be different for each group. Typically, the true value of corporations is debatable, and the "experts" are quick to defend their divergent opinions. The Holly Sugar case is no exception.

TOM DEAN'S OPINION

Buchsbaum's plans to take the company private met with skepticism and disbelief from Wall Street analysts, investors, and speculators. On March 17, 1982, the day after Buchsbaum announced plans to take the company private, Holly stock closed at $47.75, down $11.25. According to a broker dealer at Advest Inc., their accounts had shorted 60,000 to 70,000 shares that week and would take more short positions if the stock stayed above $50. Tom Dean, a first vice president at Advest, claimed that Holly's book value of nearly $60 per share was overstated as evidenced by Buchsbaum's failure to find buyers for some of Holly's assets that it had been trying to sell. Dean said he had heard that a plant Holly was trying to sell in California for $25 million might get an offer of only $2 million, well below its historical cost. Dean's premise of evaluating Holly's assets was that they are only worth what someone would pay for them. Officials in Washington, D.C., reinforced Dean's position stating that no sugar beet plant in the country had been sold in years. With overcapacity in the industry and global sugar prices down 70 percent in two years, Holly found it difficult to sell some of its fixed assets at their appraised values.

On June 30, 1982, trading of Holly stock was halted until stock exchange officials could meet with Holly and Tom Dean of Advest. A stock exchange spokesman refused to comment concerning the trading halt. Skeptics of the plan to take Holly private, including many of Dean's clients, had sold short nearly 300,000 of Holly's 1.6 million shares.

LENDERS EXPRESS THEIR OPINIONS

In April, Buchsbaum received information from Republic Bank of Dallas, indicating its interest in organizing a bank syndicate to extend credit to a group of investors who would take Holly private. The deal never materialized since Holly was unable to meet one of the conditions. Specifically, the deal required Holly to come up with $37 million expected to be raised by selling the nonbeet-processing assets. Other conditions required by the bank further lessened the chances of closing the deal.

In June of 1982, Buchsbaum announced that General Electric Credit Corporation (GECC) had offered his group a

$100 million loan package to take the company private. This arrangement did not require Holly to sell any of its fixed assets as did the prior offer from the Dallas bank. However, GECC required Holly to come up with $33 million in cash. Advest's Stanley Goldring said "I don't see where the company has that kind of cash at the moment." He estimated that Holly may have $6 million in cash and that it was unlikely for Holly to be able to raise the cash either through the sale of fixed assets or through the investor group. In addition, the credit offer was contingent on a thorough review of Holly's creditworthiness. When GECC withdrew its offer abruptly with no explanation, Buchsbaum said he would seek financing alternatives with other lenders. Financial professionals were skeptical of Holly's chances to raise the funds necessary for a leveraged buyout.

STOCK PRICE FLUCTUATION

Early in July 1982, Holly repurchased 198,000 of its shares for $32 a share for a total of $6.3 million. This action came in the wake of news that GECC had withdrawn its offer of a $100 million loan to take the company private at $65 a share. The bad news caused Holly's stock to fall precipitously. Holly shares had traded from 28 to 64⅞ over the 52-week period from July 1981 to July 1982. Some analysts accounted for the lows by the low prices on the world sugar market. Many analysts perceived the highs as primarily a function of Buchsbaum's effort to take the company private rather than a function of intrinsic value based on fundamental analysis.

In spite of the obstacles Buchsbaum faced trying to make Holly Sugar the most profitable sugar company in the United States, he would not admit that he didn't know what he was getting into. Running the operation from his New York office, 2,000 miles away from headquarters in Colorado Springs, Buchsbaum has been known to waken executives at 5 A.M. with his hard-charging style. He has been criticized by beet growers and employees for being a distant and perplexing leader. As a dissident shareholder, Buchsbaum, while waging the proxy fight, called Holly earnings performance dismal and criticized the size of expenditures on property maintenance. Nevertheless, soon after he took over, Holly experienced a $2 million loss. This time, as a manager rather than a dissident, he found that major expenditures on property maintenance were an absolute necessity.

Buchsbaum, still a trader at heart, traded stocks and commodities as before. He hoped to use his skills to bolster Holly's earnings by trading in the sugar futures market. A chalkboard covering the entire wall in his New York office is filled with information about numerous mergers, corporate raids, liquidations, and LBOs. The Holly deal is conspicuously missing from his "big board," but he accounts for its absence by claiming that all the details are well entrenched in his head. According to Buchsbaum, the pitchfork in his office is "for people I don't have patience with." That could include a majority of people since he claims that "99.5 percent of the people out there are amateurs and another 0.25 percent are dummies." Evidently he would include himself in the winner's circle of the remaining 0.25 percent of savvy financial professionals.

THE VALUATION DEBATE:
A SUPERMARKET OF OPINIONS

Ed Moore's Opinion—$97 per Share

Three years went by before Holly appeared in the news again. During this time Buchsbaum no doubt was not idle in his efforts to take the company private. Evidently, Brookehill Equities' partner, Ed Moore, believed that Buchsbaum would win the battle. Brookehill owned 8 to 9 percent of Holly's outstanding common. As of April 1985, using the adjusted book value approach, Moore believed that Holly had a minimum of $12 per share in an overfunded pension plan, $24 per share in LIFO reserves (market value of inventory less balance sheet value of LIFO inventory), and $10 per share in working capital adding up to $46 per share. To this sum Moore added the book value of the property, plant, and equipment of $58.6 million or close to $54 a share which results in an even $100 per share valuation. Moore suspected that potential profits from Holly's inventory were worth more than the conservative figure he gave. Therefore, as illustrated by the Adjusted Book Value Approach table, subtracting $3 per share to account for the long-term debt did not materially affect his estimate, a value of $97 per share.

Moreover, he claimed that Buchsbaum was reporting conservative earnings by reselling purchased sugar at a profit of one or two cents a pound while stockpiling a large inventory of far more profitable sugar in anticipation of taking the company private. Ed Moore said "Buchsbaum is hiding earnings in inventory...he's running Holly like a private company, generating cash but reporting what he wants to report."

Skeptics Respond—Voting by Short Selling

"No way," shouted the skeptical short sellers on Wall Street and the experienced professionals in the sugar business. Sugar executives said the scheme of reselling purchased sugar is not uncommon, but the idea of building a huge inventory of processed sugar is a dangerous game betting that sugar prices will remain high or go higher. In April

HOLLY SUGAR
The Adjusted Book Value Approach ($ per share)

	Moore's Opinion	The Over- capacity Argument	A Variation of Moore's Valuation	The Unaudited Inflation Adjusted Opinion
Book value of P.P.& E.	$54.00	$27.00	$52.16	$108.81
+ Working capital	10.00	10.00	10.90	10.90
+ Lifo reserves	24.00	24.00	19.57	19.57
+ Surplus in pension	12.00	12.00	10.82	10.82
− Long-term debt	3.00	3.00	3.49	3.49
= Value per share	$97.00	$70.00	$89.96	$146.61

1985, beet sugar sold to institutional buyers went for 24.6 to 26.75 cents a pound, a far cry from Moore's estimated selling price of 29 cents a pound.

For comparison, Wall Street professionals and sugar industry experts also looked at other LBO acquisitions in the industry. For example, Amstar, which announced an LBO in February 1984, went for $47 a share or about 1.1 times its book value and 11 times its estimated fiscal 1984 earnings. Similarly, Michigan acquired by Savannah in July 1984, went for $43.50 a share, 1.4 times its per share book value and just over 10 times previous year's earnings. In contrast, a $100 price tag on Holly shares would translate to 2 times its book value and about 14 times its 1984 earnings per share. Considering that the earnings per share were inflated by nonoperating gains and special tax treatment, $100 a share for Holly stock seemed excessive compared to Amstar and Michigan.

The Overcapacity Argument—$70 per Share

Short sellers and sugar experts alike did not buy the book value approach of valuing Holly's fixed assets. They argued that overcapacity in the industry is evidenced by the sale of Hunt International's 12 beet plants for $34 million, compared to their $105 million book value. Overcapacity implied that even Holly's well-maintained plants could not be sold for book value. Those who adopted the overcapacity argument used only one half of Moore's estimate of book value of property, plant, and equipment while using all of his other estimates. As illustrated in The Adjusted Book Value Approach table, this approach leads to a value of $70 per share.

Another problem faced by Holly and other sugar refiners was the likelihood that the current administration would cut back on price supports which have partially shielded domestic sugar companies from foreign dumping. This was expected to further exacerbate the unpredictable nature of sugar industry earnings. Highly predictable earnings and cash flows are extremely important to LBO lenders who base creditworthiness on the borrower's ability to make regular payments on the high level of debt. In addition to the cash flow, creditors also consider the liquidity of the assets that serve as collateral. Holly seemed to be in trouble on both counts, which could be the reason Buchsbaum was unable to attract the financing necessary to go private.

Add One More Opinion to the Supermarket—$89.96 per Share

Another school of thought has also applied the adjusted book value approach. However, it ended up with a value per share lower by $7 than Moore's estimate. They reported a $10.82 pension overfunding per share (compared with Moore's $12), a lower LIFO reserve ($19.57 compared with Moore's $24 per share), and estimates for other components similar to Moore's. As illustrated in the table, this approach leads to a value of $89.96 per share.

The Unaudited Opinion

A different version of the adjusted book value approach is to use the company's unaudited section of the annual report where adjustments are made to reflect the impact of inflation. Based on this approach, the most significant difference is in the value of plant, property, and equipment. Holly Sugar's 1985 annual report provides an unaudited inflation adjusted property, plant, and equipment value of $108.81 per share. This leads to a value of $146.61 per share.

Obviously, Moore's adjusted book value approach, accompanied by the other three variations of the same methodology, is a classic example of the complexity involved in valuation.

Discounted Cash Flow Valuation

Naturally, investors prefer a stream of stable cash flow rather than a volatile one. Unfortunately, Holly Sugar's cash flow does not fit this category. As illustrated in the Cash Flow History table, the year-to-year changes in Holly's cash flow are highly unpredictable.

For example, in 1984 it reported cash inflows of $16.8 million compared with cash outflows of $15.7 million in 1983. However, in 1985 it was again $5 million in the red. Given that in this case past cash flows are not a good indicator of

HOLLY SUGAR
Cash Flow History (in millions)

	1978	1979	1980	1981	1982	1983	1984	1985
Net income	($ 6.1)	($ 5.7)	$ 5.3	$14.1	($2.0)	($13.3)	$ 9.4	$4.0
+ Depreciation	6.0	5.8	6.6	6.6	6.2	5.0	4.9	5.2
+ (1 − t) × interest	1.7	2.0	4.1	3.4	1.9	1.4	2.0	4.4
± Changes in working capital	1.6	(6.1)	1.3	9.4	(9.6)	(5.7)	5.2	(9.0)
− Capital expenditure	10.9	15.6	2.2	3.0	3.6	3.1	4.7	9.6
= Cash flow	($ 7.7)	($19.6)	$15.1	$30.5	($7.1)	($15.7)	$16.8	($5.0)
Annual growth rate		−155%	+177%	+102%	+124%	−121%	+207%	−130%

future cash flows, a more thorough fundamental analysis has to be made. An example of such an analysis is the one conducted by Value Line, which estimated Holly's 1986 cash flow as $12.9 million.

As the next step, we have to derive the appropriate interest rate for discounting Holly's future cash flow. Given that Holly's cost of debt is 11.42 percent and its beta is estimated as 0.6, as stated in the Weighted Average Cost of Capital exhibit, the appropriate rate for discounting its future cash flow is 10.66 percent.

Obviously Holly Sugar's value is critically sensitive to the assumed growth rate of its cash flow. This sensitivity is clearly exhibited in the Discounted Cash Flow Valuation table.

If Holly's cash flow would decline by the same rate as it did over the period 1978–85 (averaged −23.9 percent), the value per share would be estimated as $30.06. In contrast, if Holly's cash flow is assumed to grow at a 4 percent rate, the value per share is estimated as $170.72. As illustrated in the Stock Price Scenarios exhibit, a change in the assumed growth rate from 4 percent per year to 6 percent, significantly increases the value per share from $170.72 to $245.39.

The historical evidence does not support such a growth rate. However, it does reinforce Value Line's opinion that the market is not valuing Holly on the basis of its earnings, but rather on the distinct possibility of the company going private through an LBO. If Buchsbaum is able to secure financ-

HOLLY SUGAR
Weighted Average Cost of Capital

$$WACC = \frac{Debt}{Value} R_{debt} (1 - Tax) + \frac{Equity}{Value} R_{equity}$$

$$R_{equity} = R_f + Beta \times (R_m - R_f) = .072 + .6(.155 - .072) = 0.1218 = 12.18\%$$

$$R_{debt} = Interest\ exp./debt = 5,149,000/45,091,000 = 0.1142 = 11.42\%$$

$$WACC = \frac{96,459,000}{156,085,000}(.1142)(1 - .149) + \frac{59,626,000}{156,085,000}(0.1218) = 10.66\%$$

HOLLY SUGAR
Discounted Cash Flow Valuation

I. Basic parameters:
   1986 Cash flow = $12.92 million
   Cost of capital = 10.66 percent
   Number of shares = 1,114,253
   Long-term liabilities = $3.89 million

II. Valuation framework:

$$\text{Asset value} = \frac{\text{Next year's cash flow}}{\text{Cost of capital} - \text{Growth rate}}$$

   − Long-term debt
   = Value of equity
   ÷ Number of shares
   = Value per share

III. Results

Item	Cash Flow's Growth Rate			
	−23.9%	0%	2%	4%
Value of assets ($ million)	$37.38	$121.25	$149.25	$194.07
− Long-term debt ($ million)	3.89	3.89	3.89	3.89
= Value of equity ($ million)	33.49	117.36	145.36	190.18
÷ Number of shares (million)	1.114	1.114	1.114	1.114
= Value per share ($)	$30.06	$105.35	$130.48	$170.72

ing, it will be interesting to see if his cash flows will be enough to service the high level of debt.

EPILOGUE

Volatile times were ahead for Holly Sugar. Holly's stock jumped from $83 in November 1985 to $132 two months later. But the stock settled down and by January 1987 it was trading at 105. What fueled the fire? For one thing, speculation again amounted that Buchsbaum would soon take the

HOLLY SUGAR
Stock Price Scenarios with Varying Growth Rates

Growth	Stock Price
−23.9%	$ 30.06
−15.0	41.71
−10.0	47.69
−5.0	70.57
0.0	105.35
1.0	116.57
2.0	130.48
3.0	147.92
4.0	170.72
5.0	201.42
6.0	245.39

company private. Another was the sugar subsidy finally awarded to the industry by a Congress convinced that it was needed. Still another was the removal of a large potential liability through the settlement of a $56 million lawsuit with the Wyoming growers for only $1 million.

No doubt, much of the volatility during the period was caused by the wide variation in earnings estimates for the forthcoming year. Knowledgeable estimates ranged from a high of "at least $65 million" to a much more modest $7 million. Meanwhile, internal battles continued to rage. In February 1986, John Bushnell resigned as Holly's president, chief executive officer, and as a director. The resignation came as a result of disagreements with Buchsbaum over plans to take the company private.

And interestingly, Buchsbaum did not sell beet processors as many analysts had predicted. Rather, in July 1986, Holly bought a sugar beet processor from Sara Lee. Moreover, by late 1987, Buchsbaum still had not taken Holly Sugar private. As usual, Buchsbaum continued to confound his critics.

Mary Kay's Cosmetic: Going Private

In the first week of December 1985, stockholders of Mary Kay Cosmetics approved plans to sell the company to Mary Kay Ash, the company's charismatic chairman and founder, and her son Richard Rogers, its president. The agreement provided $11 in cash and $8.25 in debentures for each of the 21 million publicly held shares, which represented 70 percent of the company's total outstanding shares. At the time the deal was struck, analysts believed that the debentures would begin trading at one half of their $8.25 face value, thus valuing the deal at around $15 per share or $315 million.

Why did Mary Kay decide to go private? What was the history of the company leading to the LBO decision? Was the deal "fair?" Will Mary Kay be able to successfully amortize its unprecedented level of debt? And finally, how can we determine the underlying value of the firm?

LBO: A COSMETIC FOR A FLABBY COMPANY

Mary Kay spokesman, Dean Meadors, says that going private gives the company "the freedom to make long-term strategic decisions—maybe at the expense of short-term profits." Some experts argue that the time, cost, and hassles of dealing with inquisitive shareholders and Wall Street analysts can push management into short-term strategies just to pacify this Wall Street constituency. "You find yourself managing your business to analysts' expectations," says a consultant at Booz Allen & Hamilton Inc. A Mary Kay spokesman also cites personal and family reasons for the Mary Kay buyout. "It's their life. Mary Kay and Richard like the idea of

---

We appreciate the research, analysis, and writing done by Eric Sullivan. Without his very significant contribution, the completion of the Mary Kay case would not have been possible.

family ownership—of having it be theirs." Furthermore, while Mary Kay Ash has never revealed her true age, she is at or approaching 70 years old which may have prompted her to want to liquidate some of her holdings for estate planning purposes.

However, the decision of Mary Kay to go public is more of an economic decision than one merely to get out of the public eye. During the 1970s and early 1980s the founder and her son have grown the company nicely and have managed to generate strong profitability. Jointly, they have insight into Mary Kay's future prospects, and they know what it takes to run the company profitably. It is plausible that their information regarding a potential turnaround in the business outweighs the information available to the market, thus potentially leading to an undervaluation of the company's stock. In 1983, Mary Kay stock hit a high of $44 per share, only to fall to a low of $9 the following year. At the time shareholders voted on the LBO proposal, the stock was traded at $14.

Carrying out an LBO when the company's stock is relatively "cheap" is quite often an incentive to go private. In addition, for a relatively small equity contribution, approximately 7 percent in the case of Mary Kay, an LBO candidate can be leveraged up to a point that the cash flows are sufficient to retire the debt and the buyer ends up owning the company by using other people's money. Finally, there is the incentive of large profits potentially generated by taking a flabby company private, getting it into shape, and going public again.

In order to set the stage for the examination of some of Kay's problems, its business will be briefly described and we will take an analyst's peek at the "Mary Kay mystique." In order to understand this buyout, it is important to first place Mary Kay in the context of its competitive environment and to analyze some of the problems associated with the climate in the cosmetics industry.

There appears to be a certain mystique surrounding Mary Kay Ash and the company she founded back in 1963 in Dallas, Texas. In many ways the company is still closely aligned with the personality of its founder. Many of the company's motivational practices and policies may be considered gimicky and corny, and prizes such as pink Cadillacs, furs, and diamonds may appear gaudy. But, for the past 20 years this marketing style has been successful in building a large motivated sales force which has resulted in more than a sixfold increase in sales over as many years.

Mary Kay Ash says that the company's financial statements don't reflect profit and loss but rather people and love. Even her corporate symbol, the bumblebee, is meant to motivate the beauty consultants who are not employees but independent salespeople. "Aerodynamically the bumblebee shouldn't be able to fly, but it doesn't know that, so it flies anyway." Furthermore, Pageant Night is held annually to give out the large awards and to further hype the "Mary Kay Experience." At these carefully orchestrated Pageant Nights the atmosphere has been described as electric and a cross between a Las Vegas revue and a revival meeting. These extravaganzas along with training films such as "Capture the Vision" (in which the founder is shown standing on the terrace of her palatial home) provide effective vehicles to embellish the mythical corporate image and to motivate salespeople to increase their productivity.

Mary Kay Cosmetics is engaged in the production and direct marketing of cosmetics, toiletries, hair care products, and related products. Its products are oriented toward skin care rather than the high-fashion makeup market. However, according to *Product Marketing* magazine, skin preparation was the only major cosmetics market segment to experience a drop in sales in 1984. But during 1985, Mary Kay increased the percentage of makeup items sold from 28 to 33 percent. Even though, skin care products still accounted for 43 percent of total sales.

DIRECT SELLING: THE PLUSES AND MINUSES

The company's sales force has been structured to consist of independent salespeople referred to as beauty consultants who work strictly on commission. They earn money from selling cosmetics at "parties" held at prospective customers' homes. The salespeople earn additional commissions and incentive prizes by recruiting additional salespeople and by reaching specified quotas. This organizational structure does not constitute the illegal practice of pyramiding since a salesperson does not have to recruit others just to stay afloat financially. Every salesperson purchases the products at 50 percent below the retail price. Some sales training courses are conducted at the corporate headquarters in Texas. However, most of the ongoing training is performed by existing salespeople during the recruitment process. These people walk the new recruits through the proper use of skin care products and teach them specific beauty techniques and makeup artistry.

The direct selling technique, employed by companies such as Mary Kay, Avon Products, and Tupperware, has some distinct advantages. First, some of the firm's inventory carrying costs are reduced since the salespeople carry their own inventory of cosmetics. These companies also enjoy very low overhead and are able to quickly alter marketing and selling strategies in line with demographic changes. They are also privy to almost instantaneous consumer and market information. Furthermore, some managers of direct selling firms believe that individuals, in addition to being motivated by incentives such as trips or furs, are willing to work harder when they feel like entrepreneurs.

All of Mary Kay's products are sold in highly competitive markets. Its strongest competitor in the direct sales cosmetics is Avon Products. However, Mary Kay also competes with numerous other cosmetics and skin care product manufacturers. As of July 1985, Mary Kay had a price-earnings ratio of 17.3 as opposed to Avon's 10.7. Even though both companies remained profitable, since 1984, sales and profitability have remained flat for Avon but decreased 14 percent for Mary Kay. This was due to a decrease in both the number and productivity of its beauty consultants. The company cited the increased availability of alternative employment due to the economic recovery as well as increased competition for recruits as the major causes of decreased enrollment.

Mary Kay's cost of sales and fixed and discretionary

expenses were held constant during 1984. However, increases in selling, general, and administrative expenses, due to additional commissions and expenses for new marketing and incentive programs, forced net income down by 33 percent from the previous year. Mary Kay's performance in the first nine months of 1985 was not much better, exhibiting an 18 percent decline in sales. Despite the increase in sales productivity resulting from the new incentive programs, the average size of the sales force continued to fall, though it appeared to be stabilizing. During 1985, cost of sales increased due to higher manufacturing costs and a shift in product mix to promotional items. However, return on sales remained constant, lending further credence to the notion that sales and profitability may be stabilizing.

Similarly, Revlon's sales and profitability remained basically flat over the three years prior to it going private, reflecting the relatively mature cosmetics market as a whole. In an attempt to promote sales growth and increased market share, both Revlon and Avon were looking aggressively toward new marketing techniques and changing distribution channels, thus intensifying the pressure on Mary Kay.

Interestingly, despite the competitive pressures and the giants' push for market shares, Noxell Corp., a firm of equal sales volume to Mary Kay, appears to be one of the few cosmetics firms to emerge unscathed by the slowdown in the industry. Noxell's niche is in the mass-merchandising market, including department stores and supermarkets. These distribution channels have produced pronounced sales growth over the last couple of years as the medium-priced market has become more competitive. The upscale cosmetics market has also been growing but the recent trend has been toward lower-priced offerings that can be pulled from the shelf by the consumer while doing other shopping.

Mary Kay and Avon have not only had to cope with the problems surrounding a maturing cosmetics industry, but are plagued with problems in the direct selling industry where companies such as Tupperware and Shaklee Corporation, a direct seller of nutrition products, have been hurt. Today 64 percent of all women age 18 to 44 are employed, a figure that is forecast by the Bureau of Labor Statistics to rise to 80 percent by 1995. With a stronger economy and more women working full-time, the availability of workers for direct selling has decreased dramatically. Sales have also been hurt by customers' reluctance to open their doors to strangers. Furthermore, more working women also means fewer women at home to answer the door or arrange "beauty shows." These women have less time and are more apt to buy makeup where they do the rest of their shopping.

According to Neil Offen, president of the Direct Selling Association, to combat some of these problems, "the direct-selling industry has gone from being sales-driven to being market-driven." Thus, direct salespeople are turning their sights toward places such as office complexes, schools, and nurseries. The companies agree that they must gear sales and recruiting toward the working woman. Also more emphasis is being placed on direct mail and advertising while firms continue to look into new product offerings to promote sales. Finally, some companies such as Avon Products have diversified. They, for example, have moved into the higher-margin health care industry and are stepping into retailing through a joint venture with Liz Claiborne to manufacture a line of designer cosmetics. Thus far these ventures have helped to stabilize sales levels for Avon, but they must still address their main business, direct selling. In contrast, Mary Kay has not yet proceeded with a diversification strategy. More specifically, Mary Kay is addressing the industry's problems by introducing changes in its discount and commission structure and incentive programs, and through changes in its product line and marketing objectives. It is too early to tell whether these changes will have a lasting impact on sales and recruitment growth.

BEAUTY HAS VALUE

Having looked at Mary Kay's historical performance and financial condition, we now turn to the issue of valuation. Two analytical measures are described in an effort to value the company. The first is the adjusted book value approach. It requires making adjustments to the historical values on the asset side of the balance sheet to reflect their likely market values.

In the Adjusted Book Value exhibit both the "value-in-use" as well as the "orderly liquidation" values are provided for fixed and intangible assets. These were developed by the appraisal firm of Marshall and Stevens. The asset valuation analysis begins with working capital; to it the value of the fixed, intangible, and other assets are added; and then other liabilities and the existing long-term debt are subtracted. Other assets such as the surplus in pensions and LIFO reserves ordinarily are also incorporated into the analysis. However, these assets are not present in the case of Mary Kay. Applying the two different appraisal methods shown in the exhibit, one obtains a range of $8 to $12.28 per share. This range is helpful in establishing a lower bound for the value of the company's common stock.

Next we apply a discounted cash flow valuation. Based on pro forma financial statements for the next nine years as provided in the Mary Kay LBO prospectus, one obtains the

MARY KAY
The Adjusted Book Value Approach (in millions, except per share data)

	Value as of September 1985	
Asset	Value-in-Use	Orderly Liquidation
Working capital	$ 72.5	$ 62.1*
+ PP&E	114.3	82.3
+ Intangibles	176.7	78.4
+ Other assets	21.8	21.8
− Other liabilities	(14.2)	(14.2)
− Long-term debt	(.2)	(.2)
= Adjusted equity value	$370.9	$230.2
Per share	$12.28	$8.00

*Based on a $0.60 per $1 liquidation value for inventory.

estimated cash flows for each period. (See Projected Cash Flow exhibit.) The average growth rate is then calculated. As is ordinarily done, the cash flows are calculated by taking the projected net income and adding back noncash expenses such as depreciation and noncash interest expense. Projected increases in working capital and anticipated capital expenditures are then subtracted.

The next step is to determine the weighted average cost of capital to be used in discounting the cash flows. For Mary Kay the cost of capital has three components: the cost of debt, the cost of equity, and the cost of its preferred stock. The cost of debt is determined by weighting the after-tax interest rate to be paid on each debt instrument by the proportion of each type of debt to total debt. This weighted average cost of debt is determined to be 7.86 percent.

Since debt is a key element in any LBO, it is important to review the financing of the Mary Kay LBO. The total debt that was taken on by the firm was $297 million, of which $81 million represented term loans from banks (with the Bank of New York as the lead bank) and $60 million were senior notes issued to institutional investors. Both of these groups had a senior security interest in virtually all corporate assets. An additional $83 million was raised from the placement of 15 percent debentures which were traded at a value of about half of their face value of $8.25 per share. These are 15-year debentures paying 15 percent. The final source of debt financing were notes from Mary Kay's holding company to family members in partial settlement of their 30 percent share of Mary Kay common stock previously owned. These notes are also 15 years in duration and pay 12.5 percent annually. As illustrated in the Cost of Debt exhibit, after accounting for the different sources of debt and their costs, Mary Kay's after-tax cost of debt is estimated as 7.86 percent.

To determine the cost of equity, the capital asset pricing model (CAPM) is used. As illustrated in the Cost of Equity exhibit, to apply the CAPM, a beta value (provided by Value Line) for the period prior to the LBO is utilized.

In essence this beta is adjusted to reflect the higher debt level that arises from the financing associated with the LBO.

MARY KAY
Projected Cash Flows (in millions)

	1986	1987	1988	1989	1990	1991	1992	1993	1994	1995
Net income	($ 7.1)	($ 2.9)	$ 1.9	$ 6.9	$10.7	$15.3	$20.6	$26.5	$33.1	$40.0
+ Depreciation	19.4	19.8	18.7	16.6	16.8	17.0	17.2	17.4	17.6	17.8
+ (1 − t) Cash interest expense	13.0	14.1	12.2	9.2	6.7	17.8	15.2	12.2	8.6	4.9
+ Noncash interest expense	12.8	14.7	17.1	19.6	22.8	0	0	0	0	0
− Increase in working capital	.1	.1	.1	.1	.1	.1	.1	.1	.1	.1
− Capital expenditures	6	6	6	6	6.4	6.7	7.1	7.4	7.8	8.2
= Total cash flow	$32.0	$39.6	$43.8	$46.2	$50.5	$43.3	$45.8	$48.6	$51.4	$54.4
% change		23.9%	10.7%	5.6%	9.3%	−14.3%	5.8%	6.1%	5.8%	5.8%

Average growth rate = 6.52% per year.

MARY KAY
Cost of Debt

	Amount of Proceeds ($ millions)	Proportion of Total Debt	Annual Percent Rate	Weighted Average Cost of Debt
Term loan	$ 81	0.27	11% (floating)	2.97%
Senior notes	60	0.20	14 (fixed)	2.80
Debentures	83	0.28	15 (fixed)	4.20
Notes from holding company	73	0.25	12.5 (fixed)	3.13
Total debt	$297	1.0		13.1(1 – .4) = 7.86%

MARY KAY
Cost of Equity

I. Adjusting the Beta:

   *Given: Pre-LBO debt-equity ratio = .34
                Pre-LBO beta (based on Value Line 7/85) = 1.3
                Relevant tax rate = 40%
                Post-LBO debt-equity ratio = 4.59

   a. Unlevering the Beta:

$$1.3 = \text{Beta}_{unlevered} [1 + (1 - .40).34]$$
$$\text{Beta}_{unlevered} = 1.08$$

   b. Adjusting for the New Debt-Equity Ratio:

$$\text{Beta} = 1.08 [1 + (1 - .40) \times 4.59] = 4.05$$

II. Estimating the Cost of Equity:

   *Given: Beta = 4.05
                Risk premium (average 1974–1985) = 7.05%
                Risk-free (T-bill) rate = 7.7%

     Cost of equity = Risk-free rate + Risk measure × Risk premium
                     = .077 + 4.05 × .0705 = 36.3%

Using an average risk premium calculated over the previous six years and the one-year T-bill rate at the time of the proposed LBO, the CAPM yields a cost of equity of 36.3 percent. The cost of preferred stock is assumed to be approximately the same as common stock since it is noncumulative.

Each of the required rates of return calculated above are weighted according to the various proportions of each type of financing to yield a weighted average cost of capital (WACOC) of 14.05 percent.

To arrive at the value of Mary Kay's assets the 14.05 percent is used to discount the anticipated cash flows, assuming a 6.5 percent growth rate. Although the 1986 cash flow projected by the company's management is $32 million, a more conservative estimate based on the company's past volatility is appropriate. As a result, we use an estimate of approximately $27.5 million. Finally, as illustrated in the Discounted Cash Flow Valuation exhibit, long-term liabili-

MARY KAY
Weighted Average Cost of Capital

	Amount ($ millions)	Weight	Cost
Debt	$297	78%	7.86%
Equity	76	22	36.3
Total	$373	100%	

Weighted average cost of capital = .78 × 7.86 + .22 × 36.3 = 14.05%

ties are netted out of this figure, resulting in a value of $12.00 per share.

While this value is somewhat below the $14.50 to $15.00 per share range that analysts assigned to the proposed Mary Kay LBO, an examination of the Sensitivity Analysis exhibit reveals the possible assumptions used by the analysts in arriving at their estimated range. The exhibit displays the results of the valuation estimates under different assumptions.

The effect on share value of changes in sales growth, operating margins, and WACOC are investigated. The analysis shows that the value is particularly sensitive to changes in the operating margin. The WACOC is also an important variable but to a lesser extent. The sensitivity analysis ulti-

MARY KAY
Discounted Cash Flow Valuation

I. Parameters:
    *Expected cash flow = $32.0 million
    *Expected growth rate = 6.52%
    *Discount rate = 14.05%

II. Valuation:

$$\text{Value of assets} = \frac{32.0}{.1405 - .0652} = \$366,300,000$$

− Liabilities	$ 3,800,000
= Value of equity	$362,500,000
÷ Number of shares	30,200,000
= Value per share	$12.00

MARY KAY
Sensitivity Analysis (value per share as a function of operating margin, WACOC, and sales)

		WACOC (%)	
		13	15
Operating Margin (%)	17	$13.55	$10.17
	19	18.75	17.34

When Operating Margin = 18% and WACOC = 14%, Value = $12.00 per share

		Operating Margin (%)	
		17	19
Sales Growth (%)	6	$10.83	$15.63
	8	13.26	18.04

When Sales Growth = 7% and Operating Margin = 18%, Value = $12.00 per share

mately demonstrates that relatively small changes in one or several key assumptions can significantly alter the analysis. It reveals the critical need to obtain reliable forecasts to input into the cash flow model.

Will Mary Kay succeed in an LBO or will it succumb to the inherent difficulties resulting from offering shareholders a price at the high end of the analysts' range of values? The firm, through 1986 and 1987, has had the benefit of lower interest rates on their mammoth debt position resulting in a significantly lower cost of capital than initially projected. On the other hand, the key factors are operating margin and sales growth. Can the company maintain margin and income growth? Can it stem the tide of declining profitability and competition in the direct sales marketplace? Only time will tell.

The Battle for Storer:
Coniston versus KKR

In the 1984 Storer Communications Inc. annual report, Peter Storer, the firm's chief executive officer and Terry Lee, its president, excitedly portrayed the year's results to stockholders: "...1984 was a watershed year setting the stage for accelerated improvements in 1985 and the years ahead.... In the latter part of 1985 we look for a strong performance in all phases of our operations, and can repeat with confidence that the long-range outlook for Storer Communications is very promising."

These were very encouraging words for a company whose 1984 income statement showed a $16.7 million loss on revenues of $537 million, and had not earned a profit since 1982. Interestingly, as illustrated in the Income Statement Data exhibit, despite the mounting losses, Storer did not eliminate its cash dividends but just lowered the annual payment from 72 cents per share in 1982 to 40 cents in 1984. Similar to the Income Statement Data, the information provided in the balance sheet data also indicated financial distress. From 1982 to 1984 Storer's long-term debt had been increased by $150 million, along with a $50 million a decline in its equity base. (See Income Statement Data and Balance Sheet Data exhibits.)

However, there were signs of hope, which these men were understandably trying to emphasize. In 1984, the Cable

---

We appreciate the research, analysis, and writing done by Mary Feddersen. Without her very significant contribution, the completion of the Storer case would not have been possible.

STORER COMMUNICATIONS
Income Statement Data: 1981-1985
(in millions, except per share data)

	Year Ended December 31			January to June	
	1982	1983	1984	1984	1985
Net revenues:					
Television	$156.6	$167.8	$184.7	$ 89.1	$ 98.1
Cable Communications:	222.7	291.1	352.1	166.9	193.0
Total revenues	379.3	458.9	536.8	256.0	291.1
Income/expense data:					
Operating income: Television	51.1	53.2	60.8	29.2	34.2
+ Operating income: Cable Communications	2.4	2.5	24.3	6.4	20.4
= Total operating income	53.5	55.7	85.1	35.6	54.6
− General corporate expense	(13.1)	(16.7)	(15.8)	(8.3)	(7.8)
− Other general and administrative expenses	(2.2)	(1.4)	(1.3)	(0.6)	(0.9)
+ Other income/(expenses)	2.8	(6.4)	5.2	0.3	(29.7)
= Income before interest and tax	41.0	31.2	73.2	27.0	16.2
− Interest expense	(51.3)	(67.7)	(86.6)	(40.7)	(39.0)
= Income before tax/(loss)	(10.3)	(36.5)	(13.4)	(13.7)	(22.8)
− (Tax liability)/credit	19.5	(3.2)	(3.3)	(1.9)	(2.0)
= Net income/(net loss)	$ 9.2	$ (39.7)	$ (16.7)	$ (15.6)	$ (24.8)
Per share data:					
Earnings/(loss)	$ .56	$ (2.42)	$ (1.02)	$ (.96)	$ (1.45)
Dividends	.72	.40	.40	.20	.20

STORER COMMUNICATIONS
Balance Sheet Data: 1982–1985
(in millions)

	Year Ended December 31			June	
	1982	1983	1984	1984	1985
Assets					
Net working capital (deficit)*	$ (13.7)	$ (32.0)	$ (34.2)	$ (35.1)	$ (22.7)
Property plant and equipment	803.9	908.4	911.6	908.8	788.0
Franchises and other intangibles	147.6	136.3	167.1	154.8	173.3
Other assets	70.1	65.8	62.7	61.7	78.9
Total assets	$1,007.9	$1,078.5	$1,107.2	$1,090.2	$1,017.5
Liabilities					
Long-term liabilities	$ 657.2	$ 757.4	$ 809.5	$ 788.1	$ 643.9
Stockholders' equity	350.7	321.1	297.7	302.1	373.6
Total invested capital	$1,007.9	$1,078.5	$1,107.2	$1,090.2	$1,017.5

*Net working capital = Short-term assets − Short-term liabilities.

Communications Division experienced continued growth in cable subscribers, resulting in a 21 percent increase in revenues. This division represented two thirds of total revenues with an operating margin of 7 percent. The Television Stations Division showed an increase in revenues of 10 percent and exhibited an impressive 33 percent operating margin. While these operating results were the hope of the company, the Achilles heel was its high leverage. Storer, as the nation's fifth largest cable company and a major television station operator, had incurred $785 million in long-term debt. This debt was undertaken primarily to finance the development of its cable systems. As a result, interest payments had increased from $7.64 million in 1980 to $86.5 million in 1984, raising the debt-equity ratio from .81 to 2.64. Such huge interest payments made it very difficult even for an highly profitable operation to result in overall company profitability.

Management's planned solution to this net loss and underlying debt problem was to sell certain cable systems which did not fit the company's operational or financial goals. These proceeds plus the increased cash flow from improving operations were expected to reduce long-term debt significantly. Based on this debt reduction, management forecasted a profit for 1985. (See Pro Forma Income Statement Data: 1985–1990 exhibit.)

On the positive side for Storer were the legal and regulatory events of 1984. Congress had passed the Cable Communication Policy Act of 1984 which benefited the industry in two ways. First, basic cable rates were deregulated, allowing rate increase programs. In addition, federal standards were set for franchise renewals which resulted in new industry stability. Furthermore, the Federal Communications Commission (FCC), continued on a deregulatory course, adopting a new 12 television station ownership limit. This represented a significant increase from the previous seven station maximum which Storer had already reached. The deregulatory measures enhanced the value of both the Cable Communication and Television Station divisions properties.

STORER COMMUNICATIONS
Pro Forma Income Statement Data: 1985–1990 (in millions)

| | Actual | | | Projected | | | |
	1984	1985	1986	1987	1988	1989	1990
Net revenues	$536.8	$602.8	$661.8	$743.3	$823.2	$907.4	$999.6
− Operating expenses	468.8	496.7	514.5	547.2	586.8	629.0	672.7
= Operating income	68.0	106.1	147.3	196.1	236.4	278.4	326.9
Net income	$ 16.7	$ 7.5	$ 88.7	$ 83.7	$113.5	$145.4	$179.9

THE BATTLE ERUPTS:
UNHAPPY SHAREHOLDERS

On March 19, 1985, a group of dissident shareholders, calling themselves the Committee for Full Value of Storer Communications Inc., announced it would try to gain control of the firm through proxy solicitation. The group's plan was to subsequently liquidate all of Storer's assets for an estimated $2 billion.

The group was led by the New York investment firm Coniston Partners, which was in turn managed by the eight-year-old investment company of Gollust & Tierney. Keith Gollust, 40, and Paul E. Tierney, 43, had met as associates in the corporate finance department of White Weld & Co. When White Weld was acquired by Merrill Lynch, Gollust left with two colleagues to form an investment firm. Tierney stayed on, rising to become managing director in charge of transportation finance. In 1978, Gollust and Tierney reunited to combine their corporate finance expertise and formed a company carrying both their names on the masthead. In 1983, they added a third principal to the firm, Augustus K. Oliver, who at age 35 had become a takeover specialist in the law firm of Skadden, Arps, Slate, Meagher, and Flom.

Gollust & Tierney had a history of investing in undervalued companies as active participants. Generally, the company bought a stake in a firm and attempted to realize the true value by selling or redeploying its assets. The principals had used this method in 1982 when they purchased Baldwin United's 32 percent interest in Bancroft Convertible fund, a closed-end investment fund whose shares were selling at 10 to 12 percent below the fund's asset value. By convincing Bancroft to become an open-end fund and make an offer to all shareholders to repurchase their shares for a value 1 percent below asset value, Gollust & Tierney made a quick $2.5 million profit on a $20 million investment.

The case of Storer was no different. Keith Gollust, both a principal in Gollust & Tierney and a partner in Coniston, believed values in the cable communication and broadcast stations industry were substantially higher than stock market prices. Assets of such companies had recently been selling privately, giving security analysts a benchmark to value other companies in the industry. For example, John Bauer, vice president of Oppenheimer & Company, valued a Storer liquidation at $90 a share while prior to the Coniston announcement the shares had been trading in the $60 range. He also stated, "You can buy cable and television assets on Wall Street for 50 cents on the dollar." The dissident group, directed by Gollust & Tierney, planned to nominate a rival slate of directors at Storer's May 7 annual meeting. Upon election of the new slate, these directors intended to immediately sell the company's assets and distribute the proceeds to the shareholders. In a filing with the Securities and Exchange Commission, Gollust & Tierney stated that it was in the interest of shareholders to get value out of Storer now through liquidation, not three years from now. Tierney claimed "it will be years before earnings are high enough to support a stock price at the liquidation value we are projecting." The dissident group further contended that management hadn't proven its ability to turn the company around. In addition, the group announced that it did not intend to accept any potential greenmail offered by the company.

After carefully evaluating Storer, in May 1984 Coniston began buying shares. In mid-March 1985, it controlled 5.3 percent or 867,500 of the company's 16.4 million shares outstanding, obtained at an average price of $48.50. The market for Storer stock heated up. On March 18, one day prior to Coniston's announced bid for control of Storer, the stock which had been trading at $45 in January, jumped 4¾ points to 64⅜. On March 19, the announcement date, it jumped another 5¾ points to 70⅛. Analysts meanwhile put a liquidation price tag on Storer between $1.9 and $2.5 billion which placed the value of the 21.5 million fully diluted shares in the range of $90 to $117 each.

A BITTER PROXY CONTEST

Management's initial reaction was to urge shareholders not to elect the rival slate. The board voted to "vigorously oppose" the takeover attempt, concluding that it was not in shareholders' best interests. A spokesman for the company stated that it was completing a "five-year billion dollar" program to build cable TV systems. Thus, he claimed that the benefits which would increase shareholder value would appear over the next few years.

Storer's second defense tactic was to use the Communications Act of 1934 in its legal battle against Coniston. This act required advance FCC approval of a change of control of any corporation holding an FCC license. Storer filed a petition asking the FCC to dismiss Coniston's application, claiming that Coniston was trying to avoid full examination of its qualifications to run a public service concern. Such a full examination and allowance of public comment would be required of the dissidents if the FCC determined that control of the company would be substantially different. Given that a full review could take in excess of two years before final consent, Storer's defense was clearly a time-delay tactic.

However, this defensive measure didn't work. On March 29, the FCC staff refused Storer's request for dismissal of Coniston's application to transfer control of Storer. The staff ruled that "control" lies with shareholders, not the board, and therefore a proxy contest to install a new board of directors would not constitute a change in control. Consequently, it was unnecessary for the dissidents to file a lengthy application and be subject to a full FCC review. Storer immediately filed an appeal, requesting a full commission review of the staff decision. The appeal was granted in early April.

Fighting for votes, Coniston's proxy statement used the following arguments to persuade shareholders. First, Storer's past and present financial problems, specifically its $785 million in long-term debt, would hold its future stock price down. As a result, the prospect of the company's market value reaching its current liquidation value which was placed at $1.9 to $2.1 billion, was not realistic in the near future. Second, the timing was ripe. As previously mentioned, the legal and regulatory climate was very positive. This no doubt enhanced values in the industry. Furthermore, excitement spread throughout the industry as a result of the merger between American Broadcasting Company and Capital Cities Communications. Other evidence was the Justice Department's allowance of the consolidation of two large cable systems through a swap of such systems between Storer and Times Mirror Corporation. In addition, in the proxy material the group claimed it would attempt to pay all proceeds in cash and to complete liquidation by early 1986. However, the group did not exclude the possibility of using notes or stocks as supplements to the cash component.

An interesting development provided the Storer management with another legal avenue to defend itself. On March 28, it was revealed that Coniston's advisory firm, Donaldson, Lufkin, and Jenrette (DLJ), had a stock interest in Storer. DLJ, along with Alliance Capital Management Corp., were subsidiaries of Equitable Life Assurance Society. Together, the three firms held 1.7 million shares of Storer, a 10.5 percent stake in the firm. Alliance controlled 758,225 shares, a 4.6 holding, while DLJ controlled 653,150, or a 3.9 percent of the firm. Storer filed a lawsuit in a federal district court in New York, alleging that DLJ and Alliance had "inside knowledge" of the pending proxy contest when they or their customers purchased the 1.7 million shares. The suit charged that Coniston Partners and DLJ worked "in concert" to acquire a significant number of Storer shares and, in soliciting stockholders they violated federal law. Storer asked the court for an injunction to prevent the dissidents from soliciting proxies or voting at the annual meeting. In response, Gollust & Tierney indicated that they had not known of DLJ's interest in Storer when the company was retained.

On April 12, the Federal Communications Commission ruled three to two in favor of the dissident shareholder group. The agency agreed that under the dissidents' proposal, control of the company would transfer. However, the commission ruled that the ensuing change would not be significant enough to require Coniston to follow the more extensive FCC rules. The decision demonstrated the agency's deregulatory stance and its determination to remain a neutral observer in takeover attempts. As expected, Storer appealed the FCC ruling to the U.S. Court of Appeals.

Meanwhile, as the battle heated up, on April 15, Standard & Poor's added Storer to its Creditwatch list, citing continued losses and high debt levels as detrimental to the BB— rating on Storer's subordinated debt.

Seeking refuge with legal and regulatory bodies proved fruitless. Storer was forced to defend itself with other methods. On April 16, the company announced it was willing to discuss a friendly merger with other firms and subsequently met with 22 potential suitors, providing financial information to 12 of them. The difficulty in finding a white knight resulted from Storer's massive long-term debt. Even at a reasonable acquisition price, the knight's earnings dilution from adding Storer's interest payments was expected to be huge.

Nevertheless, Storer did not give up. It launched an informational defense by mailing a letter to stockholders, again urging them to reject the takeover bid. At a news conference, Peter Storer, the son of the company's founder, indicated that by 1988 or 1989 Storer's debt would be reduced and operations improved to increase its asset value to around $200 a share. This $200 price was determined by Storer using a "commercially acceptable formula for a communications company" and was found to be "9 to 10 times the following year's operating cash flow less debt." The operating cash flows were taken from Storer's projections prepared in April 1985 shown in the Pro Forma Income Statement Data exhibit. Peter Storer disputed Coniston's estimated liquidation value, saying that tax considerations and the difficulty in quickly transferring broadcast and cable properties to new owners would reduce the value estimated by the dissidents from $90 to $100 per share to $63 a share. Storer argued that liquidating the fifth largest cable operator and major broadcast concern would bring fire sale prices and shareholders would not receive full value. In a letter mailed on April 20, shareholders were told to expect $63 from liquidation and were provided with projections that by 1989 Storer shares should be worth $207 to $228 a piece.

Contrasting Storer's version of its outlook, Augustus Oliver, a partner with Gollust & Tierney, reported that the negative tax consequences of liquidation would be minimized and "the proceeds would in fact be $90 to $100 a share," not

$63. He added that Coniston was "skeptical about the ability of Storer management to produce anything like the $200 a share asset values in the time frame they are talking about."

Angry with this $200 projection, on April 20, Coniston's Committee for Full Value filed counterclaims against Storer Communications and Peter Storer in the federal court in New York. The lawsuit sought to prohibit them from "repeating unsubstantiated predictions of the future value of Storer and the value of the program proposed by the Committee." In addition, Coniston sent out its own letter to shareholders, standing by its liquidation valuation.

Meanwhile, first-quarter results showed a decrease in Storer's net loss from $14.6 million a year earlier to $5.7 million. In addition, quarterly revenue increased by 15 percent from 1984, and according to management, earnings were expected to improve in the second half of the year. The stock was then trading in the $75 range and was steadily increasing.

STORER: EXCHANGE OFFER—A WEAK AND FLEETING DEFENSE ATTEMPT

When the search for a white knight as well as additional appeals to shareholders were not successful, Storer turned to more drastic measures. It realized that some shareholders wanted to maximize current value while others wished to retain equity. To meet these conflicting stockholder needs, on April 23, Storer's board approved an offer to buy back 6 million shares, a 36 percent of the total. This "exchange offer" was issued upon the advice of Storer's investment banker, Dillon, Read & Co. The exchange offer was planned to proceed in two stages with each one being 3 million shares. Payment would consist of a package of cash and securities valued by the company at $100 a share. In exchange for each share of stock, the holder would receive $40 in cash and $60 principal amount of 10-year subordinated debenture. Provisions of the debenture included: (1) no interest for three years, (2) 16 percent interest thereafter, and (3) callable after three years. In addition, the debentures were expected to be traded at a discount. The company planned to finance the exchange buyback through: (1) bank financing for the cash portion, (2) calling $100 million of outstanding convertible debentures, and thereby hoping to force a conversion and eliminate some debt payment responsibilities, and (3) the "sale of certain assets." The Coniston group dismissed the buyback plan as inadequate and not delivering full value to all stockholders.

At that time, Storer's board rejected as "inadequate" a leveraged buyout proposal from the New York investment banking firm of Kohlberg Kravis Roberts & Co. (KKR). The terms of the offer were to convert each of Storer's common shares into $75 cash and $25 in liquidating preference preferred stock. This liquidating preferred would have priority over both common stock and any other series of preferred stock issued with cumulative dividends, and would have a $25 value at the end of six years. In addition, the "preferred" wouldn't pay dividends for six years but would pay 13 percent dividends for nine years thereafter. The offer also required Storer to pay a $3 million fee for preparation and submission of the KKR offer, and $18 million if the merger were canceled for any reason other than KKR's failure to obtain financing. Storer's board deemed the offer inadequate, basing its decision on advice from Dillon Read that the cash portion was too low.

STORER AGREED TO A KKR LEVERAGED BUYOUT: A STRONGER DEFENSE

Two days later, on April 25, Storer's board withdrew its proposed stock buyback plan and approved a revised leveraged buyout plan to take the company private by a corporation to be formed by KKR. The new plan involved conversion of each Storer common share into: $75 cash, $25 face value "liquidating" preference stock described above, and an unspecified number of warrants to purchase a total of 10 percent of the common stock in the new company. The warrants which would be exercisable only if the firm made a public stock offering, would expire after 10 years. If no offering occurred, the warrants would be bought back at a price equal to the appraised value of the underlying shares in the new company. The value of the proposed transaction was estimated at $1.64 billion. The reasons for the board's agreement with the LBO proposal were its fairness to shareholders; its inclusion of warrants for the current shareholders; and finally, but most likely not least importantly, the ability of certain executives to obtain equity in the new firm. Peter Storer would remain chairman and chief executive officer of the new company.

Completion of the revised buyout depended on a number of conditions. They included arrangement of financing by KKR, approval of Storer shareholders, and approval by the FCC and other cable-franchising authorities. The remuneration associated with the second offer also changed slightly. Storer agreed to pay KKR a fee of approximately $21.2 million which amounted to $1 per fully diluted Storer share, plus expenses if the merger collapsed under any of the following conditions:

1. Storer's acceptance of another acquisition offer.
2. The election of less than five incumbent directors.
3. Acquisition by a third party of 15 percent of Storer's common stock in a tender offer.
4. Disclosure of ownership of 15 percent or more of Storer's stock, including at least 5 percent acquired after April 24.

Obviously, these terms were an attempt to prevent another party from taking control of Storer. Specifically, it would cost any "other" party a hefty extra $21.2 million if it were to acquire the company instead of KKR.

Industry reaction was positive. In general, observers felt that the leveraged buyout was superior to Storer's buyback offer because of the warrants, and slightly better than KKR's first offer. Beyond this, opinions ranged from the doubtfulness of better offers due to Storer's high leverage to the possibility that more offers would come in.

The Coniston group's response was to continue its proxy battle in order to "close a transaction which would bring the highest value to all shareholders...whether it's this transaction, a higher bid or a liquidation." The $1.64 billion value placed on the KKR offer was not as high as the dissident group had expected.

On May 3, the U.S. Circuit Court of Appeals affirmed the FCC ruling that if the dissident group won the proxy fight it would not involve a significant change in control of the company's broadcast licenses, and therefore, extended examination of Coniston was not required.

Also on the same day, amid speculation that Telecommunications Inc. would make an acquisition bid, Storer signed a definitive agreement with KKR, adhering to the terms described in the second offer above. No other bids for Storer were submitted prior to the shareholder meeting on May 7, where the intense proxy contest for the control of Storer was expected to be decided.

The friction continued even after the votes were cast. Storer filed suit in Ohio state court, arguing that the latest votes were improperly tabulated by the Coniston group. Each group had been assigned to tabulate its own proxy votes. Coniston countersued and the court rejected Storer's bid for a recount. May and June passed with little action as both sides awaited the outcome of the proxy contest.

THE PROXY BATTLE IS DECIDED

In the proxy battle the directors were elected using cumulative voting. With this type of voting each share controlled nine votes, one for each director position. Each vote could then be distributed as the shareholder wished. The result of the voting was the seating of five incumbent directors and four newly elected dissidents. The plan to be taken private by KKR through the newly formed corporation, SCI Holdings Inc., was not affected. A representative for the dissidents, Paul Tierney, Jr., assured the company that they would not try to upset the buyout but would continue to look for higher offers, attempting to gain fair value to shareholders which the dissidents figured to be between $90 and $100 a share.

In early July, amendments concerning SCI Holding's decision to use public offerings of securities to finance the merger were submitted to, and then approved by, the Storer board. SCI Holding's $1.9 billion financing package included the following:

- Issuance of $1.2 billion in securities including: (*a*) $600 million of serial zero coupon senior notes; (*b*) $500 million of 12-year senior subordinated debentures; and (*c*) $100 million of units consisting of 15-year subordinated debentures and interests in a KKR-limited partnership.
- Commitments for $740 million in financing from a banking syndicate led by Citibank.

To complete the buyout, SCI had to obtain definitive financing by October 10. But at this time, speculation arose that Comcast Inc., the 16th largest cable-television company, would also bid for Storer. In mid-July, the stock price was still rising, and on July 12 it closed at $81.50.

A NEW BIDDER

As it turned out, the speculators were right. On July 16 Comcast did indeed bid for Storer. The offer was valued by Comcast at $97 a share, and included cash, stock, and warrants for a total value of $1.84 billion. The terms of the offer called for making Storer a subsidiary of Comcast and provided shareholders with $82 per share in cash, 1.2 shares of $25 liquidation preference stock in the new subsidiary, and 1.2 warrants to buy the new subsidiary common stock.

Comcast had arranged $2.3 billion in financing. It included $200 million cash, $900 million in loans, and $1.2 billion from Merrill Lynch which would manage the sale of Storer's seven television stations and underwrite the issuance of the subordinated debt in Comcast's new subsidiary.

Industry analysts generally agreed that this new offer was superior to KKR's proposed leveraged buyout, noting it would pay $7 more a share in cash and that the paper issued by Comcast would be more valuable than that issued by KKR.

Meanwhile, the then successful Wall Street risk arbitraguer Ivan Boesky and a group of companies bought a 9.6 percent stake in Storer, attempting once again to gain arbitrage profits.

After reviewing both the Comcast bid and KKR's second offer, the Storer board advised both bidders that on July 29 it would reconvene to consider any proposals either party wished to present.

On Monday, July 29, both bidders returned with sweetened offers, each anticipating that its rival would increase its bid. According to Comcast, its new offer had a value of $98 per share. The package offered to shareholders included:

1. $83.50 per share in cash.
2. $35.00 face value of subordinated zero coupon debentures in the surviving company.
3. .353 shares of "liquidation preference" stock with a face value of $25.
4. The right to receive, within 180 days of the merger, the proceeds from a sale underwritten by Merrill Lynch Capital Market of an additional .52 shares of the "liquidation preferred" stock, or $5.25 in cash at Comcast's option.

Storer's investment banker, Dillon Read, valued the offer at $95 to $96 a share. This valuation was based on the capitalization of the surviving company, the interest rate at the time of the closing, and the uncertain proceeds which would be realized from the proposed sale of preferred stock.

KKR's revised offer was for $90 cash and one merger warrant per common share and also included certain options to be given to KKR. Valued by Dillon Read at $92.50 a share, the board favored this bid if certain modifications could be effected to increase the value of the offer.

In reaching the decision that the KKR offer was superior to Comcast's, the board cited numerous reasons including the following:

1. The higher cash component of the KKR offer compared to the slightly higher, although less certain, value of the Comcast package.
2. The greater uncertainty and complexity of the Comcast bid, including the uncertainty of the market value of the securities offered.
3. The possible delay of up to 180 days after the merger in realizing the cash proceeds from the sale of preferred stock, and the unknown amount of these proceeds.
4. The greater likelihood that the KKR transaction would be completed on a timely basis, considering the significant progress already made in applying for necessary regulatory approval.
5. Potential diminution of Storer's business value if key personnel departed following acceptance of Comcast's offer, and the risks to the company if the Comcast transaction did not close.

KKR agreed to certain adjustments and the resulting offer was $91 cash and one merger warrant with an exercise price of $4.72 to buy common stock in the new company. The modified agreement was valued by Dillon Read at $93.50 a share for a total of $2.51 billion. As part of the deal, Storer agreed to give KKR certain lockup options exercisable if Storer were acquired by another party. These included the right to buy three of Storer's most profitable television stations for $635 million. The value was adjusted upward at Storer's request to reflect the new higher value offer, and the option to purchase up to 3.5 million, or 16 percent of Storer's common shares at $90 each. As illustrated in the Financing of the Deal exhibit, seven different types of financing vehicles were used. The largest amount was bank loan financing, followed by notes, subordinated debentures, preferred stock, common stock, working capital credit line, and warrants.

The seven nonmanagement directors rejected the Comcast offer and voted to approve the deal with KKR's offer. On October 23, shareholders were mailed a proxy statement for approval at the November 22 special shareholder meeting.

STORER COMMUNICATIONS
Financing the Deal (in millions)

Sources of funds:	
Bank debt (7½-year senior revolving credit)	$ 740
Working capital line of credit	50
Issuance of notes	600
Issuance of the senior subordinated debentures	600
Issuance of the preferred stock	261
Issuance of holdings common stock	227
Issuance of the warrants	5
Total	$2,483

Uses of funds:	
Payment for shares of Storer common stock	$1,929
Available for payment of fees and expenses incurred in connection with the consummation of the merger, and repayment of certain indebtedness of Storer and for working capital	554
Total	$2,483

Comcast's reaction to the board's decision was strong and bitter. Bernard Gallagher, vice president and treasurer of Comcast, stated that his company would not make another bid for Storer because of the lockup options or "poison pills" granted to KKR. He stated that a hostile tender offer "may have been a possibility" before these options were awarded. "I think they've effectively spoiled the company for future bidders." This reaction was echoed by Wall Street analysts who agreed that the new deal made it highly unlikely that anyone else would buy the company. John Bauer of Oppenheimer and Co, summed up Wall Street thinking by saying that the higher cash portion in the KKR bid, and top officials' concern at possibly being replaced, influenced Storer's decision to reject Comcast's offer. Finally, he referred to the options granted to KKR, saying that Storer had "built in some awesome poison pills."

On November 22, shareholders approved the merger and thus the Committee for Full Value of Storer Communications Inc. achieved its objective of obtaining between $90 and $100 per share. Each shareholder received $91 cash, and a merger warrant valued at $2.25. As illustrated in The Events and the Common Stock's Market Price exhibit, Storer's shareholders did very well. Just 11 months before the approval of the merger the stock changed hands for $45 a share.

After completion of the merger, 97.2 percent of the new common stock was held by KKR associates, and 2.8 percent by management investors. On a fully diluted basis, the ownership was 83 percent KKR associates, 7 percent management investors, and 10 percent original Storer common stockholders.

Although top management lost the battle for independence, it was able to preserve its position in a going concern, and positioned itself with 7 percent equity in the new company.

STORER COMMUNICATIONS
The Events and the Common Stock Market Price

Date	Event	Stock Price
January 1985	—	$45.125
3/18/85	One day prior to dissident group announcement	$64.375
3/19/85	Coniston announces proxy solicitation to obtain control of Storer	$70.125
4/19/85	FCC sides with dissident group*	$74.875
4/22/85	Storer offers stock buyback for: $40 cash $60 debenture*	$76.25
4/25/85	KKR LBO accepted by Storer, approximate value: 1.64B/21.2M shares = $77.40 a share	$77.75
5/02/85	Speculation Telecommunications will make an acquisition bid	$75.75
7/12/85	Speculation Comcast Inc. will bid for Storer	$81.50
7/16/85	Storer's board of directors votes to approve revised offer by KKR valued at $93.50 a share, provide lockup options to KKR	$85.875
November 1985	Shareholders approve LBO by KKR	$93.25

*Indicates event occurred approximately at cited date.

EPILOGUE

A month after the LBO, Peter Storer, chairman and chief executive officer of Storer announced his retirement. KKR, in August 1986, after arranging the buyouts of Storer and Wometco, another major cable operator, now arranged the buyout of Wometco by Storer. Ironically, it also announced that it might once again offer Storer's shares to the public

A Pantry Raid at Revlon

August 1985: "It's clear they intend to take [Revlon] apart like you take apart a chicken, chew on the bones, and spit out the pieces." This was the complaint of one Revlon executive describing the intentions of its hostile suitor, Pantry Pride, Inc. Revlon had long been rumored on Wall Street as a prime takeover target. In August, Pantry Pride approached Revlon intending to "buy the company cheap and bust it up," according to Revlon's much maligned Chairman and Chief Executive Officer Michel C. Bergerac.

THE QUEEN OF BEAUTY

Revlon, based in New York, was started by Charles Revson in 1932. By 1985, it was involved in two main businesses: health care and beauty products. The health care division manufactured and sold a broad range of products including ethical pharmaceutical products, vision care products, and medical diagnostic systems. These businesses were Revlon's fastest growing segments and required large capital expenditures in order to assure continued growth. The beauty products business consisted of both manufacturing and distribu-

---

We appreciate the research, analysis, and writing done by Lisa Stavro and Raj Chandaria. Without their very significant contribution, the completion of the Revlon case would not have been possible.

tion. The products included cosmetics, fragrances, beauty care and treatment products which were sold worldwide. Some of its well-known brand names included Charlie and Scoundrel fragrances, Flex Shampoo, Custom Eyes, and Natural Wonder Super Nails beauty care products. Even with these well-known brands, from 1982 to 1984 the beauty care division of the company experienced a 20 percent decline in operating profit. Nevertheless, Revlon was an attractive takeover candidate. In 1984, it reported a $300 million operating profit on $2.4 billion sales. In addition, with $1 billion equity and $470 million long-term debt it had a low debt-equity ratio, an important characteristic for any group contemplating the use of leverage in taking it over. Obviously, such investors found Revlon as a firm with many desired features. In addition to its low leverage, it paid out 63 percent of its earnings as dividends to the holders of its 38.3 million shares outstanding. Any group considering taking Revlon private could incorporate savings resulting from discontinuing these payments in its pro forma cash budget. The following pie charts summarize Revlon's health care and beauty businesses and their contribution to Revlon's 1984 sales and operating income. (See Revlon Selected Financials—1984 exhibit.)

REVLON
Selected Financials—1984

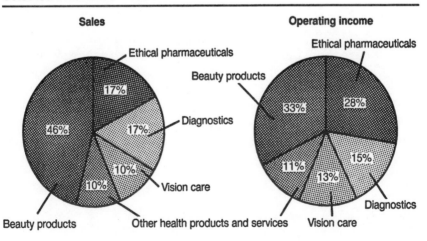

As illustrated in the chart, the various business segments vary significantly in their profit margin. For example, the beauty products contribute 46 percent of Revlon's sales, but only 33 percent of its operating income. In contrast, ethical pharmaceutical products contribute only 17 percent of Revlon's sales but 28 percent of its operating income. This type of information is crucial for the investing group. On one hand it is tempting to liquidate the low-margin units and use the proceeds to pay back part of the amount borrowed for the buyout. On the other hand, if a low-margin segment is also a low-risk (stable) business, it might be worthwhile retaining it. A stable cash flow is a crucial ingredient in a successful post-LBO plan.

DEFENSIVE ACTIONS AND TAKEOVER SPECULATION

At the May 1985 annual shareholder meeting, Revlon passed certain antitakeover amendments to discourage any potential hostile bids. These included:

1. Golden parachutes for Revlon executives.
2. Staggered terms for Revlon directors.
3. All stockholder actions must be taken at an annual or special meeting.
4. The size of the board can be changed only by a majority vote of the directors.
5. Revlon directors can be removed only by approval of at least 80 percent of the shares.

Revlon officials stated that these measures were not in response to any specific takeover threat. They were taken strictly as defensive measures for possible future hostile bids. Yet, Revlon had been rumored as a takeover target, primarily because of the attractiveness of its health care business. The health care division was made up of independent units that could be spun off and sold separately. If sold off, these units could likely be sold for more than the entire division. The high value of these units was based on the present value of future cash flows that each unit could generate. Additionally, the market value of each unit was driven up by the unit's value to another firm specializing in its line of business. As a result, the sum of the Revlon parts were worth more than the whole. This, in addition to criticism of Bergerac by some analysts, made Revlon a valuable takeover candidate.

Below are estimated values of each Revlon unit if sold separately made by Wall Street analysts.

Business Unit	Estimated Value (in millions)
Vision-Care Business	$ 380–$ 400
National Health Labs	220– 300
Medical Diagnostic Division	421
Norcliff Thayer	180
Reheis Chemical Company	170
Prescription Drugs	600
Technicon and Other Health Care Units	79
Beauty Care Division	900
	$2,950–$3,050

On August 14, 1985, Revlon takeover speculation began. Rumors filled Wall Street that Revlon had been approached by Pantry Pride attempting to buy the health care and beauty products company. Later, Michel Bergerac admitted attending three meetings with Pantry Pride—one in June and two in the week of August 12. He said that Pantry Pride didn't make a specific offer, "but the indication was that they were trying to buy the company cheap and bust it up...the bust up artist [would] sell anything [he] could sell." The speculation that such meetings occurred was reflected in Revlon's stock price. On August 14, following heavy trading, Revlon's stock increased by $1.50 closing at 45³⁄₈.

THE HOSTILE SUITOR

Pantry Pride, Inc., based in Florida, was controlled by MacAndrews and Forbes Holding Inc. It took control of Pantry Pride in 1985 with a $60 million preferred stock purchase—37 percent controlled by MacAndrews and Forbes's corporate interest, and 63 percent owned by the public. Pantry Pride was a retailer and supermarket operator whose assets included 112 retail stores, 419 drugstores, and 40 supermarkets. It had been looking for an acquisition for some time.

According to Ronald O. Perelman, chairman of MacAndrews and Forbes, "We look for companies that are strong cash flow generators and are free from major capital expenditure requirements." The *New York Times* commented about Perelman's strategy: " . . . He has built a successful mini-conglomerate . . . by borrowing heavily to buy a stable of companies, then putting his own brand of financial wizardry to work on each by selling off just the right assets and squeezing the remainder of the business to produce hefty cash flows."

Pantry Pride said it was "actively seeking to dispose of substantially all of its assets and businesses and to acquire new ones." To raise cash, Perelman planned to sell off its supermarkets and other retail chains. This would come on top of the $700 million obtained by Pantry Pride through the July 1984 sale of high-yield, low-rated junk securities. Perelman's objective was to create a corporate shell out of Pantry Pride. This takeover war chest could then be used to buy up businesses with greater money-making potential. Furthermore, as of July 1984, the company had tax loss carryforwards of about $330 million, leading to a search for firms with profitable operations whose income could be sheltered. One mutual fund executive summed up Perelman's maneuverings as "He's absolutely brilliant in using leverageability of smaller companies and buying bigger companies."

THE BATTLE BEGINS

On August 19, 1985, the official battle for Revlon began. Revlon ended talks with Pantry Pride and immediately adopted two additional antitakeover measures:

1. A buyback offer to its shareholders for 5 million of its 38 million outstanding shares. Revlon negotiated bor-

rowings of up to $1 billion which would give it the flexibility to buy back up to 62 percent of the shares outstanding. Because of this plan, both Moody's and Standard & Poor's said they were considering downgrading Revlon's debt rating.

2. The adoption of a poison pill provision. Revlon's variation of the poison pill stated, "if someone acquires 20 percent of Revlon's shares, other holders can exchange their shares for $65 face amount of 12 percent one-year Revlon notes; the hostile acquirer is barred from doing so." Additionally, the rights given to Revlon shareholders to participate in this exchange were "redeemable by Revlon for 10 cents each, anytime prior to a 20 percent acquisition." The aim of the poison pill was "to increase the amount of securities outstanding and make an unwanted takeover bid prohibitively expensive."

In response to Revlon's defensive actions and the adjournment of its meetings with Pantry Pride, Pantry Pride announced a $1.9 billion hostile tender offer for Revlon. The offer included $47.50 for "any and all" outstanding common shares and $26.67 for all preferred shares. To finance the takeover, Pantry Pride planned to use its $750 million currently held in cash and marketable securities, $500 million worth of funds made available by Chemical Bank, and $650 million through another issue of junk bonds. Two days later, the $650 figure for the junk bond issue was revised upward to $900 million. Pantry Pride's offer was conditional on the success of this debt issue. But many felt this condition raised doubts about Pantry Pride's ability to raise enough money for the transaction. The junk bond offering was to be handled by Drexel Burnham Lambert, Pantry Pride's investment banker. The Pantry Pride transaction was to be a "departure in tactics for Drexel" because the offering would be to the public rather than to institutions and wealthy individuals to which Drexel had been accustomed.

Pantry Pride also conditioned its offer on the removal of the poison pill. Ronald Perelman called Revlon's poison pill "a blatant attempt to deny its shareholders their right to decide for themselves whether or not to take advantage of our cash tender offer."

THE LEGAL BATTLEFIELD

Within a day of Revlon's receipt of the hostile tender offer, two lawsuits were filed.

1. Revlon filed a suit against Pantry Pride and MacAndrew and Forbes in the U.S. District Court in Delaware. Revlon charged that Pantry Pride manipulated the price of Revlon's stock by spreading "materially false and misleading statements to the investing public and certain selected market professionals." Revlon claimed that Pantry Pride failed to say it was raising money to buy Revlon during their previous meetings. Bergerac commented, "We are being met with poison so we are applying the necessary antidotes."

2. Pantry Pride filed against Revlon in the U.S. District Court in New York. The suit was filed "to prevent Revlon and [the] New York state attorney general's office from enforcing the state law on takeovers." The state law said that one who makes an offer cannot "omit to state any material fact necessary in order to make the statement made...or to engage in any fraudulent, deceptive or manipulative acts or practices, in connection with any tender offer...." Pantry Pride claimed that it did not hold back any information or act in a manipulative manner. The enforcement of this law was likely to delay Pantry Pride's offer. Two days later, another suit was filed.

3. Pantry Pride filed against Revlon in the Delaware state court. It asked the court to declare the poison pill measures adopted by Revlon as "invalid and unlawful." It claimed that the poison pill "effectively transfers" the power of takeover proposal considerations away from the shareholders and gives it to the directors. This would be a "breach of fiduciary duty" by Revlon. The hearing was scheduled for September 10, 1985.

PANTRY PRIDE'S PLANS

Pantry Pride planned to sell Revlon's health care units individually for a breakup value of $1.95 billion. All of Pantry Pride's borrowings would be repaid by the sale of these units and from other sources such as the $88 million in surplus assets from Revlon's employee retirement plan. It would keep the domestic beauty products line, estimated to be worth approximately $900 million.

Bergerac felt that $65 per share "would be the price at which the board would consider something." Security analysts speculated that $50 to $55 per share might be a fair price for the company. To these estimates Bergerac responded that "I respect the [analysts'] opinion... but it isn't necessarily mine."

On August 19, 1985, the day of Pantry Pride's hostile tender offer, Revlon common stock jumped 87.5 cents closing at 45⅝. By the end of the week, the stock increased to a closing price of 46⅞.

Pantry Pride apparently sought Revlon because of its high breakup value and its comparative bargain basement stock price. Daniel J. Meade, an analyst at the First Boston Corporation, commented: "If a split-up of Revlon is worth so much, then why is its stock trading below Pantry Pride's [$47.50] offer? One main reason is that investment bankers are assuming that Revlon's parts can be individually retailed for top dollar, which has yet to be seen. Purchased in its entirety by a 'wholesale' buyer, the company is worth no more than $49 per share."

REVLON FIGHTS BACK
BY RESTRUCTURING

Revlon's board reacted strongly to Pantry Pride's $47.50 per share offer, noting that it was "grossly inadequate" and "detrimental to Revlon's interests." On August 26, Revlon decided to replace its buyback plan for 5 million common shares with a new defensive measure. It concluded that the buyback proposal wasn't sufficient to "deflect the Pantry Pride bid." The new plan called for financially restructuring Revlon in hopes that "combined with the poison pill... [it] will be enough to sink the Pantry Pride offer."

Revlon's proposed restructuring included a swap for 26 percent or 10 million of the common shares outstanding. Under this offer, a shareholder who converted 10 Revlon common shares would receive in return 10 notes with a face value of $47.50 apiece. These notes would pay 11.75 percent interest each year for 10 years, after which they would be redeemed. In addition, the shareholder would receive one share of Revlon's $9 preferred stock which had a face value of $100 and which was convertible into 1.739 Revlon common shares. At this time, Revlon shares were trading at around $44 per share. A Revlon shareholder who did trade in his 10 Revlon shares would thus receive $475 worth of notes plus one preferred share worth 1.739 × $44, a total of $551.52 or $55.15 worth of securities per each share turned in. Revlon's intention was to buy back 10 million of its shares in this manner, financed by an increase in debt, thus making the company less attractive to Pantry Pride.

The securities that Revlon planned to issue would be "laced with covenants." The covenants "would limit Revlon's future debt level, dividend payments and asset sales." This debt would also have a first call on the company's assets— making it particularly risky for insurance companies, pension funds and others that ordinarily might buy high-risk, high-yield junk bonds that would be used to finance the venture.

The plan also included the sale of $250 million of Revlon assets. With the financial restructuring plan, Revlon would more than double its long-term debt to a level of $956 million and would shrink its equity position by more than one half to $460 million. The new debt-equity ratio would be approximately 2:1, compared to its debt-equity ratio of .47:1 prior to the swap. Revlon hoped to increase its debt sufficiently such that Pantry Pride's issue of junk bonds would be too risky a transaction for investors. The swap offer expired a month later, on September 27, 1985.

Ronald Perelman commented on Revlon's "debt-for-stock" takeover defense as "outstandingly absurd and horrendous" for shareholders. But according to Bergerac, Revlon was acting in their best interests. "We want to make sure we don't let the company be sold at a bargain basement price, because our shareholders deserve better than that."

On August 26, after the market closed, Revlon revealed its restructuring plans. The following day its stock dropped by 1⅝ to 44¾. Many felt that the fall was due to shareholder apprehensiveness that Pantry Pride's takeover attempt would fail.

HOW FAR WOULD THE BATTLE GO?

As the end of August came around, there were differing opinions on how the Revlon-Pantry Pride battle would continue. A friend of Ronald Perelman commented, "I wouldn't plan on Ron buying Revlon." He said that the takeover battle would "drive up the price of Revlon stock and make the transaction too expensive to achieve those wonderful returns Mr. Perelman is accustomed to." Daniel Meade of First Boston also had doubts that the takeover would materialize: "I don't think it will go at all. We're telling people to at least sell half of their positions."

But on August 23 *The Wall Street Journal* reported that "the takeover story is far from over. Despite all the impediments Revlon had erected...Pantry Pride may increase its offer. This could be one of the biggest cat fights in history."

On September 12, 1985, Federal Judge Joseph Farnan of the U.S. District Court in Delaware denied Revlon's "request for a preliminary injunction to stop Pantry Pride." Judge Farnan concluded that Pantry Pride had not violated the federal securities laws by failing to disclose its plans to buy Revlon. Furthermore, the judge said that the federal margin regulations would not be violated by Pantry Pride's borrowing plans. The Federal Reserve's margin rules "specify that a purchaser can't borrow more than 50 percent of the value of the stock being bought."

The day following this ruling, Revlon announced that 87 percent of its total shares outstanding (33 million shares) had been tendered in its self-tender swap offer valued at $55 per share. Since Revlon would only purchase 10 million shares (26 percent of the total shares outstanding), there was a proration factor of 30 percent. This meant that by retiring 10 million shares, Revlon would accept 30 percent of the shares tendered by each holder. Revlon officials commented, "The response to [the] self-tender offer showed that shareholders clearly backed the company's management."

On this same day, September 12, Pantry Pride offered a new, lower bid of $42 a share for Revlon. This was a decrease of $5.50 from its original offer of $47.50 which was rejected by the Revlon board. Pantry Pride also terminated its offer to purchase preferred stock. A Pantry Pride adviser said, "all we did was reduce dollar for dollar our offer to purchase preferred stock, to reflect what Revlon holders are receiving from the company."

The motivation for Pantry Pride's reduced offer was the additional debt which Revlon assumed in its debt-for-stock swap. If Pantry Pride succeeded in the acquisition, it would take on the $550 million of new debt (10 million shares times $55 market value). Additionally, Revlon's common shares outstanding decreased by 10 million shares to 28.3 million as a result of the swap.

The reasoning behind Pantry Pride's offer is summarized in Panels I and II of the Revlon Swap Offer exhibit. In Panel I, the value received by Revlon shareholders in the buyback is shown to be $551.5 million. This is determined by summing the value of the notes received by shareholders ($47.50) and the value of the preferred shares received ($7.65). This sum ($55.15) is then multiplied by the number of shares to be repurchased (10 million).

The total, received by Revlon shareholders is approximately equal to the reduction in the offer made by Pantry Pride. This is shown in Panel II. Pantry Pride had previously offered $1.819 billion for Revlon. They now reduced their offer to $1.261 billion due to the 10 million share reduction in Revlon shares outstanding. The new offer was thus $558 mil-

REVLON
Swap Offer

Panel I—Value Received by Revlon Shareholders

Revlon shareholders received from Revlon:

A note worth	$47.50
¹/₁₀ of a preferred share worth ¹/₁₀ × 1.739 × $44	7.65
Total amount per share	$55.15

Total amount received by Revlon's shareholders:

10 million shares tendered × $55.15 per share	$551.50 million

Panel II—Reduction in Offer by Pantry Pride

Pantry Pride's previous offer:

$47.50 × 38.3 million common shares =	$1,819.25 million

Pantry Pride's new offer:

28.3 million common shares + 1 million preferred shares convertible into 1.739 million common shares or a total of 30.04 million shares at $42 per share =	$1,261.68 million
A reduction of:	$557.57 million

---

lion less than the old offer, an amount approximately equal to that received by Revlon shareholders in the buyback.

The only condition associated with Pantry Pride's new offer was that 90 percent of Revlon's outstanding shares be "tendered and not withdrawn." Unlike its previous offer, Pantry Pride did not condition its offer on the removal of the poison pill. However, Pantry Pride said it "would consider making an appropriate increase in the price of [its] new tender offer" if Revlon nullified its poison pill provision. A Wall Street takeover speculator commented that "Pantry Pride is still making a strong offer because Revlon's stock would probably be trading at about $38 a share if Pantry Pride hadn't launched its takeover bid."

On September 13, 1985, Revlon common stock closed down 87.5 cents at $43. Traders predicted that the decline was due to a combination of two factors: Pantry Pride's reduced offer and the oversubscription to Revlon's self-tender.

For the next week and a half, Revlon's stock price continued to fall, closing on September 23 at 41⅜. As expected, on September 24, Revlon rejected Pantry Pride's reduced offer.

PANTRY PRIDE TRIES AGAIN

Then on September 27, Pantry Pride made a new hostile tender offer of $50 per share, or $1.4 billion, claiming that it was still seeking "a friendly merger." This new offer was proposed along with the following conditions:

1. Revlon's board must redeem the poison pill rights that were issued.
2. It must waive the covenants restricting total debt and asset sale levels.
3. The board must cancel the payment restrictions included in the notes that Revlon issued in its swap offer.
4. Revlon must eliminate the debt-to-capitalization ratio covenant included in the preferred stock also issued in its swap offer.

Nancy Hall, a Prudential-Bache securities analyst who followed the cosmetics business, said Revlon would probably turn down this offer as well. She added, "the only way Revlon is going to top $50 is through a leveraged buyout or a white knight."

NEW RUMORS ON WALL STREET

On October 1, 1985, rumors covered Wall Street that Revlon was negotiating to be taken private in a leveraged buyout with Forstmann Little. As expected, such talk had an effect on Revlon's stock price, causing it to jump 3⅞ to close at 50⅜.

Forstmann Little's previous transactions had included a $416 million buyout of Dr Pepper and a $370 million buyout of 12 ITT companies. Revlon would be Forstmann Little's largest buyout transaction.

As buyout rumors began to travel, Pantry Pride took action and sweetened its bid to $53 per share. Pantry Pride didn't give Revlon much time and conditioned the offer on its acceptance by October 1, 1985. According to Wall Street sources, Revlon also received a proposal from American Home Products, a New York-based pharmaceutical and consumer products company. For the first time, Revlon was considering merger proposals. Revlon's board told management to "request that Pantry Pride continue to keep open its latest $53 cash merger proposal, [originally planned to expire October 1], so as to permit [the Revlon board] to consider it along with the other proposals." This statement was the first admission by Revlon that it was for sale. The news was reflected in Revlon's stock price by a jump of $4, closing at 54⅛ on October 2.

REVLON'S FINAL DEFENSE ATTEMPT

On October 3, 1985, Revlon announced that it would break up the company through a leveraged buyout by Forstmann Little and Revlon management for $56 a share, or a total of $1.77 billion. Revlon's plan to be taken private included the following transactions.

1. The Norcliff Thayer unit and Revlon's chemical company, the Reheis unit, would be sold to American Home Products for $350 million.
2. Adler and Shaykin, a small private investment partnership that specializes in leveraged buyouts, would lead a group that would buy Revlon's beauty products business worldwide for $900 million.
3. The Forstmann group would own the remainder of Revlon's health care businesses, valued at $1.75 billion. This $1.75 billion was the remaining value of the company given the earlier $3 billion estimate (less the Norcliff Thayer, Reheis, and beauty products units). Michel Bergerac would be the chief executive officer of the new Forstmann Little company.
4. Nothing was offered for the 105,000 Revlon nonconvertible shares outstanding, leaving them to continue trading in the market.

Investment bankers said that this buyout plan was unusual in that it involved two simultaneous leveraged buyouts, one with Forstmann Little and Adler and Shaykin, and one friendly suitor, American Home Products. Bergerac commented that the breakup plan was "obviously in the best interests of the company, its employees and of stockholders" and "clearly in keeping with my previously announced pledge to maximize shareholder values."

In order to complete the transaction, investment bankers worked through the night during the week while Revlon searched unsuccessfully for someone to buy the entire company. A Revlon source said that "everyone was afraid of what would happen [on October 3] when Pantry Pride is free to start buying tendered shares, perhaps at $53 or more if it raises its offer." Revlon's proposal was subject to shareholder approval at a special meeting to be held in late November.

With the breakup, nobody needed to feel sorry for Michel Bergerac. The event would trigger his golden parachute. It gave Bergerac $20 million if the company was broken up or if he was fired. Some analysts said they were shocked that it would be triggered by a buyout plan that Bergerac helped put together. Joseph Kozloff of Dean Witter said, "I think it's incredibly outrageous." In defense, Bergerac said, "Don't jump to any conclusions that I did this all for my personal benefit [and that] I was motivated by greed." However, only with the new breakup plan would Bergerac remain as chief executive officer. Bergerac also owned 261,633 Revlon shares which were valued at $14.7 million, giving him the "paltry" sum of $34.7 million just for stepping aside. NOT A BAD DEAL!

NOTHING STOPS PANTRY PRIDE

October 7, 1985: Pantry Pride responded to Revlon's breakup plan by sweetening its offer to $56.25 per share. The conditions of this new offer were the removal of the poison pill adopted by Revlon in August and the elimination of Revlon's covenants restricting new debt, asset sales, and dividends.

However, the offer was not conditioned on a minimum number of Revlon shares tendered.

Pantry Pride also amended its lawsuit against Revlon. Originally, it was filed to:

1. Eliminate Revlon's poison pill.
2. Eliminate the golden parachutes.
3. Prevent Forstmann Little from receiving a $25 million fee if Revlon's leveraged buyout were to fall through. This amount was agreed upon under the breakup plan as compensation to Forstmann Little.

Pantry Pride's amendment allowed the golden parachute to remain.

The advantage of Pantry Pride's bid over Revlon's leveraged buyout was that Pantry's offer would "put cash in [the investors'] pockets more than a month sooner than under Forstmann Little's proposed buyout." In fact, since the Forstmann Little buyout plan would not be voted on until late November, shareholders would have to wait at least two months to realize any gains. In contrast, Pantry Pride could immediately begin buying shares "under its tender offer which expired [on] October 21, 1985." By taking this into consideration, some analysts predicted the actual value of Forstmann Little's offer to be between $52 and $53.

"AN UNUSUAL MOVE"

October 13, 1985: Revlon's senior management dropped its efforts to take the company private through a leveraged buyout. Meanwhile, Forstmann Little sweetened its offer to $57.25 a share, or $1.81 billion. Bergerac and other Revlon executives did not plan to have any management role in the new company. This was quite unusual because management participation in a buyout is often required by lenders and equity investors. However, in explaining this move, Bergerac said he was "in the awkward position of appearing to have a conflict of interest." This conflict resulted from the golden parachute which Bergerac would receive as well as a management role envisioned in the original plan. He planned to exercise the parachute option to fund his investment in the new Forstmann Company.

Revlon encouraged Forstmann Little's sweetened offer by agreeing to four conditions.

1. *A Lockup Option.* The lockup option was "aimed at defeating a suitor—Pantry Pride" by giving Forstmann Little rights to buy valuable Revlon assets. Revlon granted Forstmann an option to purchase its vision care unit and National Health Laboratories unit for a total of $525 million. "Despite [these] latest moves, there's no assurance that Pantry Pride will be stopped." As a result, if a bidder other than Forstmann Little acquired 40 percent of Revlon's stock, Forstmann could exercise the lockup option. Since Lazard Frères valued these units at between $600 and $700 million, the lockup option offered the units at a very low price.

2. *Removal of the Poison Pill.* Revlon agreed to withdraw the poison pill for Forstmann Little and any other bidder that matched its $57.25 a share offer.

3. *Removal of Debt Covenants.* Revlon waived its antitakeover debt covenants as long as the buyer assured that the 11.75 percent notes would trade at face value. Forstmann Little agreed to swap the 11.75 percent notes for a new senior subordinated note due in 1995 and paying an interest rate that would grow to 17 from 14 percent. The notes were designed to trade at face value.

4. *Adoption of No-Shop Clause.* Revlon promised that "it wouldn't seek any competing bids for the company or negotiate with any other bidders."

PANTRY PRIDE DOESN'T GIVE UP

In reaction to Revlon's lockup option with Forstmann Little, Pantry Pride immediately filed suit in Delaware Chancery Court to void the use of the lockup. On October 15, Justice

Joseph T. Walsh granted a temporary restraining order, blocking Revlon from proceeding with the lockup option. He granted this order pending a hearing on Friday, October 18. Because of this order, Revlon faced a delay in proceeding with the Forstmann Little buyout.

In the meantime, Pantry Pride took advantage of this delay and sweetened its hostile tender offer to $58 a share or a total of $1.83 billion. Pantry Pride appeared determined to buy Revlon and...sell off the health care [units] to any one of several big companies waiting hungrily in the wings."

The $58 a share offer was conditional on the removal of both the lockup option and the poison pill provision. Since Pantry Pride's $58 bid was greater than Forstmann's $57.25 offer, Revlon was required to remove the poison pill according to the conditions in its latest buyout proposal with Forstmann Little. Pantry Pride also said it was "prepared to match Forstmann Little's offer to swap new, higher yielding notes for Revlon's 11.75 percent notes, or to pay holders cash." This action would meet Revlon's condition on the removal of the debt covenants. Pantry Pride's offer was set to expire on November 1, 1985.

Some Wall Street sources believed that Forstmann wasn't prepared to raise its bid again. If this proved to be true and the lockup option was voided, Pantry Pride would be the "victor in the bidding war." Perelman complained that Revlon continued to "exhibit a blatant disregard for shareholder value" which Pantry Pride had always been ready to offer.

THE LAST BLOW TO REVLON'S DEFENSE

October 23, 1985: The Delaware State Court invalidated the lockup option. It appeared that Pantry Pride finally won the battle for control of Revlon. Justice Walsh's ruling included:

1. The invalidation of Revlon's lockup option agreement with Forstmann Little.
2. An injunction against the no-shop clause adopted by Revlon.
3. The validation of Revlon's poison pill.
4. The validation of Revlon's restrictive debt covenants.

The last two rulings essentially had no effect on Pantry Pride's takeover success. As part of Revlon's attempt to complete a leveraged buyout, conditions were developed by which the poison pill and debt covenants could be lifted. It was not difficult for Pantry Pride to meet these conditions.

The court charged that Revlon "failed in its fiduciary duties to the shareholders." Revlon agreed to the lockup and no-shop clauses in exchange for Forstmann Little's sweetened bid as well as its promise to exchange new senior subordinated debt for Revlon's 11.75 percent notes. Judge Walsh stated that "the board's self-interest in resolving the noteholders' problems led to concessions which effectively excluded Pantry Pride to the detriment of Revlon shareholders." He found that Revlon was protecting the rights of Revlon's noteholders, not shareholders, when it agreed to the lockup and no-shop clauses.

Revlon attempted to use the lockup option to secure the leveraged buyout deal with Forstmann Little. Theodore J. Forstmann, general partner at Forstmann Little, said, "We wouldn't have entered the bidding or raised it without inducements" like the lockup. However, Judge Walsh said that as a defense tool the lockup "must advance or stimulate the bidding process, not retard it." By stimulating the bidding process, the judge claimed that the interests of the shareholders would be best served through encouraged competition.

The Delaware court decision has implications for the use of lockup options in future defensive battles. Lawyers said, "the Chancery Decision doesn't prohibit lockups but curbs indiscriminate use of them. Also, it [implies] new limits on the use of the poison pill." The lower court "suggested that directors who adopt poison pills will be held to a higher standard of accountability by courts to assure that fair bidding for the company takes place."

The ruling placed primary importance on the issue that competitive bidding is in the best interests of the shareholders. Firms had frequently adopted lockups and no-shop clauses purely as defensive tools—no matter what the cost. This ruling changed their use. Bruce Wasserstein at First Boston said the ruling "is a blow to companies who thought there could be a defense at any cost." One takeover expert commented that it would now be impossible to employ a lockup option as soon as there are two or more bidders for the company. A general partner of Lazard Frères best summarized the implications of the court decision: it "changes the rules very seriously and tips the balance in favor of the bidders. [The ruling] can really limit the freedom of directors to take some [defensive] actions in face of competing bids."

Forstmann Little announced it would appeal the court ruling which in turn would delay Pantry Pride's purchase of tendered shares. Justice Walsh did agree to stay his order, giving Revlon and Forstmann Little time to appeal.

November 1, 1985: The Delaware state court upheld its October 23 decision breaching "Revlon's antitakeover defenses." This was Revlon's final defeat; there was no hope left to keep the company from falling into the hands of hostile suitor Pantry Pride. Perelman said the decision was "a great victory for shareholders [which] clears the way for Revlon shareholders to participate in Pantry Pride's generous offer." He continued with his claim that "the shareholders have the right to obtain the best price for their stock." However, if Pantry Pride had succeeded with its first bid of $47.50, this price would have been "the best price," not the final $58. Immediately after Justice Walsh's announcement, Pantry Pride began purchasing Revlon shares at its last hostile tender offer of $58. Meanwhile, the nonconvertible preferred shares remained outstanding.

Revlon directors and executive officers tendered their shares to Pantry Pride stating that they wouldn't "do anything to impede Revlon holders from tendering their shares." The board didn't prevent Ronald Perelman from taking control even though Revlon had staggered terms for the election of its directors. Revlon's management may have lost their jobs in the bitter battle, but they gained in their pocketbooks. Bergerac alone walked away with $35.2 million—$20 million from the golden parachute agreement and $15.2 million for the 261,633 shares he owned prior to the takeover. All told, Revlon officials received a total of $82.5 million in stock options and employment contracts.

Originally, Pantry Pride planned to sell off Revlon's health care units and keep the beauty products line. By the time Pantry Pride won the takeover battle, this plan changed because of Revlon's binding contract with Adler and Shaykin to sell the beauty line for $900 million. This transaction was binding because it was specified in a contract between Revlon and Adler and Shaykin; not between Forstmann Little and the investment banking partnership. The agreement to sell the Norcliff Thayer and Reheis units to American Home Products for $350 million was made contingent upon the Forstmann Little buyout. This transaction was thought likely to fall through because Pantry Pride felt it could solicit a higher bid for these units elsewhere.

Perelman was likely to keep some of Revlon's businesses to take advantage of Pantry Pride's $350 million in tax loss carryforwards. Lazard Frères predicted that Pantry Pride could keep at least the Technicon unit and still raise approximately $1.95 billion by selling the other health care units. Pantry Pride sold the Norcliff Thayer and Reheis units to the Beecham Group PLC of Britain for approximately $400 million ($50 million more than estimated). It also sold the Ethical Pharmaceuticals Division to the Rorer Group, which makes pharmaceuticals and medical devices. This division was sold for $690 million which was also greater than the $600 million estimated value. As Pantry Pride began selling its newly acquired business units, it continued to receive significantly more than it originally anticipated.

ALMOST EVERYBODY WALKS AWAY A WINNER

During the battle, Revlon's stock price was bid up from 45³⁄₈ to 57⁷⁄₈—an increase of 28 percent. The summary of the changes in Revlon stock prices on the next page illustrates the stock market dynamics during the takeover battle.

Quite unusual was the fact that Pantry Pride's stock also increased on the transaction date. It jumped ³⁄₄ to 8¹⁄₄. While an acquirer's stock price nearly always does not increase

Date	Event	Stock Price
8/14/85	Speculation of takeover	45³/₈
8/19/85	Hostile tender offer by Pantry Pride of $47.50	45⁵/₈
8/27/85	Revlon announced financial restructuring plan	44³/₄
9/13/85	Pantry Pride lowered bid to $42.	43
9/24/85	Revlon rejected Pantry's $42 bid	41⁵/₈
10/1/85	Pantry Pride raised bid to $50 on Friday, 9/27, Exchange was closed on that day due to Hurricane Gloria.	50³/₈
10/2/85	Pantry Pride raised bid to $53.	54³/₈
10/3/85	Revlon announced LBO with Forstmann Little	54¹/₄
10/7/85	Pantry Pride raised bid to $56.25	52³/₄
10/13/85	Revlon management pulled out of LBO-Forstmann offered $57.25 for new LBO. Pantry Pride raised bid $58	55³/₈
11/1/85	Pantry Pride won battle	57⁷/₈

on the announcement of a takeover, the market must have smelled the good news in the Pantry Pride announcement.

In the end, Pantry Pride seemed to be the biggest winner of this battle for ownership. But Revlon management certainly didn't go home as losers. Revlon's golden parachute clause provided them with enough to keep them happy for some time. Those who predicted early on that this would be "one of the biggest cat fights in history" seemed to know what they were talking about! The big loser may end up being Forstmann Little. The Delaware court issued a preliminary injunction to stop Forstmann from receiving its $25 million fee, the fee to which Revlon agreed in case the leveraged buyout attempt fell through.

EPILOGUE

For Michel Bergerac, life changed after the Pantry Pride deal. He had to get used to traveling by commercial airlines. As someone who was used to circling the globe in a Boeing 727 corporate jet with fancy couches, plush carpeting, and a bedroom, it was a step into reality. It was like a deposed king having to hail a cab. But with $35 million in his pocket, including his golden parachute, he could well afford a first-class ticket.

For Revlon, the deal ended a fiercely contested battle. But half a year after the deal closed, the SEC slapped Revlon on the wrist. The agency said that Revlon did not promptly issue public notice of its negotiations with two investment firms after Pantry Pride's initial offer. They should have made the negotiations public two days before they did.

It didn't take long for the acquiree to becoming the acquirer. Revlon, led by its aggressive chairman, Ron Perelman, struck in November 1986. It offered $65 a share for Gillette. But Gillette blocked the bid by using greenmail and buying Perelman's 13.9 percent stake in the company for $558 million. In the end, Perelman and Revlon had the last laugh, walking away with a profit of $34 million. Not bad for a few week's work.

CHAPTER 3

THE PLAYERS IN THE LEVERAGED BUYOUT ARENA

For several years now, leveraged buyouts have been Wall Street's equivalent of the philosophers stone, that mythical substance that turned ordinary metal into gold. It's a game that everybody seems to win. Leveraged buyouts have produced payoffs as large as 200 to 1 for some happy investors. The deals have made syndicators rich, allowed some corporate managers to become corporate owners and helped some corporations shed unwanted divisions for premium prices. For investors putting equity money into buyouts, returns in the area of 40 percent a year and more are common.

The profit potential is the big source of an LBO's allure for most everyone involved. This typically includes the stockholders in the "target" company, who sell their shares at a premium; the lenders, for whom there are fat front-end fees; and most of all, the investors. Specifically, investors in LBOs need not put up much of their own cash, but if all goes well they can cash in their equity via a public stock offering, perhaps within three to five years or even less—at lush premiums.

Like any investor, LBO participants tend to favor companies with the prospect of stable growth, good market share, and a product line that's not likely to become obsolete. Unlike some investors, however, they shy away from firms

We appreciate the research, analysis, and writing done by Laurie Hearne, Paul McManus, Max Sherman, and Tom Sidley. Without their very significant contribution, the completion of this chapter would not have been possible.

that can promise spectacular growth, since growth is costly to finance and besides, fast-growing companies often can be outrageously expensive. Firms with major capital spending requirements are not favored since they often generate an intolerable debt burden. The ones that are preferred are companies such as Macy's that have the flexibility to sell fixed assets, if necessary, during a business turndown.

The market for leveraged buyouts has never been more robust, with the participants involved being varied in size and number. This wide variety of players has resulted from the structure of the deals and the hopes of earning high returns. The megadeals currently making news headlines have tended to focus on LBOs involving public companies being taken private. However, these are not the only LBOs taking place. The not-so-publicized deals have involved divisional spin-offs and private placements. Many of the parties financing LBOs are drawn to this type of investment because there are typically fewer bidders entering the fray.

PROFILE OF A TYPICAL DEAL— DENNY'S INC.

Denny's is in the food service business. In 1984, it operated 1,073 full-service restaurants, 853 donut houses, and 24 fast-food Mexican-style chicken restaurants. In May 1984, Denny's senior management hired Merrill Lynch to discuss the possible sale of the Winchell's Donut House Division. Denny's management had grown unhappy with Winchell's net profit growth rate of 7 percent compared with the corporate growth rate of 15 percent. During the discussions about spinning off Winchell's, Merrill Lynch presented several alternatives. One option was the potential sale of Denny's in its entirety to a private investor group including members of Denny's management. Interested in this possibility, Denny's management authorized further investigation of the buyout. On May 29, Merrill Lynch returned with an offer from the investor group to acquire Denny's for $45 per share in cash, a $13 premium over the market price. Once Denny's accepted the bid, Merrill Lynch promptly attempted to arrange financing for the investor group. But in September, Merrill Lynch advised Denny's that it was having difficulty doing the deal at any price over $43. Denny's then hired Dean Witter to evaluate the fairness of the new price. Upon Dean Witter's recommendation, Denny's directors accepted the new bid and voted to proceed with the merger.

The main reason the directors accepted the proposed deal was their belief that it was in the best interests of the shareholders, providing them with a fair price for their shares. The directors considered a whole host of reasons in coming to their conclusion. They included:

- The recent and historical prices for Denny's stock.
- The market prices of comparable stocks.
- Their knowledge of the business.
- The prices and premiums paid for similar acquisitions.
- The recommendation of their financial adviser, Dean Witter.
- The value of Denny's assets.
- The liquidation value of the company.
- The ability to operate without the pressure of the financial markets on short-term performance.

Soon afterward, in January 1985, Denny's shareholders voted to accept the $43 a share offer and Denny's went private. The Denny's Capital Structure exhibit describes the capital structure of Denny's before and after the deal.

THE ROLE OF THE INVESTMENT ADVISER

In Denny's LBO, Denny's investment adviser, Merrill Lynch, brought the financing participants involved in the deal together. Its knowledge of the investment community and, specifically, possible buyout participants allowed it to structure a deal which would satisfy all the players involved. For example, those parties participating in the post-LBO ownership are listed in the Post-LBO Ownership of Common Stock exhibit.

DENNY'S
Capital Structure (in thousands)

	Before	After
Long-term debt:		
Long-term notes:		
Mortgage	$ 91,985	$ 91,985
Other	334	334
Convertible debentures	47,939	0
Capital leases	132,007	132,007
Revolving credit loans	0	372,590
Senior fixed rate notes	0	60,510
Subordinated fixed rate loans	0	118,700
Subordinated fixed rate notes	0	16,400
Total long-term debt	$272,265	$792,526
Total preferred stock	0	35,646
Shareholders' equity:		
Denny's common	$ 15,550	$ 0
Investors class A	0	77
Investors class B	0	19
Additional paid-in capital	60,796	44,258
Retained earnings	235,856	0
Total shareholders' equity	$312,202	$ 44,354
Total capitalization	$584,467	$872,526

Source: Denny's Proxy Statement.

Company management rarely has the knowledge or contacts within the industry to bring all of the parties together. While the involvement of the adviser often stops at structuring the deal, in the Denny's case, Merrill Lynch also became an investor.

The services of an investment banker are sought in order to help management shuffle through the many complex financial arrangements that are needed to ensure a successful deal. The investment banker is able to establish the relationships with lenders and investors with much greater ease and speed than management could do on its own.

One case where the need for expert advice is essential is in the divisional spin-off. Suppose, for example, a large corpo-

Post-LBO Ownership of Common Stock

	Number of Shares	Percent of Total
Nonmanagement investors:		
Merrill Lynch Affiliate	292,529	29.25%
Morgan Guaranty Affiliate	62,896	6.29
Wells Fargo Affiliate	62,895	6.29
Other commercial lenders	178,663	17.87
Prudential	135,776	13.58
Management investors:		
Vern Curtis	26,750	2.67
David Bixler	17,500	1.75
Vincent Lambaise	8,955	0.89
Roger Mercier	18,925	1.89
Donald Pierce	5,955	0.59
John Radenbaugh	15,000	1.50
Others (49 persons)	81,275	8.10
Profit sharing plan	48,791	4.88
Options for key employees	44,090	4.41
	1,000,000	100.00

Source: Denny's Proxy Statement.

ration has decided to spin off a division and is allowing the management team to purchase it via an LBO. The potential lenders for the transaction require a complete breakdown of the division's financial performance for the previous 5 to 10 years. As is often the case, detailed financial statements are not available for individual divisions. Therefore, it is necessary to construct the statements. This is where the expertise of an investment banker is essential. The investment banker is able to develop financial statements and contact potential investors, informing them of the division's strengths and performance record.

Another function of the adviser is to conduct due diligence. The investment adviser is responsible for making a thorough check into the background of the LBO candidate to determine its viability as an ongoing business. Due diligence entails gaining complete knowledge of the division's or company's business practices, financial strengths and weaknesses, and its competitive position. This information is passed on to the lenders and investors who then decide whether or not to participate in financing the deal. Performing due diligence can be a painstaking effort for the sponsor, but it is one of the most crucial services rendered. The Due Diligence Questions exhibit provides an overview of some of the issues covered in due diligence.

Due Diligence Questions

Background:
    Financial information
    Income statements—previous 5 years
    Income statement—year to date
    Budget history
    Balance sheet—most recent fiscal year
    Balance sheet—year to date

History:
    Incorporation
    Recent changes in corporate structure
    Shareholder list
    Subsidiaries

Business information:
    Product offerings
    Pricing strategies
    Depreciation methods
    Patents
    Distribution channels
    Promotion tactics
    Customer base
        Buyer concentration ratios
    Cash position
    Accounts receivable
        Turnover
        Control
        Credit policy
    Research and development expenditures

Inventories
    Turnover
    Cyclicality
    Sources of supply
    Valuation methods
Equipment
    Age
    Condition
    Service contracts
Leases
Future capital needs
Dividend policy
Legal environment
Tax status

Property:
    Holdings
    Recent acquisitions or spin-offs
    Insurance coverage
    Expansion plans

Competition:
    Who?
    How do they compete?
    Advantages, disadvantages?
    Current relationships

Due Diligence Questions *(concluded)*

Management:
  Who?
  Experience
  Ownership
  Compensation and contracts
  Evaluation criteria

Employee relations:
  Union contracts
  Experience
  Number of employees
  Wage rates
  Benefits
  Competitive situation

Due diligence provides the background information to support the analysis and evaluation undertaken to make the lending decision. The following factors are considered in the decision-making process.

1. Are income statement projections realistic? Does the sensitivity analysis show that the firm can mitigate the effect of higher interest costs, lower sales, reduced margins, and so on.
2. What do the balance sheet projections show? How quickly does the debt to equity relationship come back into balance?
3. Will the company be financed adequately? Do the projected sources and uses of funds show an ability to generate working capital adequate to maintain historical relationships between sales and net working capital?
4. Is the proposed capital structure appropriate? Is there enough equity to avoid the possibility of a thin capital problem: Is the mix of fixed and floating rate debt prudent?
5. Does the company occupy a particular niche? Is it a price leader or follower? Having been turned into a high-cost producer by the leveraged buyout, is it vulnerable to predatory pricing? If so, is there enough

room in the margins to meet the competition? Is the industry growing, mature, or shrinking? How large and strong are the company's competitors? Have any been sold recently? What is the level of technology in the industry? How substantial are research and development expenses? What is the cost of entry in the industry?

6. What are the key executives' knowledge of this specific company and industry? Can they make the right decisions quickly and instinctively when conditions change? Are key officers making substantial personal investments in the new company? Do they have a real stake in its success or failure?

7. Who will be a "third-party" investor? What will be this group's financial stake and relative ownership position? How much of the voting stock will it own? How closely will the group work with management? What is its expertise in consulting, in corporate development, and in recruiting new top executives should that prove necessary? Does the group have a large enough staff to oversee all its investments, even in a case in which one or more companies experience difficulties? What is the group's plan for realizing its equity return? Can it provide more equity if needed?

8. Based on all of the above, and under "worst case" scenarios, what is the range of the likely returns to the investors and lenders? Is the risk/reward relationship acceptable?

Compiling the information to conform to due diligence requirements entails an extensive amount of time on the part of the investment adviser. Naturally, this is one of the reasons for their enormous fees. When the Levitz Furniture Co.'s management team decided to take the company private, they contracted Drexel Burnham Lambert to act as the financial adviser in the deal. While Drexel acted as the buyer's agent, E. F. Hutton became the seller's agent. In virtually all leveraged buyout transactions, to ensure fairness of the deal, there will be an adviser representing each side.

From the seller's point of view, there is a desire for a

fairness opinion on the price offered by the buyer. In this case, the Levitz board required an opinion that the price offered by Levitz management was fair to the selling stockholders. If for some reason, the board felt that the price was inadequate, they might urge their adviser to seek alternative suitors. However, in the Levitz example, the sellers agreed on the price and were willing to proceed with the deal.

For their role as the buyer's adviser in the Levitz deal, Drexel received $7.2 million plus $100,000 for arranging the commitments of institutional investors and an additional $300,000 merger fee once the deal was finalized. The deal, valued at $318 million, netted Drexel over $7.6 million for work that took little more than six months.

Management's choice of an investment adviser should be done with care. The firm's lawyers and accountants are valuable sources of information on possible choices for an adviser. Though not necessarily involved in an advisory role themselves, these professionals can often refer management to a set of possible investment bankers. Once a group of potential candidates has been identified, the parties should be conscientious about checking into their backgrounds and previous involvement with LBOs. For example, if a firm is planning on using a company ESOP for the buyout, investment banker experience in doing such deals would be appropriate. Some of the leading investment bankers that have been involved in LBO transactions are given in the table.

Leading Investment Bankers Participating in LBOs

Bear Stearns & Co., Inc.
Dillon, Read & Co. Inc.
Drexel Burnham Lambert
First Boston Corporation
Forstmann Little & Co.
Goldman Sachs & Co.
Kelso & Co.
Kidder Peabody & Co.
Kohlberg Kravis Roberts & Co.
Lazard Frères & Co.
Merrill Lynch
Salomon Brothers Inc.

FINANCING THE DEAL

The next figure, The Leveraged Buyout Transaction, depicts the leveraged buyout transaction as a flow of processes. Putting the pieces of the deal together does, in fact, involve a steady flow of information between each of the participants. As discussed with regard to the investment adviser, there is a need for accurate information to ensure the success of the

The Leveraged Buyout Transaction

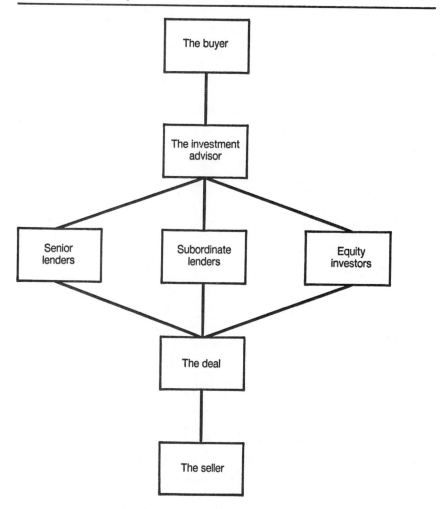

deal. Due diligence requires management to pass the information to the adviser, who in turn passes it along to the potential lenders and investors. Each investor will decide how much he wants to invest and in what layer of financing the investment will fall.

Traditional financing has given the investor the choice of putting money into the debt or equity portion of the deal. These "horizontal" layers have allowed the investor the choice of investing strictly in debt or strictly in equity. However, as the size of the deals has continued to grow and change, so too has the structure of the deals.

Vertical "strip" financing is now finding its way to the heart of many LBOs. The idea behind strip financing is that each investor holds a portion of each type of financing. With the exception of the senior secured lender who makes a secured fixed rate loan, most participants can be found to hold strips of the deals.

Merrill Lynch, in the Denny's deal, provides the perfect example of a firm holding a "strip." In this case Merrill Lynch was involved in every level of financing, excluding the fixed rate loan. The reasons for stripping the deal are twofold. As the sizes of the deals have grown, it has become

Types of Funding in Denny's LBO (in millions)

Sources of Funds:	
Revolving credit loans	$372,590
Senior fixed rate notes	60,510
Subordinated floating rate loans	118,700
Subordinated fixed rate notes	16,400
Equity:	
Preferred stock	35,646
Common stock	44,354
Total	$648,200
Plus existing cash balances	104,000
Total	$752,200
Uses of Funds:	
Purchase of Denny's common stock	$734,200
Payment of fees and expenses	18,000
Total	$752,200

Participants in Denny's LBO

Senior Fixed Rate Notes
Prudential Insurance Company

Revolving Credit Loans
Merrill Lynch
Morgan Guaranty
Wells Fargo

Subordinate Debt
Merrill Lynch
Morgan Guaranty
Wells Fargo
Westpac Banking Corp.
Bank of New York

Preferred Stock
Merrill Lynch
Prudential

Common Stock
Merrill Lynch
Prudential
Management
Profit Sharing Plan

---

necessary to bring in a larger number of financial participants. (See Types of Funding in Denny's LBO and Participants in Denny's LBO tables.)

In order to meet the needs of this growing investor base, it became important to have securities which would have both protection from downside risk such as debt instruments, and earnings potential on the upside. The second reason that explains the increased use of vertical stripping is the move toward financial deregulation. As the distinction between various financial institutions becomes hazier, it is difficult to discern what different firms can and cannot do.

Previously, some banks and financial institutions were prohibited from holding both a debt and equity position in a company. The theories of equitable subordination and conflict of interest were often cited as reasons for keeping the holdings to one side. However, in the current market, prominent players in the LBO marketplace, such as Morgan Guaranty and Manufacturers' Hanover, hold both debt and company stock. Once again, the reason comes back to earnings potential. The regulatory environment does not prohibit banks, insurance companies, and pension funds from holding both positions, so these institutions have jumped at the opportunity to increase their earnings.

In order to visualize how stripping an LBO might work, consider a $150 million buyout. Including $60 million of bank debt, the deal will be made up of $40 million additional unsecured debt, $20 million in subordinate debt, and $30 million of equity. Stripping a deal:

- $60 million—asset-based bank debt
- $40 million—unsecured debt
- $20 million—subordinate debt
- $10 million—preferred stock
- $20 million—common stock

The investor in a "stripped" deal might hold a piece of each type of security. The larger firms putting deals together, such as Kohlberg Kravis Roberts & Co., will determine exactly what the strips will look like when they set up an LBO. They will inform the investors of the financial breakdown of the strips, and the investor will buy into these instruments. However, in the smaller deals, the investors themselves can have some say in the matter of what types of securities will be in the strips. For example, if PruCapital were putting together the financing, they might discuss what the vertical strips might include with the bankers and other financial participants. This is not generally the case in the larger dollar deals. It is quicker and easier for the adviser to put the strips together prior to bringing the deal to the market. The strips might resemble the following:

- $5 million—Unsecured Debt
- $1 million—Subordinate Debt
- $1 million—Preferred Stock
- $3 million—Common Stock

In stripping deals, many firms feel that it is important to be involved in all levels of financing. They are looking at companies that may be brought public again in a few years, and want to share in all of the benefits that stripping brings.

The three basic types of leveraged buyout financing are senior debt, subordinate debt, and equity financing. The combination of the three is what forms the financial structure of every LBO. Analyzing each level will present a picture of what lenders and investors are seeking when investing at each level.

SENIOR LENDERS

Senior lenders fall into one of two categories, secured or unsecured lenders. They are predominantly commercial banks and finance companies. The loans made by the senior lenders have on occasion constituted up to 75 percent of the total value of an LBO transaction. The average amount, however, falls somewhere between 40 to 55 percent of the deals' total dollar value.

Secured lenders are the most conservative participants in LBO deals. However there is competitive pressure on financial institutions to abandon a conservative position in attempting to increase the value of their portfolios.

Most asset-based lenders do not look solely to future cash flows as the sole source of repayment. They generally have liens on specific assets for collateral (i.e., accounts receivable or inventories). All secured lenders make their loans based on the value of the firm's assets, at times lending up to 85 percent of the total company value. Asset-based lenders and other secured lenders focus on the liquidation value of the assets. Though they are not looking to liquidate the company, secured lenders want to be sure they will not lose their investment and that there is a source of repayment.

The rates on asset-based financed LBOs are usually prime plus 1 to 3 percent. There is also an up-front fee ranging from 0.5 to 1 percent of the loan amount. Generally, the asset-based lenders will advance funds both through a revolving line of credit called a "revolver" on accounts receivable and inventory and also on a term loan based on the firm's fixed assets.

The term loan is based on the economic life of the assets, but generally equipment is financed over 5 to 7 years and real property over 10 to 15 years. The loan value is based on the liquidating market value of the assets. In other words, it is based on the expected proceeds they would bring in a distress sale, as determined by professional outside appraisers. The upper advance rate on equipment is 80 percent of the liquidating value and 70 to 75 percent on real property. Liens and mortgages are filed against the fixed assets and generally require maintenance of insurance coverage and other conditions pertaining to their use and upkeep.

Accounts receivable and inventory loans are written on a "revolving" basis. This means that the loan "revolves" or goes up and down based on the collateral value of the accounts receivable and inventory. Generally the borrower is obligated to turn over all sales receipts to the bank to be applied against the loan. New advances are then made against the updated value of the collateral. Both accounts receivable and inventory loans are written on a demand basis, meaning they can be called at any time, and are cross-collateralized with the term loan. Cross-collateralized loans have assets pledged against one loan that are also secondarily pledged against another. Therefore, a default on the revolver will also cause a default on the term loan and vice versa.

Advance rates on accounts receivable and inventory differ. Inventory advance rates are dependent on the marketability of the inventory and in most cases do not exceed 50 percent. Generally, only finished goods are eligible for financing. Asset-based lenders are generally only interested in financing inventory which is readily liquidated, easy to get a hold of, and has a relatively high value per item. Accounts receivable advance rates are generally 80 percent on receivables not older than 60 to 90 days from the date of invoice. Accounts receivable that are eligible for financing are those that don't include contracts, extended warranty requirements, holdbacks, potential offsets, or any other factor that might preclude their collection.

Unsecured lenders, on the other hand, do not require liens on specific assets. They focus on the borrower's future cash flow estimates as a basis for repayment of their loans. They also look to see if there are additional assets which can be sold off in the event the firm has trouble meeting its debt payments. Lenders generally examine basic company information when considering investment in an LBO. There are typically five sources of information they will look to in deciding whether or not to go ahead with the deal. These include:

1. Characteristics of individuals involved.
2. Management's commitment of capital.
3. Cyclicality of the industry.
4. Quality of the assets.
5. Need for future capital infusion.

But the decision is primarily based on the forecasted cash flows of the firm. While the unsecured lenders are technically unsecured, they take a number of steps to protect themselves. If the firm defaults, they have the ability to sue under the terms of the note and attach the assets. Since, the senior unsecured lender requires the other lenders to subordinate their interests, the senior lenders along with the trade creditors will get first crack at the assets. Additionally, the senior unsecured lenders require the borrower to sign terms and conditions which preclude pledging any assets as collateral to other lenders as well as other negative pledges and restrictions.

Negative pledges are covenants agreed to by the borrower that prohibit certain actions by the firm. These include, for example, taking on more debt, acquiring additional assets or making investments. Furthermore, it is not unusual to attach restrictions to the firm, governing minimum levels of tangible net worth or working capital. Violations of these covenants could trigger clauses which allow the lender to come in and take over the firm.

Generally, unsecured lenders offer terms of payment of 7 to 10 years. It is not uncommon for the amortization process to start only after the second year, to allow the firm to "get on its feet." The interest rate is usually 1 to 3 points over prime with a 0.5 to 1 percent fee collected up front.

Lenders will generally perform some type of sensitivity

analysis to examine the effects of various economic and business scenarios. Most lenders will run a "what if" spreadsheet program. This allows the lender to view the company's financial fitness under both adverse and optimistic circumstances. Since most lenders are conservative in nature, they will be apt to concentrate on the company's position under the most pessimistic circumstances. This will allow them to determine whether or not they will proceed with the venture. A business proposing an LBO should be prepared to defend itself completely under such scrutiny.

In addition to securing loans to reduce their risk, many lenders will also form syndications with other banks and financial intermediaries. Morgan Guaranty, for example, was the senior lender in the management buyout of American Sterilizer in 1984. The bank provided two short-term secured credit agreements for $88 million and $66 million. The total value of the deal was $230 million. In addition to Morgan Guaranty, many other banks participated in the "pool" to raise the necessary funds. Morgan Guaranty acted as the agent while other participants included First National Bank of Boston, Mellon Bank, Continental Illinois, The Bank of New York, Marine Bank, Security Pacific, and The Canadian Imperial Bank of Commerce. Many banks involved in syndications will be willing to share unsecured loans as well as secured loans because of the reduced amount of risk they are taking on. Since they are not the sole financial backer for the deal, they feel they can afford to take on a greater amount of risk. If they were the sole participant, they might be more reticent about putting up such large amounts of capital without some type of security to back their investment.

SUBORDINATE LENDERS

The second tier of LBO financing consists of the subordinate lenders. Participants in this level of financing are usually insurance companies, pension funds, large finance companies, and some specialized LBO funds. Generally subordinate debt consists of senior and junior subordinated notes. Subordinate creditors are second in line to collect in the event of a failed transaction and therefore will often require a higher return to compensate for their risk. The loans offered by this creditor tend to be longer term in nature and will carry an interest rate of up to four percentage points above the prime rate.

Initially lured by the high earnings attainable when interest rates rose dramatically in the early 1980s, many of the larger commercial banks became heavy investors at this level of financing. At a conference on LBOs at the Wharton School, Alan Vitule, senior vice president of Smith Barney, stated, "Commercial banks are probably the primary source of unsecured debt, with loans usually up to 80 percent of working capital needs and 100 percent of net worth."

The criteria examined by the subordinate lender include the following:

1. Management skill.
2. Low-current debt levels.
3. Physical assets in good condition.
4. Sound, steady cash flows.
5. Alternative sources of servicing debt.
6. Low or medium technology firms.

Many of the larger insurance firms, such as Prudential and Equitable Life, and large finance companies, such as General Electric Credit Corporation (GECC), have also become involved in LBO financing at this level. Insurance companies view this type of transaction as a way of hedging their fixed-income investments against inflation. In addition to seeking prime plus rates, more and more subordinate lenders are also looking to gain a small equity position to go along with their debt holdings.

Referred to as "mezzanine financing," this combination of subordinate debt and preferred stock or equity "kickers" gives the investor the opportunity to participate in company ownership as well as guaranteeing fixed earnings from his debt holdings. An equity kicker is a warrant which gives the holder the right to purchase a small portion of the stock at a specified price. Similar to strip financing, mezzanine financing also allows the players the advantage of profiting from stock appreciation, with the appeal of minimizing their downside risk by holding some debt.

The increased use of mezzanine and strip financing has served to blur the lines between lenders and investors. Many commercial banks will not enter a deal today unless they are able to hold at least a small portion of the company's equity. In a growing number of the larger deals, it is imperative that these players become involved. Of course, there are still many investors who are only interested in holding an equity position. Their primary objective is capital appreciation. Indeed, most equity investors are betting that the company will once again be taken public. Going public allows management, venture capitalists, and LBO specialists to realize substantial gains on their investments.

EQUITY INVESTORS

As a result of declining markets for certain financial instruments, and to ensure the execution of LBOs, investment bankers are playing a merchant banking-type role in that they are taking equity positions in the acquisition. This was evidenced in the management-led buyout of Dr Pepper. In the purchase of the third largest soft drink firm in the nation, Forstmann Little managed the takeover by buying a part of the company's stock and arranging $100 million of financing through subordinated debt and equity. Parties investing in this debt were pension plans of major corporations such as General Electric and Standard Oil of Indiana.

The leveraged buyout of Dr Pepper illustrates the major attributes an investment banker has to offer. In particular, it offers its experience and ability to negotiate for the acquiring firm. To effectively negotiate and value a firm's worth requires an outside party. This is more than just a second opinion or a free estimate. In negotiating a deal, investment bankers approach many acquisitions with the idea that the buyer is willing to pay so much and no more. A second feature of Forstmann Little's role was the ability to access funds. The parties interested in taking over a firm rarely have relationships with pension and money managers. Investment bankers also have access to insurance companies which seek ways to increase returns on their own investment portfolios.

While raising money has often involved the issuance of junk bonds, Forstmann Little has become one of the premier LBO players to compete with fully financed, no junk bond offers. Indeed, the fact that they come to the table with an unconditional deal has won them business against higher competitive offers. In December 1986, for example, Forstmann Little won Lear Siegler, even though Wicke's bid was a full dollar higher. How did they do it? They were the only bidders to go to the board with a fully financed offer not relying on the issuance of any junk bonds.

Involvement in leveraged buyouts goes beyond arranging debt and long hours at the bargaining table. Involvement in these deals now includes investment bankers investing their own money in exchange for ownership or equity.

The fact that Forstmann Little invested their own money to buy part of the 23.5 million shares is not a long-standing trend on Wall Street. But major players such as Forstmann Little are now putting up large sums of their own money; the statistics tell the story. The table below, for example, shows the stellar returns Forstmann Little has had on its LBO investments.

	Year Bought	Year Sold	ROE (annual)
Dr Pepper	1984	1986	101%
Unicom	1983	1986	62
Beverage Management	1983	1985	27
All-American Bottling	1982	1983	49
Union Ice	1981	1984	147
Kincaid Furniture	1980	1983	51

One dealmaker at First Boston portrayed one of the conditions for entering an acquisition with his firm's money as requiring the deal to have a minimum annualized return of 35 percent per year over a five-year period. First Boston has extended this investment concept to the point where they are now guaranteeing 100 percent of the financing for certain leveraged buyouts. For example, they were recently involved in financing the $112.9 million Avondale Mills LBO. Here, First Boston took an equity position in Avondale Mills, and in doing so, assured the seller that the deal would go through. This assurance is not only guaranteed by the investment banker's money, but is also assured by large sums of money pooled together by firms like First Boston.

Fueling this wave of big deals has been the increased competition among financial institutions and the climate in which investment bankers do their business. For years, corporations and investment bankers have maintained long-term relationships aiding clients in various financial matters. Specifically, corporations have relied heavily on their investment bankers to arrange funds to support daily operations and expansion. The need for this service has diminished greatly as a result of a 1982 Securities and Exchange Commission regulation that instituted shelf registration for new issues. Now companies have the ability to register large amounts of new securities at one time, and issue portions only when needed. Lessening the need for help in issuing securities may have been only the starting point in encouraging investment bankers to fight for other forms of business. The battle for the almighty buck has become so heated that several firms have been accused of instigating deals on their own. Indeed, with the number of big transactions going on, some Wall Street observers expect investment bankers to continue initiating deals and acting aggressively.

There are many who say that Kohlberg Kravis Roberts & Co. is synonymous with the buyout phenomenon. This 10-year old firm, which guards its clients better than the Pentagon guards its secrets, has come to the forefront of the LBO world by managing the largest going private deal to date. It involves the $6.2 billion agreement with Beatrice Foods. Complementing the size of this monumental deal was the equally monumental $45 million fee KKR received for its efforts. KKR has not made it to the forefront on luck alone. The resourcefulness of this firm is reflected in KKR's efforts to accumulate a $2 billion fund, the fifth of its kind, to finance its LBO operations. This $2 billion fund provided investors such as Equitable Life Insurance, Yale's endowment fund, and others a return of 46.8 percent for those deals that reached a payback stage. Partaking in a KKR fund is not difficult. The only requirement is the commitment of a minimum of $20 million.

Many financial officers question the value of these deal-makers who make millions of dollars per deal for what requires only a working period ranging from eight days to several months. Few parties dare to go out on their own without investment bankers. One such brave soul is Warren Buffett, the chairman of Berkshire Hathaway, who represented Capital Cities Communication in acquiring American Broadcasting Companies. Buffett, with the assistance of merger lawyer Martin Lipton, went head to head with Bruce Wasserstein of First Boston. When the confrontation between the parties was over, Capital Cities emerged as ABC's owners and Buffett, a 19 percent stakeholder in Capital Cities.

There are still many companies that consider the services offered by investment bankers invaluable in maneuvering their way through the world of acquisitions and takeovers. In the Dr Pepper deal, the board hired Lazard Frères to look for buyers and exploring possible investment alternatives. Lazard Frères's advice to the board to accept Forstmann Little's buyout offer generated a new owner for Dr Pepper and $2.5 million for Lazard Frères. The services of investment bankers are also beneficial in warding off hostile suitors. Eric Gleacher of Morgan Stanley, an ex-Marine and former Lehman executive, defended Union Carbide from being acquired by GAF Corporation. GAF, a relatively small chemical company, had designs on purchasing Union Carbide and selling off its two most profitable divisions Eveready Battery and Prestone Antifreeze for a hefty profit. Gleacher's defense for Carbide was to sell off its consumer division and use the proceeds as a dividend to shareholders.

Morgan Stanley's services also include locating and acquiring viable target firms. This was demonstrated when Robert Cizik, chief executive officer of Cooper Industries in

Houston, received a visit by Gleacher and was sold the idea of acquiring McGraw Edison, a maker of electrical consumer products. After an hour-long presentation, Cizik found himself involved in a $1.1 billion acquisition.

Why Involve Nonmanagement Equity Investors in the Deal?

Equity investors bring many attributes besides money to the deal. To the seller, they provide a way to cash out of a business, usually with swift action and quick decisions. To the buyer, they provide management expertise, usually in the form of seats on the board and key contacts in the business community. In sound operations, equity investors tend to leave things alone and to avoid upsetting the continuity of profitable operations. In poorly performing operations, equity investors typically have the resources to bring in new talent and spearhead new strategies. In return for these services, equity investors expect to realize a 50 to 60 percent annual compounded return on their portfolio.

Who Are the Equity Investors?

The most active equity investors fall into two main categories: independent venture capital firms and LBO funds. Insurance companies, commercial and investment banks also participate as equity investors, but these investments are generally made through their venture capital arm.

The venture capitalists are traditionally associated with an investment role in the start-up and early stage financing of high-growth, capital-intensive businesses. In recent years several of these firms have become involved in acquisitions by financing part of an LBO. (See Venture Capital LBO Players chart.)

Consider, for example, the experience of Brentwood Associates, a venture capital firm which helped fund Apple Computer. In mid-1984, Brentwood assisted Ideal School Supply in its LBO. Brentwood's equity stake of $1 million was worth $25 million by early 1987. That 25-to-1 return is almost

Venture Capital LBO Players

Venture Lending Assoc.
First Chicago Venture Capital
Security Pacific VC Group
Warburg, Pincus, Cpa. Corp.
Citicorp Investing
BT Capital
Narragansett Capital Corp.
The Hillman Company
TA Associates
Manufacturers Hanover VC Corp.
Welch, Carson, Anderson & Stowe
Stephanson Merchant Bank
Norwest Capital
First Venture Capital Corp.
Allstate VC Division
Brentwood Associates

---

exactly what they earned on the far riskier and more complex Apple deal. It's no wonder that venture capitalists are attracted to the safer financing of existing firms rather than to risk their money on new companies.

The pooled funds are generally groups of venture capitalists and the venture capital arms of financial institution that have combined their resources for the purpose of executing LBOs. (See Active Major Pooled Funds table.) Pooled funds are attractive to venture capitalists for two reasons: They allow firms to participate in deals that are much larger than they could have executed individually, and also allow them to reduce risk through portfolio diversification. The directors of these pooled funds often take the lead role, stripping the deal in return for a percentage of the equity investor's profits when they are realized.

ATTRACTIVE TARGETS

Companies that are attractive to the equity investor generally possess two important features. First, the nature of the firm's business is reasonably understood by the investor. Sec-

Active Major Pooled Funds

AEA Investors
Carl Marks & Co.
Clayton & Dubiller Inc.
Forstmann Little & Co.
Gibbons, Green van Amerongen
Kohlberg Kravis Roberts & Co.
Thomas H. Lee Company
Wesray

ond, the firm has a 5- to 10-year record as a going concern with consistent sales growth and quality earnings.

Once an attractive firm is identified, a closer look at the financial aspects of the deal is taken. As in the analysis conducted by the lenders, the equity investors also examine financial statements, cash flows, and future capital needs.

Understanding what makes a company attractive for an LBO, we can construct a description of an ideal target. It might look something like this:

1. Current equity holders that are willing to participate.
2. Slow but consistent growth through all phases of the business cycle.
3. Low capital intensity.
4. Low debt level.
5. Low average receivables.
6. Fast turning inventory.
7. Low level of owned fixed assets.
8. High level of leased fixed assets.

Needless to say, the ideal candidate is rarely found. When found, it is often a closely held, older firm which is generating substantial cash flows by possessing a large market share in a mature manufacturing or service industry. It is rare that a young, entrepreneurial, high-technology company in a volatile, high-growth market, needing heavy investment in R&D will be presented as an LBO candidate.

THE DEAL STRUCTURE

Equity investors will put up as little as 3 percent of the purchase price from their own funds. This is typically matched by an additional 2 percent contributed by the participating management group. As much as 50 percent of the purchase price may be provided by a commercial bank as a working capital loan or as an asset-based loan with a typical maturity of five years. The remainder of the funds required for the purchase may come from an SBIC, pension fund, or an insurance company, in the form of subordinated debt with a maturity of from 5 to 15 years and will usually carry warrants or be convertible to stock.

PROFILE OF A CONTRARIAN'S DEAL— GUILFORD INDUSTRIES

Slow steady growth. Low tech. Low capital requirement. These are the characteristics of a company that is attractive to an equity investor, unless that equity investor is Thomas H. Lee Company (THL). The investment portfolio of THL contains a diverse group of companies ranging from food processing and building supplies to robotics and computer systems. Although fast growth and high investments seem to pale most investors, THL believes they provide opportunities for high rewards. THL's acquisition of Guilford Industries, Inc., is a good illustration of this philosophy.

In 1981, 65-year-old King Cummings—founder, chairman, and chief executive officer of Guilford Industries—was interested in selling the company to settle his estate. Although he wanted to sell Guilford, Cummings, as well as some members of the senior management, wished to retain an equity interest and remain active in the company after the sale. An additional factor stimulating the sale was the need for funding to pursue a capital expenditure program on the order of $15 to $20 million to support growth. These issues created problems for most corporate bidders. They were unwilling to make commitments to Guilford's management about the future of the company or its personnel. Moreover, they were not interested in making the necessary substantial cash outlays. THL entered late into the bidding but immediately saw the opportunity. In November 1981, a letter of intent was signed with Guilford spelling out the resolution of all the firm's conditions of sale. After 12 weeks of due diligence, the deal was structured. The following exhibit lists the details of the new capital structure:

Capital Structure of Guilford after the Acquisition

Floating rate notes	(PruCapital)	3,500,000
10% notes	(Seller)	1,000,000
18% subordinated notes	(PruCapital)	4,000,000
12% subordinated notes	(Seller)	2,000,000
Equity	(THL Capital)	2,500,000
Equity	(PruCapital)	2,500,000
		15,500,000

After the acquisition, Guilford's performance improved dramatically while pursuing an investment strategy of capacity expansion and backward integration.

Based on the firm's success and the strength of the market, an initial public offering was considered to raise capital for additional expansion. In February 1983, eight months after the acquisition was completed, Guilford was offered in the public market and netted $4,025,000. In August of that same year, Guilford had a secondary offering and netted an additional $4,073,000. In these transactions, PruCapital liquidated approximately 38 percent of its holdings, realizing a 227 percent return on its equity investment in less than one year. PruCapital's remaining holdings were valued at $13 million at that time. THL liquidated a portion of its equity position, recovering its original investment of $2.5 million. THL's remaining holdings were valued at $38 million, a 1,000 percent increase.

The Guilford case clearly demonstrates that mature, slow-growth companies are not the only targets in town when it comes to LBOs. If you know what you are doing and link up with experienced players, you can realize substantial returns in the LBO game.

CHAPTER 4

THE LBO NUMBER JUNGLE:
FINDING YOUR WAY

In spite of the tremendous public interest in leveraged buyouts, relatively little has been written about the financial characteristics of acquired firms. Several benefits can be realized from such a discussion. First, if one contemplates a buyout, the buyer might want to know whether the particular firm under consideration is a typical buyout target or very different from other buyouts. If it is atypical, the buyer may have no reason to be concerned. Yet, additional research, explaining why it is different from other buyouts, is justified. Second, opportunities faced by buyout investor groups may be assessed. For example, a comparison of the profitability between buyout firms and firms not involved in buyouts can lead to a conclusion as to whether the typical buyer's intention is to turn around an underperforming firm. Third, information on the differences between the two groups' financial characteristics can be useful in predicting which companies can successfully be bought out. Obviously, developing such a prediction framework is beyond the scope of this book.

In analyzing financial data, different types of analyses are available for different purposes. For example, the analyst may be a banker considering whether to grant a short-term loan to the investing group. Naturally, a banker is primarily

---

We appreciate the research and analysis done by Obiyathulla Ismath Bacha. Without his very significant contribution, the completion of this chapter would not have been possible.

interested in the firm's near-term liquidity position, and as a result would focus on ratios that measure liquidity. In contrast, creditors that have taken a longer term subordinated debt position (e.g., an insurance company), would place far more emphasis on the firm's long-term solvency. They know that unprofitable operations erode asset value and a strong current position is necessary but no guarantee that funds will be available to repay a 12-year bond issue. The group of nonmanagement equity investors is interested in long-term profitability and efficiency. Of course, management, which in most leveraged buyouts holds a significant position in the firm's equity, is concerned with all aspects of financial analysis. It must be able to repay its debt to both long- and short-term creditors as well as to earn a profit for stockholders.

The buyouts are taken from a *Business Week* listing of deals, and to the extent possible, a control group is matched by sales, assets, and industry. A final sample of leveraged buyouts and a matched control group are presented in the LBO versus Non-LBO Firms table.

LBO versus Non-LBO Firms

LBO Firms	Non-LBO Industry-Matched Firms
Beatrice	Sara Lee
Eckerd (Jack)	Walgreen
Levi Strauss	Oxford Industries
Macy (R. H.)	Allied Stores
Mary Kay Cosmetics	Noxell Corp.
Metromedia	Capital Cities/ABC
MGM/UA Entertainment	MCA
MultiMedia	Belo (A. H.)
National Gypsum	U.S. Gypsum
Republic Health	Charter Medical
Revlon	Avon Products
Storer Communications	Taft Broadcasting
Sybron	Bard (C. R.)
TWA	Pan-Am
Uniroyal	Goodrich
Warnaco	West Pt.—Pepperell

In the following paragraphs we briefly review some of the most relevant financial ratios and compare them for both buyout and nonbuyout firms. In doing so, we find it useful to classify the financial measures into six types of basic categories: liquidity, leverage, profitability, utilization of assets, cash flow generation, and risk.

LIQUIDITY ANALYSIS

As its name implies, the focus of liquidity analysis is on the firm's ability to meet its maturing obligations. Although a thorough liquidity analysis requires the use of a detailed pro forma cash budget, ratio analysis, by relating the amount of cash and other current assets to the firm's current obligations, provides a quick and easy-to-use measure of liquidity. The most commonly used measure of short-term solvency is the current ratio. This ratio gauges the ability of a business to pay current debt using only its current assets. The ratio is computed by dividing the firm's current assets by its current liabilities. Current assets usually include cash, marketable securities, accounts receivable, and inventories. Current liabilities consist of accounts payable, short-term notes payable, current maturities of long-term debt, accrued income taxes, and other accrued expenses. Quite often the current ratio is further adjusted to account for the possibility that some current assets are actually not readily available for liquidation. For example, consider the case of a banker assessing the possibility of granting a loan to a steel foundry. In doing so, the banker typically develops a "what-if" analysis. In the analysis, under the worst case scenario, the banker is likely to assign a high value to the inventory of basic metals used in the process, assuming that in liquidation the inventory can be sold to other steel companies. But the banker is likely to disregard in his liquidation value assessment the value of any semifinished products in process. The situation is even more extreme in the case of hi-tech companies where customers may well require follow-up service. Therefore, when granting a loan to a hi-tech leveraged buyout, a creditor is fully aware that in a case of financial distress the inventory of finished products would not have much value in liquidation. At best, only some of the basic components with a reasonable secondary market would be assigned a material liquidation value. By taking such an approach to its extreme, creditors are measuring liquidity by using the quick ratio rather than the current ratio. The quick ratio, popularly called the acid test ratio, measures the firm's ability to meet its short-term obligations from those assets immediately convertible to cash. Following this rationale, it is calculated as the ratio of the current assets excluding inventory to the firm's current liabilities. As illustrated by the Liquidity Analysis exhibit, the liquidity position of the sampled LBO firms is in general better than that of the nonbuyout firms.

The top panel of the exhibit indicates that when the current ratio is used as a measure of liquidity, the LBO candidates are clearly more liquid. For example, in 1981 60 percent of the buyout firms had a higher current ratio. With the exception of 1983, this relationship holds throughout the entire investigation period. This conclusion is also supported when the quick ratio, rather than the current ratio, is used. For example, while in 1981 60 percent of the LBO firms exhibited a higher current ratio, as illustrated in the second panel of the Liquidity Analysis exhibit, the proportion is increased to 65 percent when the quick ratio is used. Furthermore, while in 1982 there were more nonbuyout firms with a higher current ratio, the relationship is reversed when the quick ratio is used. Interestingly, it seems that investors are able to locate buyout candidates that are more liquid than their industry averages.

Another way to measure the firm's liquidity is to derive the ratio of its net working capital to sales. Net working capital is defined as current assets minus current liabilities. In general, the concept of working capital refers to a firm's investment in short-term assets. Once the ratio is derived, two things should be kept in mind. First, similar to the interpretation of the current ratio, the larger a firm's working capital, the larger its liquidity. However, the size of working

Liquidity Analysis

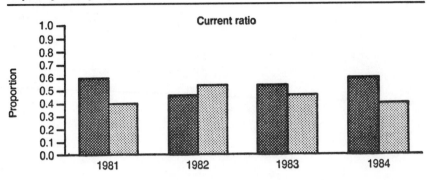

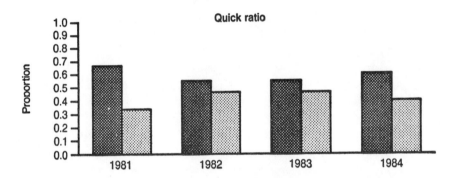

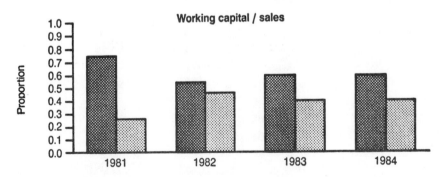

▓ Proportion of matched pairs where LBOs have a higher ratio

▓ Proportion of matched pairs where LBOs have a lower ratio

capital per se is not a sufficient indicator. It should be measured relative to the firm's sales. Second, the ratio of working capital-to-sales also indicates the firm's ability to facilitate growth. For example, consider a company that purchases raw materials for $1,000 per unit, processes them, and sells the final product for $4,000. Obviously, the firm does not get any credit from its employees. They want to collect their paychecks at the end of each month. At best, the company arranges some credit from its suppliers. However, while selling its products, it is likely that, just for competitive reasons, it has to provide its customers with credit on sales. The credit gap is clear. It obtains credit for the $1,000 material purchases, and provides credit for the full $4,000. Even if these two transactions have identical credit terms (say 30 days), the higher the firm's growth rate, the greater the requirements for net working capital. Therefore, in evaluating a candidate for a leveraged buyout, the investing group should assess the available resources to support growth in sales by deriving the firm's ratio of working capital-to-sales. As illustrated by the third panel of the Liquidity Analysis exhibit, the typical LBO candidate has more working capital per dollar sales than its industry-matched counterpart. Though high-growth companies, because of their high risk profile, are traditionally not on investing groups' "buy" lists, it seems that LBOs have more working capital to facilitate growth.

LEVERAGE ANALYSIS

The focus of this analysis is the comparison of funds supplied by the owners with the financing provided by the firm's creditors. In general, the concept of leverage has several implications. First, the creditors look to the equity to provide a margin of safety. If the equity is only a small proportion of the total financing, the risks are borne mainly by the debt holders. Second, the leverage plays a major role in determining the level and volatility of the return earned by equity holders. If the firm earns more on its borrowed funds than it pays to creditors, then the higher the leverage, the higher is the return on equity. However, if for some reason the firm is having difficulties effectively deploying its assets, and the return on the borrowed funds is lower than the cost of these funds, higher leverage will further worsen the bottom line, and the return on equity will be even lower than that of a comparable company with lower leverage. In addition, the pre-LBO leverage is particularly important for the investing group. In many cases, this group might have assessed the debt level of the potential target as being "too low." In other words, in such cases the management of the target is perceived by the investing group as following an overly conservative financial policy given the firm's industry and business risk. By acquiring the underleveraged firm and utilizing its financial slack by restructuring its capital mix (debt replacing an equal amount of equity), the acquiring group might be able to generate value equal to the present value of the newly acquired tax shields. This will lower its overall after-tax capital cost.

In practice, in evaluating the extent of leverage, two sources are used. One of them is the firm's balance sheet, where it is possible to determine the extent to which borrowed funds have been used to finance the firm. The second source, the firm's income statement, is useful in determining the number of times interest charges are covered by operating profits. In comparing the buyout with nonbuyout firms, three balance sheet–based leverage ratios and one income statement–based leverage ratio have been calculated. The first balance sheet–based leverage measure is the debt-equity ratio. This measure analyzes the firm's capitalization, and is derived by dividing the long-term debt by equity. These two items represent the more permanent sources of capital.

The same information is often obtained by deriving the ratio of debt-to-total capitalization, where the total capitalization is defined as the sum of the firm's long-term debt and equity. Despite the financial slack argument that leads one to expect buyout firms to have a lower pre-LBO leverage, the results for the firms that we look at don't support such a proposition.

As illustrated by the Leverage Analysis exhibit, the LBO

Leverage Analysis

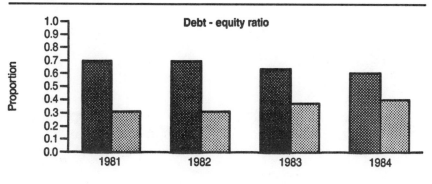

Debt - equity ratio

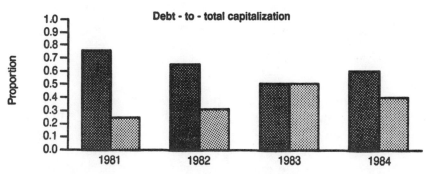

Debt - to - total capitalization

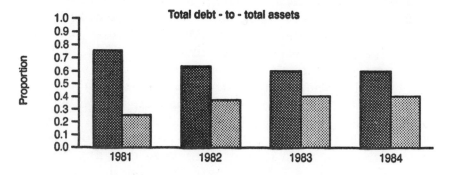

Total debt - to - total assets

. Proportion of matched pairs where LBOs have a higher ratio

Proportion of matched pairs where LBOs have a lower ratio

Leverage Analysis *(concluded)*

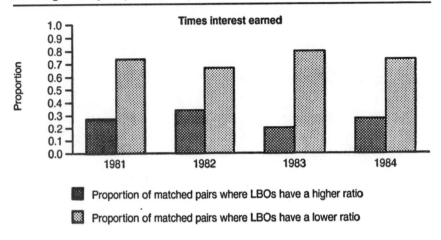

Proportion of matched pairs where LBOs have a higher ratio

Proportion of matched pairs where LBOs have a lower ratio

firms are on average more leveraged than their industry-matched firms. The top two panels of this exhibit clearly show that when leverage is measured by the firm's debt-to-equity ratio, or debt-to-debt plus equity, a higher leverage is observed for LBOs in every year throughout the investigation period. While the debt-equity ratio and the debt-to-total capitalization ratio focus on the firm's long-term sources of capital, a more general balance sheet-based measure is the total debt-to-total assets ratio, often referred to as the debt ratio. This ratio measures the firm's total debt burden, reflecting the company's ability to meet its short- and long-term debt obligations. Quite arbitrarily, accountants divide the firm's liabilities into short-term liabilities (those obligations that have to be met within 12 months), and long-term liabilities (with maturity longer than one year). The importance of the debt ratio is that it treats as debt any type of liability, independent of its maturity. The debt ratio is derived by dividing the firm's total liabilities by its total assets. Creditors prefer moderate debt ratios, since the lower the ratio, the greater the cushion against creditors' losses in the event of liquidation. However, as illustrated by the third panel of the Leverage Analysis exhibit, when leverage is measured using total debt rather than just the long-term debt, the group of buyout firms also reveals higher leverage than its industry-matched group. As shown in the exhibit, this holds true in every year during the four-year investigation period. The most popular income statement–based leverage ratio is the times interest earned ratio, which equals the earnings before interest and taxes (EBIT) divided by interest charges. The ratio measures the extent to which operating earnings can decline before reaching the point where the firm is unable to meet its annual interest costs. Inability to meet interest obligations can bring legal action by the creditors, with bankruptcy as a possible outcome. It is important to note that the numerator in the ratio is earnings before interest and taxes, since all of EBIT is available to pay interest. Therefore, when a creditor or an investor evaluates the firm's ability to pay annual interest on its debt, the relevant income statement item to look at is the firm's earnings before interest and taxes rather than its net income. In the extreme case where interest equals EBIT, times interest earned would be 1.0; the company could just pay its interest and would pay no corporate income taxes (since taxable income is derived by subtracting interest charges from the EBIT). One has to keep in mind that EBIT fluctuates from year to year, and it may in the future fall far short of current EBIT. Therefore, a current times interest earned ratio greatly exceeding unity is desirable because even if EBIT falls it means that interest on currently outstanding debt will likely be paid in coming years. As with the other leverage ratios, an ideal LBO candidate should have a high pre-LBO times interest earned ratio, creating an opportunity for the investing group to buy out the firm, adding significant interest charges, and obtaining an EBIT high enough to support the servicing of the new debt. Although it is clear how an "ideal" LBO candidate's times interest earned ratio should look, the numbers indicate that reality is quite different. As illustrated by the fourth panel of the Leverage Analysis exhibit, the LBO firms, prior to the buyout, had significantly lower coverage ratios. In fact, when this measure of leverage is used, the comparison leads to much more extreme results than the ones implied by the other three leverage ratios. The LBO firms had lower times interest earned ratios in each of the years in a sizable majority of the cases. In sum, drawing from the leverage analysis, it seems that in reality, low pre-LBO leverage has not been a key factor in the selection of companies on which to do LBOs.

PROFITABILITY AND ASSET UTILIZATION ANALYSIS

While there are many measures of profitability, each of them relates the returns of the firm to its sales, to its assets, or to its equity. Since maximizing shareholders' wealth is the ultimate objective of the firm, sustaining long-term profitability is an important goal. But analyzing a firm's profitability is a tricky task. One might observe two firms, one of them exhibiting a higher return on equity than the other. By just looking at the popular bottom line, not much can be deduced regarding the difference between the two firms' asset utilization, profit margin on sales, or degree of financial leverage. In other words, for a group contemplating a leveraged buyout, the fact that one of the companies reports a higher return on equity obviously cannot serve as an indication of better performance. In particular, it is possible that the company with the higher return on equity is less efficient in employing its assets and also has lower profit margins on its sales. Indeed, only because of the higher proportion of borrowed funds on its balance sheet, it reports a higher return on equity. In such a case, the investing group is more likely to buy the firm that historically reported a lower return on equity, and change its capital structure by replacing some of its equity with new debt, which will lead to a significantly higher return on equity. The message is clear; you cannot just look at the bottom line.

In order to find our way in the jungle of profitability-measure jargon, we will first review the individual measures and then evaluate the measures reported by both buyout and nonbuyout firms. Only then will we discuss the relationship between them.

An important question is how much the firm earns on its sales. One approach is to first focus on the determination of the firm's gross profit margin. It is derived by taking the firm's net sales, subtracting from this the cost of goods sold and dividing the result by net sales. The gross operating margin indicates the percentage of each sales dollar remaining after the firm has paid for its goods. A second sales-based profitability measure is the net operating margin. It equals net sales minus the sum of cost of goods sold and operating expenses, all divided by net sales. This measure indicates the profitability of sales before taxes and interest. In fact, this indicator which is actually the ratio of the firm's EBIT to its

Sales Profitability and Asset Utilization

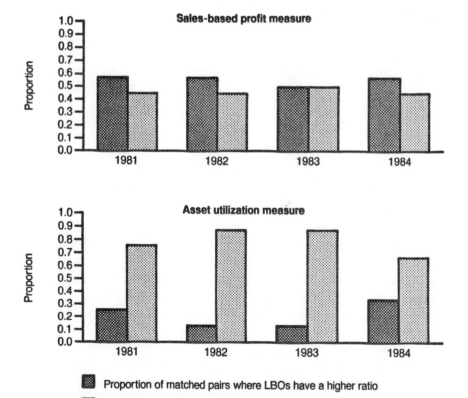

Sales-based profit measure

Asset utilization measure

■ Proportion of matched pairs where LBOs have a higher ratio

▨ Proportion of matched pairs where LBOs have a lower ratio

sales, measures the effectiveness of the company's product line in generating pre-tax profits for the firm. Given that a buyout group which evaluates an LBO candidate will anyway change the firm's leverage, and as a result also the company's tax liability, the net operating margin is by far the most relevant sales-based profitability measure. Indeed, as illustrated in the first panel of the Sales Profitability and Asset Utilization exhibit, investing groups are aware of this relevance.

The chart on page 209 indicates that, in general, the net operating margins of the LBO candidates are somewhat higher than those of the industry-matched non-LBO group. The third sales-based profitability measure is the net margin on sales, often referred to as return on sales. This measure, which is derived as the ratio of after-tax net profits-to-sales, by itself provides very little useful information since it mixes the effectiveness of sales in producing profits (reflected by the net operating margin) with the effects of the method of financing on profits (reflected by the amount of interest deduction). However, as will be shown, the return on sales measure, in combination with an asset utilization measure, is often used in computing return on assets.

The asset utilization measure linking the return on sales with the firm's return on assets is the total asset turnover. Often classified as an activity ratio, this measure is calculated by dividing sales by total assets. It indicates the efficiency with which a firm is able to use its assets to generate sales dollars. In general, the higher a firm's total asset turnover, the more efficiently its assets have been used. However, a group evaluating an LBO candidate should remember that generally, no single ratio provides sufficient information to judge the overall performance of the firm. This is in particular the case with total asset turnover. For example, consider the case of a firm that recently decided to move into new and profitable products, and as a first move already assembled appropriate production lines. Even if this investment is justified based on its expected future cash flows, at least in the short term the firm's assets have been increased at a higher rate than sales, which implies that total asset turnover is temporarily depressed. The lesson is that whenever an LBO-investing group evaluates a buyout candidate and observes a low total asset turnover, it should further dig into the firm's financial reports in order to determine whether it is a result of poor asset utilization or simply a short-term phenomenon resulting from a recent asset expansion. In addition, one of the key factors determining the long-term viability of an LBO is the ability of the post-LBO management to turn around an inefficient business and bring it up to industry standards. From this perspective, an LBO-investing group might see an opportunity in buying out a firm with a low total asset turnover, liquidate the unnecessary/nonproductive assets, use the proceeds from the asset liquidation to pay off part of the debt, and try to improve the utilization rate of the remaining assets. A comparison of asset turnover ratios of the two groups is illustrated in the second panel of the Sales Profitability and Asset Utilization exhibit. The results are striking. The LBO candidates, prior to their buyouts, are significantly less efficient in utilizing their assets. The matched pairs where LBOs have a higher ratio are outnumbered by a factor of 7 to 1 in two of the years and by similar factors in the other years. Given that we did not observe lower leverage for the LBO candidates, it becomes clear that locating a firm with "too many assets" is the dominant factor in finding an ideal candidate.

As mentioned earlier, the firm's return on sales and total asset turnover are the two components used in calculating the firm's return on assets. The return on assets (ROA), which is often called the firm's return on investment (ROI), measures the overall effectiveness of management in generating profits with its available assets. Given that the firm's ROA is derived as the ratio of net income-to-total assets, it can also be obtained as the product of the firm's return on sales and total asset turnover. This relationship, often referred to as the DuPont formula, is described as follows:

$$\left(\frac{\text{Net income}}{\text{Sales}}\right) \times \left(\frac{\text{Sales}}{\text{Assets}}\right) = \left(\frac{\text{Net income}}{\text{Assets}}\right)$$

By using the formal names of the ratios, it can be presented as:

$$\text{(Return on sales)} \times \text{(Total asset turnover)} = \text{ROA}$$

This relationship allows the group conducting the analysis to break down the firm's return on assets into a profit-on-sales component and an asset efficiency component. In analyzing an LBO candidate it is of special interest because the investing group is, in general, more likely, in the short run, to improve the firm's asset utilization (via a partial liquidation) than to drastically change its profit margin. In the short run, profit margin is likely to be predetermined and difficult to adjust because prices are typically set in competitive markets, labor cost agreed upon in union contracts, and other cost components such as raw material prices, and existing long-term lease contracts on buildings and equipment are often fixed contractually. In this sense, the DuPont formula indirectly also conveys information on how likely it is to turn around the firm and improve its return on assets. The three panels of the Return on Asset Measurement exhibit illustrate the various types of asset profitability measures.

The top panel compares the two groups' net return on assets. The second panel provides the comparison of the two groups' return on assets when income is measured after interest payment but before taxes. Similarly, the third ratio is derived by dividing the firm's earnings before tax and interest by its assets. Independent of the measure used, the LBO candidates exhibit lower asset profitability. Despite their higher net operating margins, the LBO group generated a lower asset profitability throughout the entire investigation period. This confirms the conclusion derived from the asset turnover discussion, that the LBOs' asset base is excessive, and in the post-LBO period the investing group is highly likely to "cut some of the fat" by liquidating underperforming business lines and improving the efficiency of the remaining ones.

Once the profitability on sales and assets have been determined, an investing group should conduct a return on equity (ROE) analysis. First, it is useful to define the terms involved. Also called net worth, equity is the claim of the owners on the assets of the business. In a proprietorship or

Return on Assets Measurement

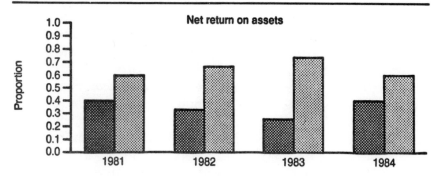

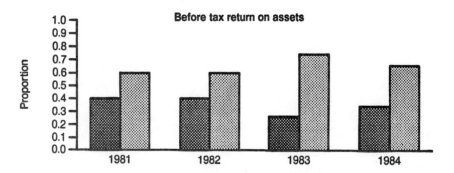

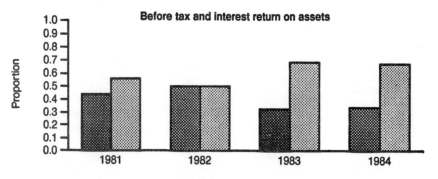

■ Proportion of matched pairs where LBOs have a higher ratio

▨ Proportion of matched pairs where LBOs have a lower ratio

partnership, equity is each owner's original investment plus any earnings after withdrawals. In a corporation, the owners are the shareholders, those who have invested capital (cash or other assets) in exchange for shares of stock. The corporation's equity is the sum of contributions plus earnings retained after paying dividends. The ROE, which is calculated as the ratio of net income-to-equity, indicates the return earned on book value of the common stockholders' equity. If the firm has outstanding shares of preferred stock, the measure commonly referred to as the return on common stock equity is derived as the ratio of net profits after taxes minus preferred dividends-to-total stockholders' equity minus preferred stock equity. In general, owners are concerned with ROE since it indicates success for the company in generating earnings on their behalf. However, for an investing group evaluating an LBO candidate, this measure is much less important in making its buyout decision. As mentioned earlier, such a group is likely to significantly change the firm's asset-mix, and is almost certain to drastically change the firm's capital structure. Therefore, the buyout group is likely to focus on the expected return on equity in the post-LBO period, as derived from a set of pro forma financial reports, rather than evaluating historical ROEs. This can be better understood once the relationship between the firm's return on assets, degree of financial leverage, and return on equity is set forth. The following relationship determines the firm's return on equity:

$$\left(\frac{\text{Net income}}{\text{Total assets}}\right) \times \left(\frac{\text{Total assets}}{\text{Equity}}\right) = \left(\frac{\text{Net income}}{\text{Equity}}\right)$$

This relationship can be also written in terms of the ratios' formal names as:

$$(\text{ROA}) \times (\text{Degree of leverage}) = (\text{ROE})$$

By reviewing the components of ROE it becomes obvious that an investing group which is planning to change the firm's assets and leverage will be better off focusing on liquidity and profit margin analysis rather than relying on the popular ROE bottom line. Given that we reported a lower asset turnover and a lower return on assets for the LBO group, the observed ROE of this group is clearly expected to be under that of the non-LBO group. Indeed, as illustrated by the Return on Equity Measurement exhibit, the LBO group's ROE, when calculated on both a before and after-tax basis, is lower than that of the non-LBO group throughout the examination period.

Once again, the investing group's intentions to buy out a firm and turn it around are revealed. In light of the inferior measures reported for both asset turnover and asset profitability, it seems that the typical buyout group will achieve

Return on Equity Measurement

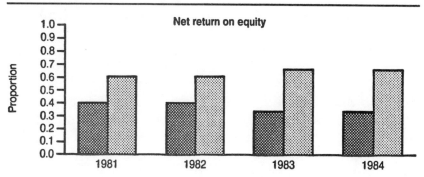

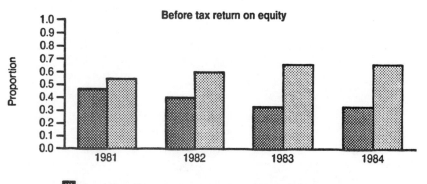

▨ Proportion of matched pairs where LBOs have a higher ratio

▨ Proportion of matched pairs where LBOs have a lower ratio

such a goal only by implementing a well-defined post-LBO plan consisting of both asset liquidation and drastic cost cutting measures.

CASH-FLOW GENERATION ANALYSIS

Unfortunately for a group evaluating an LBO candidate or a lender assessing a firm's financial strength, analyzing financial statements is a nontrivial task. On one hand, the buyout group is provided with numerous reports featuring terms such as operating income, net income, and earnings per share. On the other hand, they all look for the firm's true ability to generate cash flow to repay its debt and compensate the equity holders for the assumed risk. The difficulty in analyzing financial statements is compounded by the fact that Company A might have a higher net income than Company B, but actually generates less cash. Does it sound strange? The need to distinguish between earnings and cash flow is a result of an accounting approach called the accrual method of accounting. By this long-established and widely used principle, revenue and expenses are recognized when a service is performed or goods are delivered, regardless of when payment is received or made. This method allows, what the accountants call, the matching of revenues and associated expenses. If, for example, a computer company sells $50,000 worth of computers, $50,000 of revenue is earned and entered in the books even though the proceeds of the sale may not be collected for a month or longer. Therefore, to translate the income figure to cash flow requires an adjustment, subtracting any increase in net working capital from net income or adding to net income any reduction in that parameter. In addition, a second adjustment is needed to account for the fact that some of the figures categorized by accountants as "expenses" don't represent actual cash outflows. The largest component in the noncash expenses category is depreciation. A universal accounting assumption holds that all fixed assets—with the exception of land—deteriorate, wear out, or become obsolete. This process represents a decline in value and is called depreciation. It is calculated by apportioning an asset's original acquisition price, less any expected salvage value, over the asset's expected years of useful life. The important thing is that on the income statement, depreciation incurred during the accounting period is deducted as an expense from the firm's revenues. However, depreciation is only an accountant's approach to reflect a decline in value. It is not an actual out-of-pocket cash flow. It affects the cash flow only through its impact on taxes. Therefore, from a cash flow standpoint, given that the objective is to assess the LBO candidate's ability to generate cash, the firm's depreciation expense as well as any other noncash expenses should be added back to net income in order to derive the firm's cash flow. A simple numerical example is illustrated in the Net Income versus Cash Flow table. Both firms have $1.0 million sales, but firm A has lower expenses other than depreciation and a higher depreciation expense than firm B. As indicated by the popular net income bottom line, firm B reports a higher net income which also leads to a higher return on assets. However, a wise lender and an educated investing group would realize that once the equipment has been bought, the depreciation expense is relevant only through its impact on the tax bill. Therefore, it is useful to derive the cash flow generated by each of those firms rather than rely heavily on the ROA figures. Given that this example does not involve a change in working capital, the cash flow can be derived by simply subtracting the sum of all expenses (other than depreciation) and taxes from sales. Alternatively, we can derive the cash flow figure by simply adding back the depreciation expense to net income. As illustrated in Panel III of the Net Income versus Cash Flow table, both methods lead to the same result, indicating that despite its lower ROA, firm A has generated $70,000 more in cash than firm B. So far, in comparing the pre-buyout financial ratios of LBO candidates with a group of industry-matched firms, the results, in general, are surprising. The LBO firms have higher financial leverage, lower asset turnover, and lower return on both assets and equity. The only positive observations were the fact that they are slightly

Net Income versus Cash Flow

	Company A	Company B
I. Income Statement		
Sales	$1,000,000	$1,000,000
− Expenses (excluding depreciation)	600,000	650,000
− Depreciation	150,000	50,000
= Taxable income	$ 250,000	$ 300,000
− Taxes (40%)	100,000	120,000
= Net Income	$ 150,000	$ 180,000
II. ROA Analysis		
Assets	$1,500,000	$1,500,000
ROA	150,000/1,500,000 = 10%	180,000/1,500,000 = 12%
III. Cash Flow Analysis		
Method 1:		
Sales	$1,000,000	$1,000,000
− Expenses (excluding depreciation)	600,000	650,000
− Taxes	100,000	120,000
= Cash flow	$ 300,000	$ 230,000
Method 2:		
Net income	$ 150,000	$ 180,000
+ Depreciation	150,000	50,000
= Cash flow	$ 300,000	$ 230,000

more liquid and they have a small edge in terms of net operating income. But here comes the important piece of good news. The LBO candidates generate significantly more cash than the members of the non-LBO group. As illustrated in the top two panels of the Cash Flow Generation Analysis exhibit, when noncash expenses are added back to the figure of reported net earnings, the minor edge reported in net operating margin is widened to clearly qualify the LBO candidates as solidly desirable targets.

These results confirm a proposition made earlier in this chapter that selling specific segments of the business, which immediately will reduce the firm's asset base and required equity, can be the first and most desired plan of action adopted by the buying group. Relative to its level of sales, the typical LBO seems to generate a reasonable margin and a healthy cash stream. It is only when the return is measured relative to total assets, the LBO candidate appeared to have underperformed. This conclusion is again supported by the results presented in the third panel of the Cash Flow Generation Analysis exhibit. The outstanding performance implied by the top two panels of the exhibit reverses itself when assets replace sales as the denominator of the various ratios. These results again show that the typical LBO candidate is loaded with excessive assets. Furthermore, when comparing these cash flow-based exhibits to those based on conventional measures of profitability, the lesson is clear. A focus on cash flow rather than on earnings per se is a key ingredient of an appropriate cash flow analysis.

RISK ANALYSIS

In evaluating an LBO candidate, a risk analysis provides the investing group with indicators on the volatility of the firm's overall operations, earnings, and cash flows. When one runs a business with a 10:1 debt-equity ratio, a slight deviation from the "base-case scenario" might very quickly turn out to be a nightmare. Therefore, volatility and its implied risk play a major role in the analysis. Information required to

Cash Flow Generation Analysis

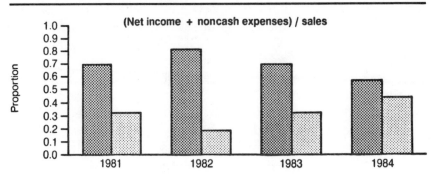

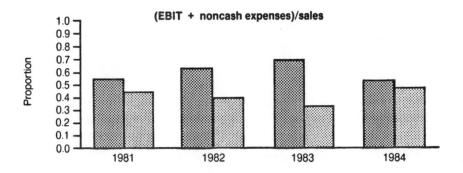

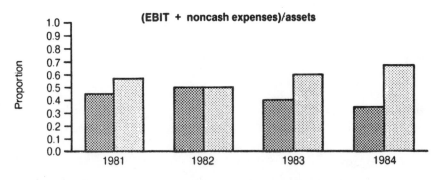

Proportion of matched pairs where LBOs have a higher ratio

Proportion of matched pairs where LBOs have a lower ratio

analyze risk can be obtained from the firm's financial reports as well as from data on the rate of return on its publicly traded stock. The financial reports can be used to calculate the variability of both earnings and cash flow generated per share. Typically, we first calculate the year-to-year percentage change in earnings and cash flow. Then, by using a simple formula, we derive the standard deviation of the earnings and cash flow for each firm. The standard deviation is the most commonly used measure of spread. In general, it measures how far the numbers in a set of data tend to be from the average of the data set. Though the standard deviation is quite sensitive to extreme values (say, one year with unusually low earnings or cash flow), it does serve as a useful indicator of dispersion. The results of comparing the standard deviation of the two groups' year-to-year changes in earnings and cash flow are presented in the top two panels of the Risk Analysis exhibit. In general, the non-LBO firms exhibit lower earnings and cash flow variability. Another interesting observation is the fact that the gap between the two groups' variability is slightly smaller when cash flows rather than earnings are used. For example, in 1984, about 70 percent of the LBO firms reported higher earnings volatility. For the same year, this indicator is reduced to 50 percent when cash flow volatility is measured.

Similarly, as indicated by the results presented in the third panel of the Risk Analysis exhibit, the observed market risk as gauged by the beta measure is in general higher for the firms in the LBO group. As described earlier in this book, the market risk assesses the percentage change in a stock typically associated with a 1 percent change in the overall market. This relative volatility is important because it is associated with the nature of the firm's products, a characteristic not likely to be changed by the investing group.

Nevertheless, one should employ certain judgment while evaluating the results reported in our risk analysis. On the positive side, a group buying an LBO candidate should be able to identify areas of excessive volatility for a potential sell-off, and leave a core of stable businesses in the company. For the sake of illustration, suppose that a group considers

Risk Analysis

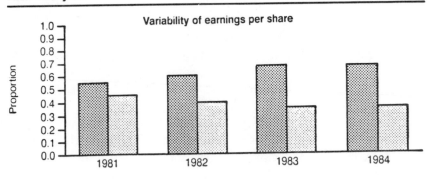

Variability of earnings per share

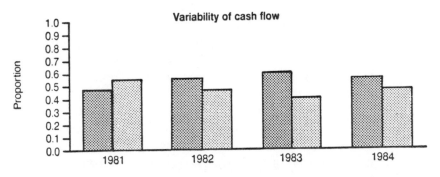

Variability of cash flow

▨ Proportion of matched pairs where LBOs have a higher variability

☐ Proportion of matched pairs where LBOs have a lower variability

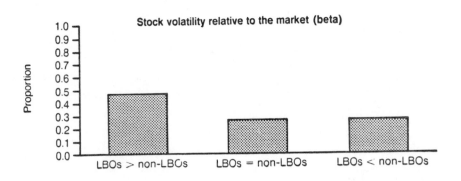

Stock volatility relative to the market (beta)

borrowing a large amount to buy Boston-based Gillette. First, it is clear that the blades and razors segment is both important and stable. Furthermore, although this segment is only one third of Gillette's sales, it contributes two thirds of Gillette's bottom line. As a second step, in trying to sell off assets, such an investing group will assess the risk-return profile of the other segments. For example, given that Gillette's toiletries and cosmetics group contributes approximately 30 percent to Gillette's sales but only 15 percent to the bottom line, the investing group will have to evaluate whether this business segment's volatility is low enough to justify such a low margin. A similar analysis should be performed on Gillette's line of writing instruments and office products which contribute 11 percent of Gillette's sales but only 2 percent of its bottom line. Obviously, if the group sells these lines in the post-LBO period, Gillette's earnings and cash flow variability will be very different from the pre-LBO values. Therefore, in conducting a formal risk analysis one should concentrate on the variability of the relevant retained core businesses.

On the negative side, any increase in financial leverage (given all other things equal), will likely be associated with an increase in the variability of earnings and cash flow per share as well as in the market risk. The good news is that already at the planning stage of a buyout, once the mix of the financing package is known, the investing group should attempt to estimate the expected variability in the post-LBO period. In fact, such an analysis has been performed in several of the valuation cases discussed in this book. For example, as part of the process of finding the appropriate discount rate for discounting Macy's cash flow, we were equipped with the information that prior to the LBO, Macy's beta was estimated as 1.10. By using information on Macy's debt-equity ratio prior to and following the buyout, and the appropriate tax rate, it has been shown that Macy's revised beta in the post-LBO period is 6.15. The lesson is clear. Analyzing pre-LBO volatility is important. The lower the cash flow volatility, the easier it is to manage the firm's cash and meet the huge loan payments. However, leverage is a two-edge sword.

It does increase the expected payoffs, but it also has the potential to completely change the level of variability. While it is very tempting to overlook this effect, successfully managing cash flow volatility is one of the key success factors in implementing a profitable LBO.

CHAPTER 5

THE LBO AND THE LAW: PROTECTING MANAGEMENT FROM LITIGATION

The 1980s will be remembered for more than Prince Charles and Princess Diana, airline wars, and Larry Bird. The economic activity during this age of the yuppie will be characterized by the popularity of takeovers and leveraged buyouts. The momentum of the trend of public companies going private is now at an all-time high, and it is safe to say that before this decade is complete, many more such deals will occur.

Managers who are considering participation in a leveraged buyout obviously will have to do their homework on the financial and behavioral implications of these acquisitions. But it does not end here. As with any high stakes activity, leveraged buyouts exist in the same universe as the omnipresent attorney, with an ever watchful eye centered on the manager. Of course, life would be wonderful if one could complete a leveraged buyout without having to worry about being sued at any moment. Since this will never be the case, management must be aware of the legal issues of leveraged buyouts and understand what actions must be taken to reduce their risks of legal confrontation.

We appreciate the research, analysis, and writing done by Larry Richardson and Bill Garrett. Without their very significant contribution, the completion of this chapter would not have been possible.

We will discuss several issues frequently arising in LBO litigation: equitable subordination, indemnification, fraudulent conveyances, fairness/business judgment, Acquisition Agreements, and key rules, restrictions, and due diligence. The purpose of this discussion is to provide information in "nonlegal" jargon that will enable a group of managers to take those steps necessary to avoid having their leveraged buyout attempt decimated by the bang of a gavel.

These legal issues have grabbed recent attention primarily because of litigation in a large number of leveraged buyouts. This litigation, which typically involves lawsuits against the management team attempting the buyout, can occur even if management is fully prepared for it, regardless of how smoothly the deal goes. There is nothing that management can do to completely eliminate the risk of being sued. If a deal goes "bad," it doesn't matter what management has done; someone can, of course, always sue. The real question then becomes: What can management do to minimize the risk of the plaintiff prevailing once they bring suit?

In this discussion we will assume that management has taken the preliminary steps to reduce this risk at the time the offer was made by complying with the tender offer statutes in terms of required disclosure, form of the offer, and accuracy of the proxy statement which accompanies the tender offer. We will therefore deal with structural infirmities sometimes found in leveraged buyouts and, within this context we will describe how management can guard against the possibility of a successful suit.

EQUITABLE SUBORDINATION

To the extent that creditors are playing an increasingly important role in LBOs, it is entirely likely that management might find itself in a position where a lender has both a debt and an equity position in the company after it has gone private. For example, a banker might agree to fund a venture if the bank were to receive a certain percentage of the company's equity. Let us assume that the bank's degree of influence in its equity position is significant and that the company's board of directors recognizes that without the banker it is limited in setting corporate policy and decision making. The banker's attitude in this instance is along the line of "I'll loan you the money, but by doing so, I get to call the shots." If this company can operate to management's and the banker's satisfaction and, more importantly, can remain solvent, the potential problems in this scenario would be limited to those of clashing personalities. Naturally, this is inherent in all companies and, so it seems, in many relationships involving bankers. In the event of bankruptcy, however, this situation instantly becomes one characterized by a conflict of interest. An important management consideration ought to be the influence of the banker's position if and when the company runs out of money. If the company cannot pay its bills, can the shrewd banker inform the naïve board of directors that, in order to satisfy its debt position, the bank will be satisfied grabbing the company's assets?

Before management proceeds with this arrangement, it needs to know the status of the banker's debt and equity positions and the priority that each would receive in the event of default. It is in this instance that the doctrine of equitable subordination would apply.

Equitable subordination occurs when a court concludes that an investment which was nominally debt is, in terms of claim priority, equal to equity. Management should be aware that the debt used for the buyout will typically not be treated as debt in the event of default. This would be regarded as good news indeed for the managers in this scenario. But consequently, it would not be well received by the banker who finds that despite his or her position of influence, is unable to go after the company's assets to pay off his or her own loan. In the event of bankruptcy, under the doctrine of equitable subordination, the court would rule that the banker's investment, despite the title and appearance of debt, would be deemed equity because "circumstances within such creditor's control [would render] it inequitable for such creditor to be treated on a par with other creditors." In other words, the court would recognize the conflict of interest between the debt position and the board position where it has responsibility for looking after the interests of the firm's equity holders. In order to be fair and protect the other creditors that do not have this influential position, it would likely deem the bank's investment as equity rather than debt.

If the investment is considered equity, it generally stands on par with all other equity, even in the event of a bankruptcy situation where there are a number of different claimants. The general hierarchy of claims is secured creditors first, unsecured creditors second, and equity third. The banker would find that each of his or her positions would receive identical treatment. The banker would also find that, if there were a default and the assets of the firm were not sufficient to pay back the investors, he or she would fall in line behind the secured and unsecured creditors. It should come as no surprise that in an LBO, the lenders look to the assets and the cash flows of the acquired business itself as the source of repayment of the loans, rather than looking to the purchaser. Indeed, the purchaser generally has no legal commitment to invest funds beyond the initial investment.

INDEMNIFICATION

Management must be aware of the issue of indemnification and the amount of legal protection to which it is entitled when doing a leveraged buyout. Specifically, management would need to know how it can minimize the probability of being held liable for possible lawsuits against the company. Since these liabilities cover such a broad spectrum, it might be best to examine one particular example, paying close attention to the nuances of the law.

Suppose that the managers of a holding company have decided to buy out a firm that manufactures children's plastic toys. Also suppose that this firm has a reputation for producing dangerous products because, several years ago, a child became very ill from the toxic material in the plastic after placing a toy in her mouth. Should management proceed with the buyout despite the obvious dangers associated with owning the toy company? Would it be more appropriate for them to seek out a company with less exposure? If management has indeed determined that such plastic toys represent a good investment, how can they be isolated from past or future litigation?

Every state statute has a provision dealing with indemnification, as does any good set of corporate bylaws. When contemplating a leveraged buyout, management must make sure that these bylaws provide adequate protection. These provisions should allow the corporation to advance funds to management to defend any suit, provided that management has not acted negligently. This line of defense is, of course, only as good as the corporation's assets.

Some corporations have what is called director and officer liability insurance which is designed to protect them against personal liabilities. Unfortunately, the cost of this insurance has become prohibitive for many companies. Yet, in the dangerous toy example, the holding company should at least consider the cost/benefit trade-off of obtaining product liability insurance. Now let us suppose that six months after management has acquired the toy company, another child becomes ill for similar product-related reasons and that this incident occurs after the buyout. If the managers have taken adequate protection, they would have been satisfied with the coverage provided by the bylaws of the toy company and with the director and officer and product liability policies provided by their insurance company prior to the completion of the deal. If the plaintiff (in this case, the child's parents) were to prevail, the holding company (of which the toy company is now a part) would recover from its insurance company under its product liability insurance, and the individual defendants (each of the managers) would be entitled to receive payments from the toy company under the indemnification provisions inherent in the bylaws.

In addition to this coverage, management should also take preventive measures by dealing directly with the seller of the ongoing business. Even if there had not been a history of liability problems associated with the toy company's products, the holding company's managers should consider the possibility that there might be such cases in the future and address this issue before proceeding with the deal. There used to be a doctrine of law which said that if you purchased assets of a business, you would not be responsible for any liabilities not expressly assumed. That doctrine has since fallen by the wayside in many jurisdictions, including Delaware. Now, if a company buys an ongoing business and continues doing business under the same name, often it will be held liable for the activity of its predecessor, even if it did not expressly assume liabilities as part of the purchase agreement. The way the managers of the holding company would guard against these liabilities would be to establish an indemnification provision in the purchase agreement with the previous owners of the toy company. This provision would require the sellers to indemnify the buyers for some scope of claims. This indemnification often involves a holdback of part of the purchase price. When the holding company's managers buy the toy company, they should hold onto a certain percentage of the purchase price for a specified period (usually not longer than two years), to be used in the event of a claim against the toy company. This will assure that there will be a ready pool of cash available as an insulation to product liability. This "security fund" provision is often the primary focus of the discussion of the purchase agreement between the buyer and seller. Among the chief issues of this provision are the detailed risks that management desires to be indemnified against, the amount of money that will be held back, and the amount of the deductible—or that amount that the buyer will be responsible for, which usually is somewhere between 1 and 3 percent of the purchase price.

FRAUDULENT CONVEYANCES

It is safe to say that whenever management proceeds with a leveraged buyout, one legal matter that will simply not go away is the issue of fraudulent conveyances. By the very nature of LBOs, management uses borrowed funds to pay for the transaction. Often this is the only way in which the transaction can take place. Otherwise, management would be unable to afford the buyout.

In essence, a can of worms is opened whenever an LBO takes place. To the extent that communication between so many parties (such as the buyer, the seller, the lender, and the insurer) is required and, given that lawsuits are won and lost over something as subtle as the wording in a purchase agreement, it would seem reasonable to label this can "Potential Fraudulent Conveyance Litigation." It must be kept in mind that all parties (including management) are affected. The majority of litigation in leveraged buyout cases has been and will continue to be over this issue. It will therefore behoove management to understand fraudulent conveyances and recognize what must be done to minimize its probability of occurrence.

Fraudulent conveyances are governed by the Uniform Fraudulent Conveyance Act which has been enacted to date by 25 states, including Delaware. It is a law which says that a transaction which is fraudulent can have its security set aside. This means that when one party sells or grants interest to another in a transaction where it knows or should know that the transferor is insolvent or will become so, then the party that received the interest may not necessarily be entitled to keep it and can have the money set aside to its own detriment.

For example, suppose I am a bank and I loan you money which you, as management, use to acquire the assets of Company A. Suppose also that I receive from you a security interest in Company A to secure payment of that debt in what you tell me in the loan agreement is "the unlikely event that Company A defaults." If Company A does default, it could be determined by the courts that I participated in a fraudulent conveyance because I should have known that you and Company A would, after the acquisition, become insolvent. If this were to occur, the grant of the security interest that I received can be set aside, shoving me down with the great unwashed unsecured creditors. In plain English, I could lose my shirt. This is also your concern as well because I would most certainly, given this occurrence, instruct my attorney to go after yours and Company A's assets to ensure that I retain my security interest on the grounds that your fraudulent conveyance was the catalyst behind my granting you the loan. I could surely argue that your assurance and documented pro forma statements suggested that the only way that Company A could become insolvent was through lackluster management that had little regard for its position of indebtedness. The floodgates for additional lawsuits under this claim would open up, resulting in a mass of litigation of which there would appear no probable winner.

To a great extent, selling shareholders may be dragged into fraudulent conveyance litigation by knowing or because they should have known that the management team proposing the tender offer would become insolvent following the acquisition. The shareholders participating in this transaction can be held accountable for losses which arise after the transaction. What this means is that even though a transaction is complete, it is possible that the shareholders may be required to return a portion of the price paid to them if the company defaults. It also implies that the shareholders would likely take legal action against management in an attempt to retain this money. This would be done on the same basis that the bank in the previous example countersued management for fraudulent conveyance and the negligent manner in which Company A was run. Even if the shareholders do not prevail in this instance, the unwanted exposure, time, and legal expense that management would incur as a result of this litigation would certainly be to management's detriment.

Management must make sure that it avoids making inaccurate and gratuitous statements about the financial well-being or expected financial performance of the target company. This is a critical area of concern for banks as well, since if they participate in financing transactions which may be deemed to violate the Fraudulent Conveyance Act, they can, as we saw in the above scenario, lose the entire loan.

The way management can avoid fraudulent conveyance claims (other than to make sure that they do not develop an insolvent company) is to prepare the transaction in a proper way. By doing appropriate due diligence when it prepares the proxy statement, management can significantly minimize this risk. In addition, management must structure the transaction in such a way that there will be adequate cash. Given that the acquired business must generate enough cash to repay the borrowed and/or deferred purchase price, a realistic analysis of the business's potential cash flow is crucial to an evaluation of whether a leveraged buyout acquisition can succeed. In a successful leveraged buyout, the acquired business will pay for itself out of cash. By examining all of the various cash flows and the accounting nuances each one entails (depreciation schedules, for example), management can in fact determine if the deal is structured in a way that will enable it to proceed in a "business as usual" fashion without having to worry about missing its next payroll. Once a payment is missed, it is really much too late. Management, or management's investment banker also needs to take steps prior to the closing of the transaction to create the necessary insolation against the claims that they were destined to become insolvent once they entered into the deal, or that they were left with inadequate capital and unable to meet their debts as they matured. These steps are discussed in the following "Fairness/Business Judgment" section.

FAIRNESS/BUSINESS JUDGMENT

Closely related to fraudulent conveyances is the issue of fairness in terms of the price offered to the shareholders. The fair price issue is very sensitive in leveraged buyouts because of management's entangling allegiances. On one hand, it has a duty to the target company's shareholders to get the best possible price for the company; yet on the other hand, it wants to buy the company at the lowest possible price.

An important question that management should consider is to what extent shareholders can contest the decision that something is fair. Can they sue management over the price that they received, and will management be obligated to increase that price if the shareholders prevail?

This is really an inquiry as to the extent that the courts will respect the director's business judgment. The courts have traditionally shown a great deal of deference to this judgment, though there have been some cases which have shed caution in the area. In most of those cases, the facts suggested that the directors had not done an adequate job of seeking any independent evaluation of the transaction. One recent Massachusetts case, for example, involved a multimillion dollar proposed transaction where the directors considered the proposal for only 20 minutes. After the deal was completed, the shareholders contested the transaction, indicating that the price they received was not fair, and they prevailed.

Certainly, one would think that responsible managers would have given this proposal more deliberation, even given the time constraints that are often imposed in these kinds of transactions, or have sought some outside expert counsel. Managers should definitely hire an independent outside adviser or investment banker to do an appraisal. This can be important in reducing exposure in any future litigation. It is very unusual that a court will substitute its own judgment for that of an investment banker's, or even the directors' if it is determined that the directors have exercised proper caution and diligence in reaching a price. Management should, however, have some record of having done this, even if the deal is open for only a short period of time and there is maximum pressure.

In order to provide protection against a possible fairness claim by the shareholders, several steps are recommended. First, appraisals should be obtained on all of the target's assets. Inventory and plant and equipment should be appraised at auction value, liquidation value, and fair market value. Receivables should also be closely scrutinized. Second, recently audited financial statements should be obtained and updated. Third, management should perform a cash flow analysis and projections for several years showing an ability to stay in business and meet obligations. All of this information should be communicated in a detailed manner to the shareholders in the proxy statement.

An illustration of what was done right by management is the 1979 classic case of *Lewis* v. *Oppenheimer & Company.* In this case, the plaintiff (Lewis), who was a shareholder in a previously publicly traded company (Big Bear, which is owned by Oppenheimer), brought suit, claiming that the offered price was unfair. Lewis claimed that the proxy statement misled him because it omitted information which "a reasonable shareholder would consider important in deciding how to vote." Among these alleged omissions was the anticipated increase in Big Bear's future sales and earnings.

The court ruled against Lewis, citing that the disclosure in the proxy statement was adequate. "The financial history of the company over the preceding five years was disclosed in the proxy statement. Furthermore, management attributed the recent increase in sales to the opening of new stores." Oppenheimer was obviously specific enough in its proxy statement.

The issue of fairness raises questions involving the method of financing LBOs. The notion that there is something inherently suspect in the buyer using the acquired assets to obtain loans to finance the acquisition was also present in this same case. Lewis argued that the proxy statement did not disclose the buyers' method of financing the purchase and that he "should have been told whether the buyers intended to use the acquired assets as collateral for the purchase." This information, the plaintiff argued, is material because it would inform the shareholders of how much of their own money the buyers were using and therefore of how fair their offer was. Again, the court ruled that the proxy statement was not defective merely because it failed to disclose the buyers' method of financing. In its ruling the court stated that "a stockholder who has firmly decided to tender has no interest in the financial position of the offeror other than its ability to pay—a point not here at issue—since he will have severed all financial connections with the target." In other words, the court ruled that it was none of Lewis's business.

Finally, there is the controversy surrounding the determinants of a fair stock price relative to the market price at the time of the transaction. In almost every leveraged buyout, the shareholders have received a price substantially over the market price of the publicly traded firm. It is because of this that shareholders dream of the day when their company will be bought out, leaving them with their bucket of gold to enjoy for the remainder of their lives.

Management, on the other hand, would like nothing better than to leave the shareholder with as low a price as possible, as the new management's economic climate will be characterized by a definite need for cash. It is worth noting that the purchase does not necessarily have to be above book value to be considered fair. If a company does not earn a reasonable return on its assets, and the market price reflects this low rate of return, a purchase at or below book value could represent a substantial premium. More often than not, however, the shareholders will fare very well when their company is bought out.

A recent case that has received a great deal of attention in the area of fairness claims is *Weinberger* v. *UOP, Inc.* This case arose out of a stockholder class action suit challenging the cash-out of public stockholders of UOP through a merger with the Signal Companies. The suit alleged that the price offered to the shareholders was unfair. At the time of the proposal, UOP's stock was trading at $14.50, and Signal proposed a price of $21 per share. The court ruled, however, in favor of the plaintiff (Weinberger), stating that fairness of the price was determined by "the economic and financial considerations of the proposed merger, including all relevant factors: assets, market value, earnings, future prospects, and any other elements that affect the intrinsic or inherent value of the company's stock." The court placed emphasis on the fact that UOP did not have an unbiased opinion rendered prior to the transaction. "The result could have been entirely different if UOP had appointed an independent negotiating committee of its outside directors to deal with Signal at arm's length."

Thus, the court ruled that directors must demonstrate the utmost in good faith and the scrupulous inherent fairness of the bargain. In a going private action when the directors appear to have conflict of interest concerns, they have the burden to show that the merger was fair.

The court established that entire fairness of the transaction includes a showing of both fair dealing and fair price. The simple participation in a going private transaction will not in and of itself prove an absence of fair dealing. Issues such as when the transaction was timed, how it was initiated, structured, negotiated, disclosed to the directors, and how the approval of the stockholders and directors were obtained, are factors which are used to determine fairness of dealing.

Although fair dealing cannot be assured, there are basic procedures which the court recommended in the Weinberger case. Upon receipt of a tender offer or bid, a committee of independent directors should be established. The committee should retain independent counsel and an independent financial adviser. The financial adviser or legal counsel's fee should not be contingent on the consumation of the buyout since it is likely to undermine the establishment of independence. If the financial adviser demands a contingency fee, it must be disclosed in the proxy statement and elsewhere.

Naturally, board members who have a vested interest in the deal should not vote or participate in the merger or buyout proceedings. Interestingly, corporate bylaws which require a majority vote of the minority stockholders to authorize a merger (which is often the case) are not sufficient to establish fair dealing. Indeed, the Weinberger court was skeptical as to the protections such bylaws provide. However, such bylaws would shift the burden to the stockholders to prove that the buyout was unfair.

Fair price is not to be determined by accountants sitting in a back room. It incorporates the entire economic and financial picture of the proposed merger. Not even a large premium will be conclusive of a fair price. The various factors will include such characteristics as types of assets, market value (current and historical), past and present earnings, future prospects, and any other elements that would affect the intrinsic or inherent value of the company's stock. Such elements include the going concern value, the liquidation value, the price of stock paid by the issuer or an affiliate over the past two years, and any reports, opinions, or appraisals of the fairness of other offers over the past 18 months. Other bid prices will be taken into account to determine fairness. Thus, Weinberger liberalized and broadened the approach to valuation, for Delaware had previously always used market value, book value, and investment value as the main measures.

The financial adviser plays an important role in valuation. He or she needs to have complete information and fully evaluate the price. The buyout should not go ahead if the adviser gives an unfavorable opinion as to the fairness of the acquisition. In Weinberger, the financial adviser completed work in little over a weekend, an effort the court viewed as much too superficial. A finding by the court that fair dealing has been established will not necessarily lead to a finding of fair price, although the likelihood of such a finding is increased.

The overriding implication of all of this is that management must consider the possibility of a fairness claim against them and must prepare for it accordingly. As illustrated in both the Oppenheimer and Weinberger cases, communication to the shareholder in the proxy statement is very important. A rule of thumb is to provide more information than required. The proverb "better safe than sorry" definitely applies in the leveraged buyout context. While this does not suggest that a group of directors can in this way avoid a fairness claim, they can at least avoid being caught off guard when and if a claim is made.

THE ACQUISITION AGREEMENT

Between the time of the initial public announcement and the proxy statement, an Acquisition Agreement will be drafted. The Acquisition Agreement is a written contract between the target corporation and the acquiring group. This agreement sets forth the terms of the proposed buyout, conditioned upon the occurrence of certain events. Examples of these contingent clauses include agreements that the proposed buyout will not occur if the target receives a better bid or if the acquiring group cannot raise the necessary funds. A proxy statement is then mailed to all shareholders seeking their support on a given issue. The proxy statement mailed in anticipation of a merger or takeover is required by corporate law and a majority of shareholders must approve. The proxy statement must disclose all relevant information about the proposed deal and the players involved.

The initial bid documented by an Acquisition Agreement might contain certain clauses that could be construed as violating fiduciary duties owed to minority stockholders. These clauses can be generalized into four groups: requiring the target not to shop the company; granting of stock and/or asset options to the bidder which can be exercised if the acquisition is by a rival company; reimbursing expenses and/ or paying breakup fees; and other various clauses that might be considered fraudulent or inequitable. The existence of these clauses may provoke concern that the directors are not looking after the best interests of the stockholders. Rather, the clauses imply that they are seeking to protect their own interests. An independent committee should consider several factors before accepting these clauses. They ought to include the price offered for the company, the financing during the time needed to complete the buyout, the need for regulatory approvals from the Securities and Exchange Commission and other regulatory bodies, and the prospects of other buyers paying a higher price for the company. Yet, managers beware. The importance of these clauses in a fairness claim relates to whether the buyer is a group of incumbent managers or directors.

A no-shopping clause may be included in an Acquisition Agreement to prohibit the target corporation from actively soliciting alternative bids. The acquiring corporation may want such a clause in order to prevent a bidding war. The target often uses a no-shopping clause as a strategy to negotiate a higher price. Courts have generally determined that no duty exists for the independent committee to obtain alternative bids to determine the adequacy of the buyout group's offering. However, the inclusion of such a clause will undoubtedly increase the probability that litigation will occur. Although the opportunity to solicit bids may be prohibited by the clause, the agreement should not prohibit the committee from giving information to other bidders who were not solicited. The withholding of information would probably be found to be self-dealing or management entrenchment.

Fiduciary-out termination provisions should be considered mandatory clauses. In a fiduciary-out termination provision, the target reserves the right to terminate the agreement if a more favorable offer is received at a later date. This provision confirms the board's standing fiduciary duty. It prevents the board from recommending the buyout proposal to shareholders if a better offer is received. However, The Ninth Circuit, in the 1984 case involving Jewel Companies and Payless Drug stores, held that the target's board may forgo considering competing bids, even if they offer a greater price, until the stockholder vote of the initial proposal takes place.

Reimbursement expenses and breakup fees are usually written into the Acquisition Agreement at the buyout group's request. Reimbursing the bidder's costs when a buyout deal falls through is usually deemed appropriate and legitimate by the court. These expenses find support in the proposition that the initial bid attracted better offers; thus the ensuing competition increased the final offering price. Also, the termination of its offer was not due to the buyout group's failure to perform but a result of the receipt of a better offer. Therefore, the losing group should be reimbursed for its expenses and such a practice is not unfair for the target to assume.

The inclusion of stock and asset lockups in Acquisition Agreements presents a more controversial provision. These lockups provide a disincentive for alternative bidders to approach the target. Stock lockups grant the buyout group an option to purchase authorized but unissued shares of the target upon receipt or acceptance of a competing bid. Dr Pepper, for example, granted Forstmann Little an option to purchase 4.15 million shares and a right to "put" these shares to Dr Pepper for $8 million in the event that an alternative bid was accepted. Because various exchanges place a limit on how much stock may be issued without shareholder approval, there is a limit to the use of stock lockups. The New York Stock Exchange places this limitation at 18.5 percent of the total number of outstanding shares, and the AMEX at 20 percent.

Asset lockups operate essentially the same as stock lockups but instead give a favored bidder an option to purchase a significant portion of its assets or its crown jewel. For example, in Mobil's attempt to take over Marathon Oil, Marathon gave U.S. Steel an option to purchase the Yates Field, Marathon's crown jewel, exercisable in the event that Mobil's takeover was successful. However, the Sixth Circuit in 1981 decided that this lockup attempt by Marathon and U.S. Steel violated the Williams Act.

Lockups have not always been determined by the courts to be unfair. In *Data Probe Acquisition* v. *Datatab,* the Second Circuit decided that a stock option to purchase yet unissued stock that would amount to 200 percent of the target's present outstanding shares was not manipulative within the federal takeover regulations. Data Probe brought this action to enjoin the merger of Datatab and CRC Information System, Inc. Their merger agreement stated that Datatab would become a wholly owned subsidiary of CRC. Data Probe itself was attempting to gain control of Datatab through a tender offer. Management should be aware, however, that since the bidding group usually has no firm commitment to buy, and since the purchase is usually conditioned upon obtaining financing, lockups can be viewed as manipulative and unfair to outside bidders. A court taking this position could lead to the prevention of the buyout.

A litigation-out provision states that the Acquisition Agreement will or will not be terminated in the event of litigation. The provision could state that the deal would proceed only if litigation is limited to private suits, governmental action, or both.

KEY RULES, RESTRICTIONS, AND DUE DILIGENCE

Management must bring a knowledge of federal rules and regulations that govern leveraged buyouts to the deal. Among the two most important of these rules is Regulation

T, or the margin restriction, and the Going Private Rule (Rule 13e-3). Regulation T says that the extension of credit for the purpose of purchasing publicly traded securities for a proposed leveraged buyout (i.e., a tender offer) is restricted. These restrictions are numerous and typically do not allow management very much flexibility when it comes to borrowing or structuring the transaction. Based on the regulation, in order for the deal to take place, management would have to structure the merger as an asset purchase for fear of violating the margin regulations. Given its complexity, Regulation T is yet another reason for an LBO not to proceed without an investment banker.

Rule 13e-3, or the Going Private Rule, is related to disclosure. It requires that management's offer to the shareholders be in good faith and constitutes fair value as determined by two qualified independent people. The factors that management must address in this disclosure are quite specific and center on how the transaction will ultimately affect the shareholder. The proxy statement must include very detailed information on the elements of the transaction that will both educate the shareholders and satisfy this rule. The information would include the following:

- Future plans for the company.
- Financing details of the transaction.
- Financial projections.
- Purpose of the transaction.
- Disclosure of any report, opinion, or appraisal.
- Alternatives to the transaction.
- Structure of the transaction.
- Effects of the transaction.
- Fairness of the transaction.

This information actually serves as a due diligence checklist which will enable attorneys and management to pursue any analysis that normally accompanies a leveraged buyout. Above all, the information must be worded in a way that shows why the transaction will be in the shareholders' best interest. In essence, adhering to Rule 13e-3 will show the shareholders the benefits of the deal and, at the same time, cover the buyout group legally for any potential litigation in the future.

The issues described in this chapter are far from a comprehensive list of legal matters associated with leveraged buyouts. Obviously, a discussion on that subject would require many, many pages of text, in addition to the equivalent of several years of research. However, equitable subordination, indemnification, fraudulent conveyances, fairness/ business judgment, Acquisition Agreements, Regulation T, and Rule 13e-3 do represent the areas of the law that receive the most attention in leveraged buyout litigation. To ignore these issues is potentially dangerous and costly. Management should prepare for their appearance as a preliminary step to the acquisition.

CHAPTER 6

STRUCTURING THE DEAL: MAKING IT WORK

Let's review the basics of a leveraged buyout. In its simplest form it is the acquisition of a company or subsidiary by an investor group financed primarily by debt. The investor group includes an investment banker who orchestrates the deal, the buyers, and a host of financial institutions. The assets of the firm to be acquired serve as collateral for borrowings which are used to purchase the assets or stock of the target company. Frequently the "borrower" is the target company itself or a shell corporation established for the purpose of the transaction. In this way, LBO financing allows for the acquisition of a target company with little equity investment relative to debt and no liability to the parent company if the borrowing is not repaid.

The LBO is becoming an increasingly popular financial tool. Many of the same firms doing LBOs have also influenced the structuring of these agreements.

The economic climate of the late 1970s resulted in an abundance of acquisition candidates. Inflation, high interest rates, and a maturing U.S. industrial base led many companies to consider divesting portions of their businesses to improve liquidity or for strategic reasons. Persistent inflation and gradually declining interest rates in the early and

---

We appreciate the research, analysis, and writing done by Kimberly Haynes and Jay Liska. Without their very significant contribution, the completion of this chapter would not have been possible.

mid-1980s once again made debt financing an attractive source of funds since interest payments could be made in inflated dollars. Financial institutions also began to reassess their attitudes toward risk. In 1981, Drexel Burnham Lambert began selling high-interest, high-risk, noninvestment grade "junk bonds" to finance LBOs. Given the importance of interest rates and debt instruments in LBO financing, it is difficult to overemphasize the importance of changes in the financial environment and their effects on the structuring of an LBO.

FINANCIAL STRUCTURE

All acquisitions involve one or more of the following forms of financing: the buyer's capital, funds obtained from third-party lenders, an installment note from the seller, or equity capital from outside investors. The difference between the size of the firm's collateral base and the transaction size determine how large the financing gap will be between the buyer's ordinarily available funds and the deal's cost. This financing requirement in turn will dictate the players involved. Their interests, which must be mutually satisfied from both a legal and financial standpoint, will determine the deal's structure. For example, if the transaction involves a single buyer putting up a small amount of capital and a company whose assets do not have much collateral value, venture capitalist support would be necessary. These venture capitalists would then negotiate for terms favorable to themselves, thus affecting the deal's structure.

Trends in LBO structuring include the following. While hundreds of small deals get done each year, the large deals are becoming larger and larger as evidenced by the $6.2 billion ex-management and Kohlberg Kravitz Roberts & Co. buyout of Beatrice. The sheer size of these deals will increase the amount of institutional funds necessary to complete such transactions. Perhaps in a quest for yield, or because of an increased acceptance of the high-yield market, institutions such as pension funds, mutual funds, and insurance companies have been receptive to securities bearing the increased risk generated by an LBO. Equity and subordinated debt investors are now often one and the same. This has occurred as venture capitalists, in response to the increased risk of these deals, have often required all players, with the exception of secured lenders, to take a proportionate share of each layer of the financing; that is, senior debt, subordinated debt and equity. The result of this requirement is a comparable risk exposure for all players and a simplified financial process with less conflict between the players.

DETERMINING FINANCIAL STRUCTURE

Ideally, a transaction will be buyer financed. In reality a buyer will rarely have sufficient funds and will have to turn to either secured or unsecured lenders to fill the financial gap. Provided the target company has an asset base consisting of good collateral, the buyer will first approach a secured lender. Collateral ratios for secured lenders are generally about 80 percent for accounts receivable, 25 to 50 percent for inventory, and 65 to 80 percent for machinery, equipment, and real estate. A secured lender will generally tolerate higher leverage if it is needed, but unless the deal is very large the buyer should not have to borrow sizable amounts from unsecured lenders. When the target company has a strong collateral base and borrows sizable amounts from secured lenders, there is less equity dilution than if warrants and/or options are provided to the unsecured lenders. The result is greater control to the buyer. But because the company's assets have been pledged as collateral, the buyer will have little flexibility to finance working capital or capital expense requirements. For example, shopping centers comprise some of the bank's collateral in the Macy's buyout. If Macy's sells or refinances any of its shopping centers, the proceeds generated by these transactions must be submitted to the banks unless the funds are needed for ongoing business operations. This covenant obviously restricts Macy's ability to finance capital expenditures.

If the company's asset base is small and cannot be used as collateral, or the LBO transaction is large, the transaction will be unsecured. Subordinated lenders and equity investors will be necessary to complete the deal. In this case, the senior, but unsecured lender, will want a subordinated debt and equity cushion. For example, in the Beatrice buyout, the $650 million of senior notes have a subordinated note and preferred stock cushion of about $2.7 billion. The company's ability to generate cash flow is very important as the debt service payments are the lenders' only form of security. Advantages of a deal structured with unsecured senior and subordinated debt, together with equity are twofold: (1) the seller is generally paid cash up front for his or her shares; and (2) the company retains its ability to borrow against its inventory and accounts receivable. Disadvantages include the fact that outside equity investors will dilute management's interest and control, and that the equity investors' desire for a quick and high rate of return could result in policies detrimental to the company's long-term potential. For example, equity investors sometimes reissue their shares in a public offering within a few years in order to realize their return. This move returns control to the general public and may force management to focus on short-run results.

CONSIDERATIONS OF THE PLAYERS— ASSET TRANSACTION

There is no "best" structure for all leveraged buyouts. An LBO can be structured as either an asset-based or a stock-based transaction. The medium of exchange will dictate whether the transaction is considered taxable or is granted tax-free status. Current tax law has determined that cash given in exchange for a target company's assets or stock constitutes a taxable transaction while an equity for equity swap qualifies as a tax-free merger. Each structure offers relative advantages in the areas of tax obligation, legal liability, and ease of transaction. The unique nature of a particular buyout situation will indicate whether tax, legal, or other considerations predominate. Should taxes be the major issue to buyer and seller, then a tax-free merger would likely be the optimal structure. Should limiting legal liability be of overriding concern to the buyer, then possibly an asset-based acquisition would likely be preferred. Should the buyer wish to guarantee the continuation of valuable legal contracts postacquisition, then a stock deal might be most appropriate. While specific situations favor particular structural options, some generalities can be made.

An asset-based acquisition differs from a stock-based deal in that it is the target's assets, not its stock, which is purchased by the buyer. The deal is typically financed with loans secured by the assets of the firm to be acquired. Yet, the explosive growth in the stock market has resulted in the acquisition of companies trading at many multiples over book value using predominantly stock, not assets, as the basis for the deal. These include such huge deals as Storer Communications, Levi Strauss, Northwest Industries, and Uniroyal. The main reason for doing the stock deals is that asset deals are too costly and time consuming. In an asset-based deal, a bill of sale must itemize each asset to be transferred and allocate a value to it. The time and money required to negotiate such a transfer are exorbitant when compared to a stock deal.

While asset-based acquisitions are becoming more scarce, they do take place. For example, former Treasury Secretary, William Simon's famous 1982 leveraged buyout of Gibson Greeting Cards was asset based. Indeed, because of the enormous profits reaped by Simon, it has been one of the most discussed LBOs of all time.

Issues to Consider

A complete evaluation of alternative LBO structures should include an assessment of their legal consequences. It may well be that legal considerations favor the selection of one structure over another.

The degree to which the acquiring company is exposed to the legal liabilities previously incurred by the target corporation should be of concern to anyone contemplating a buyout. Structuring an LBO as an asset-based transaction provides the acquirer with a unique shield against unforeseen liability claims. Unlike a stock deal or corporate merger, an asset-based deal limits the buyer to liabilities which have been discussed in the acquisition agreement. Limited liability is important not only to the buyer but also to lenders who are, in a very real sense, partners in a venture. As such, creditors are likely to require less security, offer better terms, and impose less restrictive covenants on loans which are used to finance asset-based deals.

Another concern which management has when considering a potential acquisition is how quickly and easily a fully functional target firm can be assimilated into the parent corporation. Ideally, the structuring of the buyout should facilitate this assimilation. As previously stated, compared to a stock deal, an asset-based transaction is neither fast nor does it facilitate the transfer of operations.

Complex documentation is required to execute an asset-based transaction. A bill of sale containing all assets to be purchased must be drawn up, allocation of the purchase price to the assets of the target must be negotiated, and consents, collateral agreements, and waivers of liability must be signed. Furthermore, the Uniform Commercial Code requires that the buyer inform all creditors of the target firm of the proposed acquisition. This requirement not only invites competitive bids by drawing attention to the target company, but it further limits the usefulness of an asset-based transaction as a tool for engineering a hostile takeover.

An asset-based transaction may impede the orderly assimilation of the target company by the acquiring firm. Unlike an LBO based on stock, a firm acquiring a target using an asset-based acquisition structure may lose valuable contracts, leases, and mortgages. The need to renegotiate agreements is generally a disadvantage to this type of structure, the possible exception being that of an acquired company which was saddled with expensive labor contracts which could now be subject to renegotiation.

By definition, a leveraged buyout requires that a lender

Asset-Based Transaction—Borrower as "Owner"

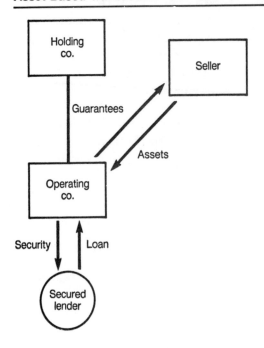

be an integral part of the acquisition team. Its willingness to participate in the deal is determined to a great extent by the riskiness of the venture, which is then determined by the structure of the acquisition. Given a choice between financing an acquisition structure as an asset-based transaction and an identical deal structured as a stock-based transaction, a secured lender would choose the former. The reason is that in an asset-based transaction the loan is being issued to a borrower who is also the "owner" of the assets which are being used for collateral for the loan. This is illustrated in the Asset-Based Transaction—Borrower as "Owner" figure.

The lender's position is thus much more secure than in a stock deal. Nevertheless, a security guarantee is still required.

STRUCTURING THE DEAL—
ASSET TRANSACTION

It has been said that the financing required in a leveraged buyout, to a large degree, dictates the players that will be involved in the transaction. Before buyer and seller can consummate a deal, a consortium of banks, insurance companies, venture capital firms, and individuals typically might be called upon to lend considerable financial support. The stakes are high; each player has interests which must be protected. The structure of the deal often dictates the security of each party's position; therefore buyer, seller, and investor will attempt to structure the transaction to minimize exposure to risk while maximizing return.

By examining the alternatives available for structuring a leveraged buyout, it becomes evident that these deals have been designed with the players' interests in mind. No one structure protects all interests evenly. While the optimal structure for an LBO will depend on the situation, a general understanding of the strengths and weaknesses of the alternative formats will help to explain why, in practice, one structure is chosen over another.

The figure on page 252 illustrates the structure of an asset-based transaction.

Once a company has been targeted as an attractive buyout candidate and the decision to acquire it has been made, the buyer's next task is to form a holding company and an operating company to be used as vehicles for the transaction. The buyer has several reasons for channeling the transaction through these shell companies.

1. The most important reason is related to the concept of legal liability. By using shell companies to conduct the LBO, the buyer is able to shield the parent corporation from liabilities incurred by the acquired company. Should a failing acquisition slip into insolvency, its assets would be subject to liquidation. The assets of the parent, on the other hand, would be protected from hungry creditors by the principle of limited liability. There is another legal reason why buyouts

Structure of an Asset-Based Acquisition

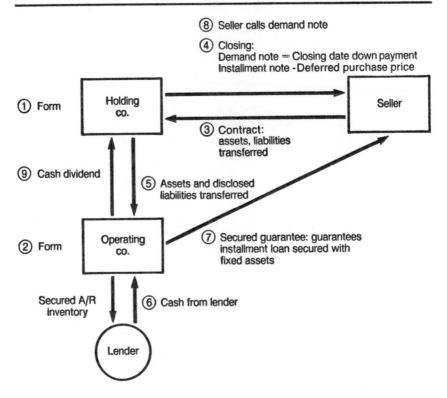

are structured in this manner. Most acquiring groups are set up as partnerships, yet tax law restricts the election of asset step-up to corporations. For this reason, if an LBO is contemplated and step-up desired, it is necessary to set up shell corporations to execute the acquisition.

   2. Another reason for establishing shell companies is due to the advantageous accounting treatment given LBOs structured in this manner. When this is done, it is often referred to as a two-tier acquisition. By utilizing shell companies, the deferred acquisition debt is kept off the nonconsolidated balance sheet of the postacquisition company. Furthermore, the debt on the new corporation's balance sheet appears simply as working capital debt under a revolving credit agreement. Finally, the guarantee of the deferred purchase price extended to the sellers by the new corporation and secured with its assets is not shown on the balance sheet, but merely reflected in footnotes.

These accounting advantages of the shell company structure typically do not materially affect the investment decision nor are likely to deceive the careful investor.

3. Under the terms of the contract between buyer and seller, the purchase price, terms of payment, allocation of purchase price, and liabilities incurred will be specified.

4. Upon agreement of terms, the buyer initiates closing by issuing two notes to the seller. The first, a demand note, defines the closing date down payment. The other, an installment note, specifies the terms of any deferred purchase price. In some situations deferred payment is preferred by the seller since it allows for the deferral of tax liabilities.

5. At this point the assets and disclosed liabilities of the seller are transferred to the buyer's holding company. From there they are conveyed to the subsidiary in what is termed a contribution to capital.

6. The lender funds the transaction with loans issued to the newly formed subsidiary. Even though an asset-based transaction is viewed as "safer" than a stock-based deal, the lender will invariably insist that the loan be secured with accounts receivable or inventory. Negotiating the terms of the loan must balance the conflicting demands of buyer and creditor. The buyer's insistence on minimizing cash outflow immediately following the acquisition must be reconciled with the creditor's desire to minimize exposure by demanding loan repayment as soon as possible. To conserve cash, the buyer might suggest that instead of a 5-year loan, the lender extend the payment term to 10 years, but include a balloon payment in the final year of the loan. Another cash conservation strategy might be to negotiate a payment schedule which is similar to a home mortgage; for example, heavy interest payments in the early years of the loan which generate substantial interest tax shields. Of course, the lender will insist on adjusting the interest rate, loan schedule, or security guarantee to adequately compensate his or her institution for its risk exposure.

7. Following negotiations regarding debt structure, the operating company must issue a secured guarantee to the sellers of the target firm. This action guarantees the terms of the installment loan and is secured with the assets of the company.

8. The seller now calls the demand note previously issued by the buyer. This triggers the payment of a "cash dividend" which satisfies the down payment requirements. This "dividend" is filtered through the holding company and paid to the seller. With the down payment delivered, the deal is consummated—now it is the newly formed company's challenge to meet its payments!

Example

Although asset-based LBOs are less common than stock-based deals, they do occur. An example of a leveraged buyout using this structure was the acquisition of the Printing Equipment Sector (PES) of the Harris Corporation (HC) by Harris Graphics Corporation (HGC) in March 1983.

Management of PES considered the division an attractive buyout target for a number of reasons. PES enjoyed 26 percent of the worldwide printing equipment market and 40 percent of the North American market in 1982. The industry was mature and exhibited fairly noncyclical earnings. Furthermore, PES's printing process was not considered to be subject to technological obsolescence since the company was a leader in product innovation, spending $10 million annually in R&D.

The structure of this asset-based management buyout in the Structure of HGC-PES Acquisition exhibit is shown on page 255.

The ability to structure the deal in this manner generally requires an uncontested sale, a close working relationship between buyer and seller, and a flexible timetable to negotiate the transfer of assets.

In 1983, the Harris Corporation was involved in two lines of business: the manufacture of advanced printing equipment, and state-of-the-art electronic information technology. In order to permit each of these business areas to achieve its

Structure of HGC-PES Acquisition (asset-based transaction)

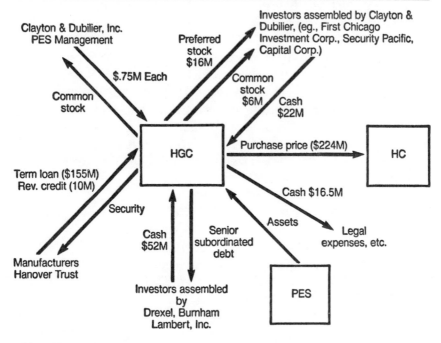

Note: M = millions.

potential, the management of Harris had determined that Harris should be restructured such that PES be transferred to a newly organized corporation while the electronic business remain in the existing corporation.

Finally, since the board had given its approval to the sale, this "insider's" deal was not subject to competitive bids and as such could proceed at a comfortable pace.

CONSIDERATIONS OF THE PLAYERS—
STOCK-BASED TRANSACTION

Since the Tax Reform Act of 1986, firms have had increased incentive to do stock transactions. They are used frequently when an asset transaction involves significant tax issues or when the target company is publicly held. As in the asset-based transaction, the structure of a stock transaction will ultimately be determined by the negotiations between the buyer and seller.

There are no nonassignability problems associated with a stock transaction as these contracts are generally transferable. To the buyer this is an important advantage when the target firm holds valuable assignments such as franchises, leases, mortgages, and other contracts. The documentation in a stock transaction is quite simple requiring only the endorsed stock certificates to be delivered to the purchaser to effectively transfer title.

Issues to Consider

The most important legal aspect of a stock acquisition is that all liabilities, including contingent and unknown liabilities, become the responsibility of the buyer. While this fact makes a stock sale preferable to the seller, the buyer will insist upon some form of protection. Protection could be in the form of a provision in the purchase agreement whereby the seller puts a portion of the sale proceeds in an escrow account whose purpose is to cover claims or any undisclosed liabilities. Another possibility is that the seller can indemnify the buyer for payment of these liabilities. This protection is usually limited to a two- to three-year period, with the exception of tax claims which command protection for a longer period.

Secured lenders require collateral in the form of the target company's assets. In a stock transaction though, the target company must guarantee the acquirer's borrowings and commit its assets as collateral. Secured lenders will still be nervous with this arrangement because, under the Federal Bankruptcy Code (FBC), three cases exist where the trustee may be able to avoid a transfer of assets to the secured lender.

1. A fraudulent conveyance occurs if the target company files for bankruptcy within one year and the courts find that the acquisition was inadequately capitalized and doomed to failure from the beginning.

2. A voidable preference occurs if the target company files for bankruptcy within 90 days, or up to one year if the lender was an insider who, at the time of the transaction, had reason to believe the target company was insolvent. This rule also applies if the transaction benefited the lender or if the borrower was indeed bankrupt at the time of the transfer.
3. Equitable subordination allows bankruptcy judges to subordinate senior lenders if it is equitable to do so. This rule is generally invoked when the lender also owns a significant amount of stock of the target company and has engaged in conduct which has injured other creditors. Therefore, because security interest could be lost in case of bankruptcy, secured lenders will generally only agree to a stock purchase if there exists a substantial cushion of subordinated debt or equity.

Equity participants will generally require some form of seniority over the issuer's common stock. This requirement can be met by the purchase of convertible preferred stock whose dividends must be paid before those on common stock. In addition, in the event of bankruptcy, the preferred stock will be paid off before the common.

State usury laws fixing maximum interest rates create problems for equity investors. Some states interpret convertible notes or units of notes with warrants attached as a "loan transaction." In this case the present value of the conversion rights or warrants is considered to represent interest on this loan. If the present value of this equity feature is greater than the maximum interest rate set by the state, the state can deem the transaction to be usurious. Investors such as venture capitalists are then penalized, often losing all or a portion of their principal and interest. This issue thus presents a powerful argument for the use of convertible preferred stock which is not viewed as a loan.

Convertible preferred can have a buyback provision in the form of a put, or call on the part of the issuer, generally after a period of five years. The call feature allows the issuer to buy back the preferred shares while the put feature allows the preferred shareholder to sell his or her shares back to the issuer. Both these transactions would take place at a price stipulated when the preferred was first sold. The put provision is preferred by the venture capital investors as it allows them to redeem their securities, often at a premium, if the issuer has not generated the high return they expected. The issuer, on the other hand, may lobby for a call option which allows the issuer to redeem preferred shares, sometimes at a premium, after a period of at least five years. In effect, this allows the issuing corporation to force conversion upon the venture capital security holder. For example, in the Beatrice LBO the preferred stock was designed to be exchangeable at the company's option at any time at $25 per share.

Antidilution protection is usually required by the equity participants. This protection often takes the form of a provision stating that if the company subsequently issues common stock at a price less than the market value, then the conversion or exercise price on the current convertible or preferred issues must be adjusted proportionately. For example, consider a company which currently has a convertible preferred issue outstanding convertible to common at $17 per share. Under antidilution provisions this company cannot issue new convertible securities which are convertible at a price less than $17 per share. This provision thus protects the preferred stockholders from paying too high a price for the equity kicker portion of their security.

Convertible preferred stockholders may hold voting rights which become effective when the preferred dividend is skipped or when the proposed issue of new securities affects the seniority of their claim. Obviously, a preferred issue containing these voting rights is preferable to the preferred buyers.

A recent phenomenon in LBO preferred stock is that some issues, such as Scipsco, a company formed in the Storer Broadcasting buyout, can pay dividends in either stock or cash for five years, reverting to cash thereafter. This product, designed to help recently bought-out companies conserve cash, can result in higher yields for equity investors who take on the increased risk.

STRUCTURING THE DEAL— STOCK TRANSACTION

In a stock transaction, the buyer often forms a holding company which will be used to sign the purchase agreement and acquire shares of the target, or operating company with a cash or deferred payment in the form of debt, equity, or both. Because the acquisition debt is at the holding company level, the parent company is not liable for the deferred acquisition debt. If the acquisition fails in the future because its cash flow cannot adequately service its debt, the parent company can in most cases cut the holding company and subsidiary loose with no repercussions upon itself. Because consent of the seller's management is not necessary under a stock transaction, a contract can then be signed by the purchaser and selling shareholders. The holding company will then issue both a demand and installment note to the seller as mentioned in the "Asset Transaction" section. In return, the selling shareholders will submit their shares to the holding company to be transferred to the target company. The target company then borrows cash from a lender who makes a loan secured by accounts receivable and inventory. The target company declares a portion of this loan as dividend to the holding company which uses this dividend to liquidate the demand note called by the seller. As in an asset transaction, the target company guarantees payment of the holding company's deferred note and uses its mortgages and fixed assets as collateral on this note. The Structure of a Stock-Based Acquisition exhibit illustrates a stock transaction diagrammatically.

Example
The Conair leveraged buyout was structured as a cash-for-stock transaction where one share was tendered for $24.70 in cash. The purchaser in this transaction was Conair's chairman and president, Leandro P. Rizzuto. The sellers were the common shareholders who voted for the LBO/merger proposal at an annual stockholder meeting with a detailed proxy statement for reference. This transaction constituted a tax-

Structure of a Stock-Based Acquisition

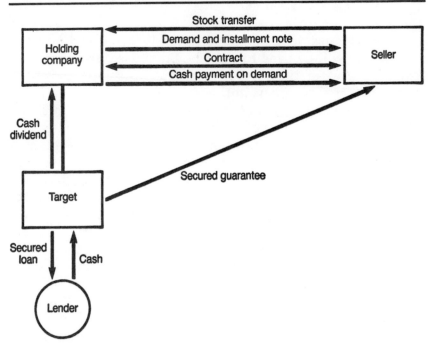

able exchange where selling shareholders recognized either a taxable capital gain or loss depending on their purchase price.

Conair Acquisition Corporation was formed to effect a leveraged buyout of Conair Corporation. The two subsequently entered into an agreement and plan of merger where, upon consummation of the transaction, Conair Acquisition Corporation was to be merged with Conair Corporation, with the latter surviving. This transaction was financed with debt securities issued by Conair Acquisition Corporation with the understanding that they would become the obligation of Conair Corporation as a result of the merger. This structure avoids the problem of a fraudulent conveyance, as the operating company actually assumes the acquisition debt.

Specifically, Conair Acquisition Corp. had access to a letter of credit from a major bank in an amount equal to the number of shares of Conair common stock outstanding times the agreed upon price of $24.70. This cash was to be paid to outstanding stockholders in exchange for their shares. A unique aspect of the Conair LBO is that Conair Acquisition Corporation never used the letter of credit. The Conair buyout was one of the first transactions in which the closing of the issuance of $80 million of senior zero coupon serial notes, $50 million of senior subordinated debentures, and $60 million of subordinated debentures coincided with the closing of the tender offer. Thus Conair Acquisition Corporation was able to use the proceeds of the debt issuance to purchase the common shares outstanding. A diagram describing this transaction is shown in the Structure of Conair Corporation Acquisition exhibit.

MERGERS

A leveraged buyout can be conducted as either an asset or stock-based transaction. Furthermore, each type of transaction can be structured as either a "tax-free" or taxable merger.

Tax-free mergers are defined by the IRS as Type A, B, or C mergers. The medium of exchange in tax-free mergers is a

Structure of Conair Corporation Acquisition (stock-based transaction)

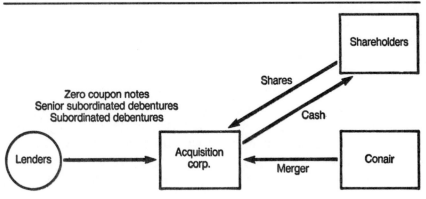

combination of stock and either cash, warrants, or debt. The nonequity portion of the seller's compensation is commonly referred to as the "boot." It is the proportion of equity to nonequity compensation which defines whether the acquisition is classified as a Type A, B, or C merger which, in turn, determines the tax and legal liabilities incurred by parties involved in the transaction. The term *tax free* is really a misnomer since under the provisions of the tax code governing these types of mergers the buyer is responsible for recapture taxes while the seller must pay taxes upon receiving the boot and deferred taxes upon the sale of equity.

Taxable mergers are more easily defined. A taxable merger differs from a tax-free deal in that the medium of exchange is either cash or debt—be it for assets or stock. When executing a cash merger the buyer is once again liable for recapture taxes, but now the seller is required to pay capital gains taxes on the transaction.

Just as the decision to conduct the LBO as an asset- or stock-based transaction depends upon the situation, so too does the decision as to whether to structure the deal as a tax-free or taxable merger. The opposing interests of buyer and seller require negotiating the structure of the deal so that it best meets the needs of both parties. For example, while the seller has incentive to prefer to structure an LBO as a tax-free merger—thereby deferring capital gains taxes—there are situations in which a taxable deal will be preferred. If an acquisition is made in which either the seller realizes a loss, needs immediate cash, or should an equity deal leave the seller with stock which is difficult to sell, a taxable merger might again be chosen. Since the tax implications of the deal's structure is usually less of an issue to the buyer, one might assume that a tax-free deal would be preferred by sellers, and offered to expedite negotiations. This is not always the case. Some sellers have been known to want to avoid the vagaries of the stock market and as a result demand cash. Moreover, since tax-free deals require that a large portion of the purchase price be made in the form of equity, this type of merger results in a dilution of ownership and possible loss of control by the acquiring corporation. By structuring the buyout as a taxable merger, the transfer of stock and therefore equity dilution is avoided and control retained. Furthermore, cash transactions are not only simpler to effect than tax-free deals, but also allow the buyer to limit his or her liability should the buyout be structured as cash for assets.

While the optimal structure for an LBO will be dictated by the unique circumstances surrounding the buyout, the considerations of the players will serve as a guideline for choosing among alternative structures.

TAX-FREE MERGERS

Considerations of the Players— Type A Mergers

This is the most commonly utilized means of structuring a merger acquisition. To qualify as a Type A tax-free merger, the Internal Revenue Code requires that more than 50 percent of the acquisition purchase price be in the form of voting or nonvoting stock. The remainder of the purchase price is termed the boot and it may either be cash, warrants, or debt. The two major subsets of Type A mergers are the forward and reverse triangular mergers. In a forward triangular merger, the target corporation is merged into the acquiring company while the opposite is the case for a reverse triangular merger.

Issues to Consider

A buyer electing to structure an acquisition as a Type A merger is not subject to an immediate tax. While taxes are not incurred by the buyer on the purchase, the acquirer's future tax burden will depend on the accounting treatment used when effecting the merger.

Should the buyer use "pooling of interests," the buyer pools the resources of the companies, and the balance sheets of the two firms are simply added together and treated as one entity. Future depreciation tax shields are thus calculated using the book value of the assets of the new corporation. Because inflation drove up the market value of company assets during the 1970s and early 1980s, this method of merger accounting became less popular. Since "pooling" prohibited the write-up of assets to market value, companies were unable to realize increased depreciation tax shields. However, the Tax Reform Act of 1986 has reduced the incentive to use the asset write-up since the amount of the write-up is subject to an immediate tax of 34 percent. Additionally, since asset liquidations are also subject to a 34 percent corporate tax on the difference between book value and market price paid for the assets, pooling offers a way to escape the effects of double taxation without the comparative disadvantage of not being able to write up assets.

A Type A merger also allows the buyer to carry over the net operating losses of an acquired company. Should the acquirer be a prosperous company with consistently positive earnings, and the proposed target a potential turnaround candidate which has suffered past losses, one means by which earnings could be shielded would be to structure the acquisition as a tax-free merger.

The tax implications to the seller in a Type A merger are somewhat complex. The equity portion of the transaction price is tax free to both the selling company and its shareholders. The boot, on the other hand, is taxable. The boot affects the tax basis of the stock which the sellers receive. The basis of the stock received is decreased by the amount of the boot and increased by the amount of the gain realized. This is shown in the exhibit depicting the Tax Implications of the Boot.

It is clear that it is not just the purchase price but the proportion of that amount in form of equity and boot which dictates the seller's tax liability. This apportioning will determine the seller's return and as such it should be an important point in negotiating the merger agreement.

In a Type A merger, the buyer assumes substantially all of the assets and liabilities of the target company. In this respect, a Type A merger is inferior to a cash-for-assets trans-

Tax Implications of the Boot

Assume:

Cost of stock	$150
Total purchase price	$200
Realized gain	$ 50
Value of boot	$ 75
Adjusted stock basis	$125 = (150 − 75 + 50)

Tax implications:

If realized gain < value of boot ⇒ Full realized gain recognized for taxes

If value of boot < realized gain ⇒ Only boot recognized for taxes

---

action in which only selected liabilities are assumed. For instance, were a buyer to consider acquiring a General Motors subsidiary with pending EPA liabilities of $100 million, the decision to structure the acquisition as an asset-based deal with indemnification through representations and warranties would likely be preferred to one financed with equity and cash.

The decision whether to structure a Type A merger as a straight or reverse triangular merger has important implications with regard to the continuity of contracts, leases, and licenses. A straight triangular merger cannot guarantee the transfer of assets which are legally "nontransferable" due to restrictive covenants built into the target's corporate charter. Examples of such "nontransferable" assets are liquor licenses, FCC licenses, and certain franchise agreements. Should a target firm possess valuable nontransferable assets, then structuring the deal as a reverse triangular merger which retains such assets would be preferred.

An advantage to structuring a Type A merger is that it allows flexibility in choosing payment alternatives and limits equity dilution relative to Type B or C tax-free mergers. An unfortunate disadvantage of Type A mergers is that they are complex, time consuming to negotiate, and require approval by the selling company's directors and stockholders. As such, this type of merger is typically not suitable for an unfriendly takeover.

STRUCTURING THE DEAL—
TYPE A MERGERS

In our discussions regarding the structuring of an asset- or stock-based deal we have already addressed the concerns surrounding such issues as the rationale for forming shell corporations, the need to balance the conflicting cash flow interests of buyer, seller, and lender, and how the structure of the deal affects the lender's implicit risk/return equation. These concerns similarly affect the structuring of tax-free mergers, therefore the following section will focus on the unique sequence of events involved in the execution of the various types of tax-free mergers.

Type A Standard Triangular Merger

In this type of transaction, target company ABC is merged into a subcorporation, which is a wholly owned subsidiary of the acquirer XYZ corporation. This structure is illustrated in the Type A Standard Triangular Merger exhibit.

To initiate this action, the parent company must first

Type A Standard Triangular Merger

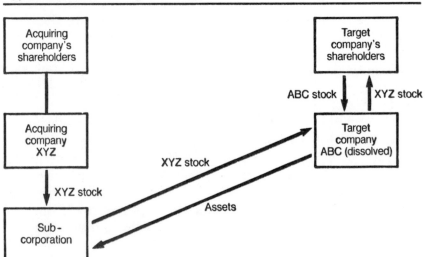

establish a subcorporation to act as a vehicle in the transfer. This shell corporation is formed for the purpose of limiting parental liability and improving the balance sheet of the new corporation postacquisition.

Upon completion of contract negotiations to establish the target's price, terms of payment and limits of liability, the acquiring company channels XYZ stock through its newly formed subsidiary to the target company in exchange for the assets of ABC. At least 90 percent of the fair market value of net assets and at least 70 percent of the fair market value of gross assets must be transferred.

At this point, the ABC corporation disappears as a legal entity and all nontransferable assets are lost. XYZ stock is then distributed to ABC shareholders by management in exchange for their ABC shares. ABC is considered, for tax purposes, to have exchanged its assets for XYZ stock.

Example

An example of an LBO structured as a forward triangular merger is the acquisition of Edgecomb Metals Corporation (EMC) by Edgecomb Steel of New England (ESNE) in June 1984.

EMC was the largest independent metal service center company in the United States. EMC was an attractive acquisition candidate for a number of reasons. First, ESNE and EMC engaged in only one line of business—the sale and distribution of metal mill products. The acquisition of EMC allowed ESNE to capitalize on its metal service industry expertise and achieve economies of scale. Second, ESNE and EMC served complementary geographical markets—ESNE operated primarily in the East and EMC in the East, South, and Midwest. Finally, ESNE's management was experienced and was expected to be able to capitalize on the opportunities available to a firm with sales in excess of $600 million.

While ESNE and EMC were not affiliated at the time of the acquisition, they shared a common founder and history. EMC was founded in Philadelphia in 1923 by Leslie Edgecomb. ESNE was spun off from EMC in 1951 with the understanding that it would not compete with EMC in its estab-

Structure of ESNE-EMC Acquisition (forward triangular merger)

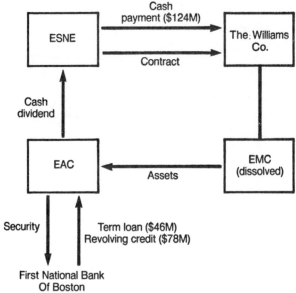

Note: M = million.

lished markets. When ESNE decided to initiate a "family reunion," all the conditions necessary for structuring a forward triangular merger had been met. ESNE and EMC's common heritage allowed ESNE to acquire EMC's substantial market share and to dissolve the newly acquired company, yet retain the goodwill associated with the Edgecomb family name. (See Structure of ESNE-EMC Acquisition exhibit.)

A consortium of lenders led by the First National Bank of Boston anted up $124 million to allow the then Edgecomb Acquisition Co. (EAC) to purchase EMC from The Williams Co.

Type A Reverse Triangular Merger

The exhibit on the following page illustrates the structure of a reverse triangular merger.

This class of transaction is, in a sense, the "reverse" of

Type A Reverse Triangular Merger

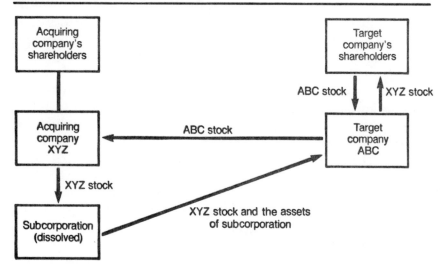

the standard triangular merger in that the subcorporation, a wholly owned subsidiary of XYZ is dissolved upon merging into target corporation ABC. (See Type A Reverse Triangular Merger exhibit.) This type of transaction is usually preferred if there is a legal need to maintain the target corporation's existence (e.g., possession of nontransferable licenses, contracts, and so on).

As with a standard triangular merger, XYZ stock is filtered through the subcorporation but instead of being exchanged for the target company's assets, it is traded for ABC stock. Should the subsidiary's stock be used as the medium of exchange, provisions are generally made in the merger agreement that upon completion of the transfer, the sub's shares automatically become shares of the target company. This action dissolves the subcorporation allowing ABC to eventually take its place.

To conclude the deal, the target company's shareholders receive XYZ stock in exchange for their stock in ABC. ABC stock representing "substantially all" of the target company is then transferred to the parent company, completing the merger, and establishing ABC as the new subcorporation.

Example

On December 5, 1985, SCI Merger Corporation, a wholly owned subsidiary of SCI Holdings, Inc., merged into Storer Communications Inc., effecting an acquisition which is representative of those buyouts termed *reverse triangle mergers.*

Prior to its acquisition, Storer had been involved in an ambitious expansion of its cable communications business. Completion of this project and recently enacted federal legislation allowing the cable industry to price its product in response to market demand was expected to result in moderate growth in revenues and operating margins. This was expected to improve Storer's credit quality significantly. An aborted attempt at an LBO by a group of dissident stockholders in March 1985 forced management into pursuing an LBO offer proposed by Kohlberg Kravis Roberts & Co. (KKR).

The acquisition was funded with cash and warrants to purchase SCI Holdings common stock. (See the Structure of SCI-Storer Acquisition exhibit.) The cash portion of the deal was raised through the issuance of bank debt, zero coupon senior notes, senior subordinated debentures, common and preferred stock. SCI Preferred Stock Co. (SCIPSCO) was established expressly for the purpose of issuing preferred stock.

The rationale for structuring the deal as a reverse triangular merger was to preserve Storer's nontransferable FCC licenses, preserve the target's net operating loss carryforwards and qualify preferred dividends for the then 85 percent dividend exclusion.

CONSIDERATION OF THE PLAYERS—
TYPE B MERGERS

The second most commonly employed means of structuring a buyout is termed *a Type B merger.* To qualify for Type B tax-free treatment, the Internal Revenue requires that 100 percent of the purchase price be paid with voting stock and

Structure of SCI-Storer Acquisition (reverse triangular merger)

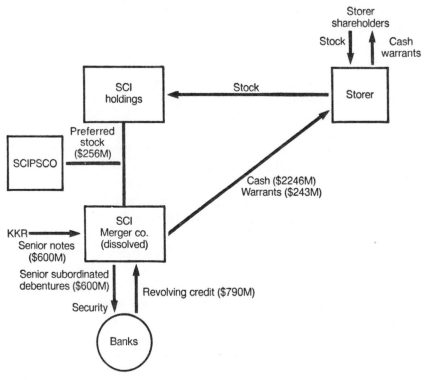

Note: M = million.

that at least 80 percent of the target firm's shares be transferred.

Issues to Consider

A Type B merger is the only truly tax-free method of structuring a buyout. As with a Type A merger, the buyout is not subject to any gain or loss on the exchange of stock.

Similarly, an acquirer using this structure is allowed to write-up assets but is subject to recapture taxes. In addition, the buyer is entitled to carryover any net operating losses generated by the acquired firm.

Unlike the Type A merger, no boot is exchanged in a Type B merger. Therefore, the transaction is truly tax free for the seller at least until the seller's disposition of the acquired shares. The tax code has determined that the basis of the stock received by the seller is equal to the basis of the stock given to the buyer to effect the merger. Since there is no change in basis as a result of the transaction, there is no gain or loss and consequently no tax liability incurred by the seller until the new shares are sold. At the point of sale, taxes on any realized gain must be declared. However, since these taxes are deferred, a Type B merger benefits the seller concerned with limiting its immediate tax liability.

A buyer which has gained controlling interest in a firm using a Type B merger will also be responsible for its accumulated liabilities. This is a disadvantage if the target corporation is suspected of having substantial undisclosed liabilities and if the seller is unwilling to limit the buyer's liability by indemnification.

A more important limitation of this type of merger is that, under the required terms of the exchange, not only is flexibility in financing the deal eliminated, but equity interest of the acquirer may be seriously diluted. If management is concerned with maintaining the current level of earnings per share, then serious consideration should be given to an acquisition structured by means other than a Type B merger.

On the other hand, an important advantage offered by the Type B merger is that it can be enacted quickly. Since the target firm's board of directors and stockholders need not approve an all equity merger, this type of transaction is usually structured when attempting a hostile takeover.

STRUCTURING THE DEAL— TYPE B MERGERS

A Type B merger is, in many ways, the simplest means of structuring a tax-free merger. It is conceptually straightforward and can be accomplished relatively quickly and without the complex tax implications which arise as a result of payment using a boot. Should XYZ corporation agree to buy target ABC using a Type B merger all that is required is that XYZ and ABC exchange stock in an amount equivalent to the agreed upon purchase price.

To qualify for tax-free status, Type B mergers are subject to certain IRS restrictions. In the subsidiary stock for stock transaction pictured in the Type B Merger exhibit, the acquiring company (XYZ) must use either its own voting stock or that of its subsidiary in the exchange—but not a combination of the two. If XYZ stock is used, it must be transferred to its wholly owned subsidiary, subcorporation, which then exchanges this stock for the target company's stock. If at least 80 percent of both ABC's total voting power and total number of shares are transferred in subsidiary stock for stock exchange, the target (ABC) becomes a subsidiary of the acquiring company's subsidiary (subcorporation).

Type B Merger

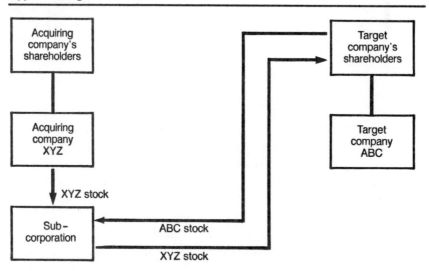

CONSIDERATIONS OF THE PLAYERS— TYPE C MERGERS

This type of merger is less common than either the Type A or B mergers. To qualify for Type C merger status, at least 80 percent of the purchase price must be transferred as voting stock of either the acquiring company or its subsidiary (but not both), the remainder being accounted for by a cash boot. In addition, the Internal Revenue requires that 90 percent of the net assets and 100 percent of the operating assets of the target firm be conveyed for the merger to be eligible for tax-free treatment.

Issues to Consider

The tax consequences to parties engaged in a Type C merger are identical to those previously discussed under the Type A merger. Neither the buyer nor the seller are considered to have realized any gain or loss on the equity portion of the exchange. The basis of the acquiring company's stock is considered to be equal to the basis of the target company's stock transferred in the exchange. However, should a boot be included in the transfer agreement, the seller will be taxed subject to the provisions already outlined in our discussion of Type A mergers.

Whether the equity of the acquiring company or its subsidiary is used in the transaction, a Type C merger is legally considered an exchange of voting stock for the assets of the target company. In this respect, a Type C merger is considered equivalent to a cash-for-assets transaction with respect to the assumption of legal liability. When structuring a deal in this manner, the buyer and seller may negotiate an agreement such that the acquiring firm assumes only selected liabilities. This gives the Type C merger a major advantage over the other tax-free alternatives, particularly if the target being considered for acquisition has liabilities which could materially affect its future performance.

The drawbacks of structuring an acquisition as a Type C merger are similar to other asset-based deals. The negotiations necessary to accomplish a Type C merger may be complex and time consuming. A detailed bill of sale must be drawn up, an allocation of the purchase price negotiated, and a determination of liability agreed upon. The fact that board and shareholder approval is required before a Type C merger can be enacted is an additional reason why this format would be inappropriate when considering a hostile takeover.

STRUCTURING THE DEAL— TYPE C MERGERS

The Type C Merger exhibit illustrates a subsidiary stock-for-assets, Type C merger between subcorporation, a wholly owned subsidiary of the XYZ corporation, and target company ABC.

In this type of transaction, XYZ agrees to purchase all of ABC corporation's assets, and through negotiations, assumes a portion of all of its liabilities.

To initiate the transaction, either XYZ or subcorporation voting stock (common or preferred) is offered in exchange for substantially all of the assets and liabilities of ABC. As was

Type C Merger

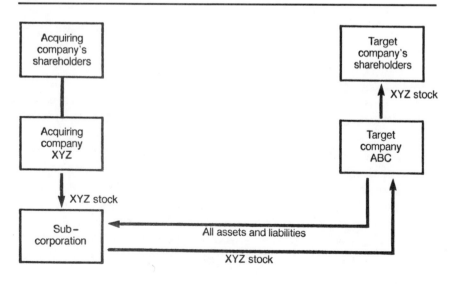

the case in Type B mergers, the equity payments transferred by the acquiring company must consist of voting stock issued by either the parent or its subsidiary—a combination is not allowed. Once again, at least 90 percent of the target's net assets must be acquired.

To conclude the deal, the target company must distribute the stock, securities and other consideration received in the reorganization to its shareholders if it is to qualify as a tax-free, Type C merger.

CONCLUSION

It has been stated that there is no "best" structure for all leveraged buyouts. Individual circumstances dictate which best fulfills the varied—and at times conflicting—interests of buyer, seller, and lender. It is the relative importance of tax, legal, and general considerations which determine the "best" structure for an LBO.

When Levi Strauss & Co. was taken private in August 1985 by a group of former company managers and family members, the Levi Strauss Acquisition Corporation was primarily concerned with maintaining controlling interest and the goodwill associated with the Levi Strauss name. Structuring the deal as a cash-for-stock, reverse triangular merger was seen as a means of satisfying these demands. By offering cash as the medium of exchange, the dilution of equity (and control) which arises with a Type A, B, or C merger could be avoided. By structuring the deal as a cash-for-stock rather than as a cash-for-assets transaction, the acquirers were assured that otherwise nontransferable assets would be retained.

Another example of an acquisition structured to meet the needs of the participants can be found in the buyout of Northwest Industries by Farley Industries, two multi-industry corporations, in July 1985. With a price tag of $1.16 million, Northwest was selling at a premium of 818 percent over book value. The deal was structured to meet the pretax reform needs of the participants. Taking advantage of the General

Utilities doctrine, Farley was able to structure the buyout as a tax-free merger and take advantage of increased depreciation tax shields by stepping up Northwest's assets to fair market value. The terms of the deal were straightforward. Farley offered Northwest cash and preferred stock. In addition, each Northwest shareholder received one share of the Lone Star Steel Co. which was spun off as a part of the deal.

These simplified examples were presented to reinforce the concept that each buyout situation requires a structure carefully selected to satisfy the complex concerns of the players involved. Future changes in the tax law and changes in legislation will require both buyers and sellers to make modifications in structuring a deal.

CHAPTER 7

THE LBO AND THE TAX MAN

The sweeping changes brought by the Tax Reform Act of 1986 make an assessment of its affects on LBO activity difficult at best. Have prices of buyout targets fallen? If so, by how much? In what ways have buyers been differently affected than sellers? Have buyers continued to favor cash as a form of payment, or has there been increased preference for tax-free stock transactions? If so, under what special circumstances? And have multibillion dollar buyouts been more adversely impacted than smaller deals? The purpose of this chapter is to try and provide a clear explanation of how LBOs have been affected by the sum total of legislative changes brought by the Tax Reform Act of 1986.

IMPACT OF THE GENERAL UTILITIES DOCTRINE ON LBO FINANCING

The major provision of the tax reform affecting LBOs was the elimination of the General Utilities doctrine. The basic impact of the doctrine was to allow companies whose assets had appreciated to avoid paying corporate tax on the sale of those assets, provided either of the following two conditions was met:

We appreciate the research, analysis, and writing done by Chet Lyons. Without his very significant contribution, the completion of this chapter would not have been possible.

1. The sale of assets was made subject to an intended total liquidation of the company. Without the doctrine, double taxation would occur if the corporation was first taxed on gains from the sale of assets, and then individual shareholders were taxed on the pro rata distribution of the remaining corporate gains. The Internal Revenue Code which reflected the General Utilities doctrine was found in Section 337 of the tax code. As a result, one often heard accountants and investment bankers speak of that well-known section.
2. The stock of a target company was acquired and the acquiring company chose to make a Section 338 "asset step-up election." The asset step-up allowed the buyer to increase the basis of the target's assets from their tax basis to fair market value without triggering a corporate tax on the gain other than recapture taxes. This would occur if the acquisition was paid for by either stock or other form of payment.

Thus, through the step-up, Section 338 allowed companies acquired through a purchase of stock to enjoy the same freedom from double taxation as companies acquired through an asset liquidation under Section 337.

The tax shield resulting from a Section 337 liquidation or 338 asset step-up election was obtained in the following way: the difference between the book value of the company's assets and the actual purchase price of the assets could be allocated to the company's tangible and intangible assets. In other words, the company's assets could be "stepped-up" from their book value to their market value. Future tax savings were then generated from depreciating the stepped-up assets. Asset step-up was of particular importance to leveraged buyouts. Any increase in future tax deductions helped to preserve the postacquisition cash flow needed to make the large debt payments resulting from the use of maximum financial leverage.

Under the conceptual umbrella of the General Utilities doctrine, the gain resulting from the stepped-up basis was not subject to corporate gains tax. However, the buyer did have to pay recapture tax, including prior benefits from depreciation, investment tax credits, LIFO inventory, and acceleration of deferred installment obligations. Acceleration of deferred installment obligations would be required if the target had sold goods on an installment basis, and had not recognized all of the income from such sales prior to the target's acquisition date. In that event, all such deferred income would be "accelerated" and recognized as part of the target's income prior to the sale of the target.

As an example of how asset step-up worked under the old tax law, let's assume that the owners of a circuit board manufacturing company were selling their business. An investor group was willing to pay the owners $50 million in cash for their stock which had a book value for tax purposes of $25 million. Because of the General Utilities doctrine, the seller's corporation did not have to pay tax on the $25 million gain resulting from the sale of the corporation's assets. While there was no corporate tax paid on the gain, stockholders did pay a personal capital gains tax of 20 percent on the difference between the cost basis of their shares of stock and payment received for shares as a result of the liquidation and sale of the company.

Our investor group (the buyers) then owned assets with a book value of $50 million. The election of Section 338 asset step-up generated both increased tax shields from depreciation and the payment of recapture taxes. The acquired company's tax shield resulting from the future depreciation of assets in this case was doubled because the book value of the assets doubled. However, the election of Section 338 also triggered some recapture costs which the buyer paid, including depreciation recapture, payback of investment tax credits, and LIFO inventory reserve. For our example, let us assume the buyers had to pay $2.3 million in recapture taxes. This immediate out-of-pocket cost was compared to the present value of the seven-year depreciation tax shield on the $25 million step-up; if it was more than $2.3 million, the decision to step up assets would be made. Since the buyers would get back almost half of the $25 million step-up as a depreciation tax shield, even though the depreciation tax shield was spread over a seven-year period, the present value of the shield might easily have been about $8 million. In our example it would have made a lot of sense—nearly $6 million worth under the old tax law—for the buyers to step up assets.

Comparing the immediate cost of recapture tax against the present value of the stepped-up portion of the company's future depreciation tax shield is still the procedure that is followed to decide whether or not to make a Section 338 asset step-up election. A number of factors affect the decision. Even before the Tax Reform Act of 1986 the decision to step up assets was not always made, or else did not provide the kind of windfall evident in our previous illustration. For example, since assets categorized as goodwill are not amortized for tax purposes, a company having to define a large fraction of its stepped-up assets as goodwill would not generate as much future depreciation as a company with little goodwill. Additionally, assets have varying useful lives, and are thus depreciated at varying rates. Because of the time value of money, shorter asset depreciation schedules generate higher present value estimates of the future tax shield. Finally, the absolute value of a company's tax shield resulting from a step-up is based on the difference between its book and market value. If, for example, a company had recently been sold and acquired, and then again sold and acquired, it may show little difference between its current book value and the latest price at which it was purchased. In that event, asset step-up would produce little added value because there is no room for a significant step-up.

REPEAL OF GENERAL UTILITIES NOW TRIGGERS "DOUBLE TAXATION"

The benefits of a Section 337 liquidation/sale and a Section 338 asset step-up expired December 31, 1986. Repeal of Section 337 and the abandonment of the underlying philosophy of the General Utilities doctrine makes the stepped-up assets resulting from a Section 338 election subject to corporate tax on the gain in addition to recapture taxes. Under the Tax

Reform Act of 1986, a liquidating company or a company acquired by another in a stock purchase is taxed on the entire gain (or loss) from the sale. The new 34 percent tax on corporate gains resulting from the sale, plus the effects of an increase in capital gains rates for individuals from 20 to 28 percent, means that the net tax on such transactions has increased from 20 percent to about 52.5 percent.

EXCEPTIONS TO THE GENERALIZATION THAT DOUBLE TAXATION CANNOT BE AVOIDED IN SITUATIONS WHERE SECTION 338 IS ELECTED

Transition Rule Exception for Closely Held Corporations

An important exception to the generalization that double taxation can no longer be avoided when Section 338 is elected is the transition rule for closely held corporations. The rule allowed treatment of Section 338 asset step-up election under pre-Tax Reform Act of 1986 terms for acquisitions occurring before January 1, 1989. A closely held corporation was fully eligible for this benefit if its market value did not exceed $5 million (with decreasing eligibility up to a value of $10 million) and more than 50 percent of its stock was owned by 10 or fewer individuals who held their stock for at least five years. This exception rule was enormously beneficial for smaller corporations, and resulted in a higher than average volume of sales of closely held companies.

Targets with Net Operating Loss Carryforwards (NOLs)

Under the revised tax law, a Section 338 asset step-up election can still be economically beneficial if the acquired company has NOL carryovers which can be used to offset the one-time gain on the sale of the assets which would occur at the close of the target's acquisition date. The following example illustrates the idea: Suppose that company A buys company

B. Company A, the acquiring company, is a calendar-year taxpayer, and the purchase takes place on February 6, 1988. Company B, the target, has a market value of $5 million, a book value of $1 million, and a NOL carryforward of $4 million. The acquiring company makes a Section 338 election for asset step-up. The target would then file two tax returns, one covering the period from January 1, 1988 to February 5, 1988, and the other, a one-day return called a "lonely return" in the accounting profession. If the target's income is $500,000 and its gain associated with the sale is $4 million, the resulting total gain subject to recapture tax is $4.5 million. The $4 million NOL would offset most of it, and the target would pay taxes on only $500,000 of income. At a 34 percent tax rate, the target would pay just $170,000, a cheap price to pay in exchange for a $4 million write-up in assets.

Restrictions on NOL Utilization of a Loss Company

Under the old tax law, the availability of the NOL of a target company to an acquiring company depended on the form of the acquisition. If shares of stock were acquired in a taxable purchase, business operations would have to be continued for a two-year period to avoid a complete disallowance of the losses to the acquiring company. In addition, after the shares of a loss corporation were acquired in a tax-free purchase, shareholders of the loss corporation would still have to own at least 20 percent of the stock of the surviving corporation, otherwise a reduction of the losses would occur. In an effort to bring consistency to these rules and to place stricter limits on the use of NOLs, Congress adopted a tough new approach to this area of the tax law. The 1986 tax law imposes a number of conditions on utilization of NOL by acquiring companies.

Under the revised tax law, changes in ownership and reorganizations of a loss corporation trigger additional limits on the rate at which new owners can use the NOL carryforward of the acquired company. In general, the Tax Act of 1986 provides that if there is more than a 50 percent change in ownership of a loss corporation over a three-year "testing period," the NOL carryforward of the loss corporation is subject to a limitation from and after the date on which the (more than) 50 percent change in ownership occurred.

The 50 percent change in ownership can result in a variety of ways. For example, either one shareholder could sell his or her stock to another shareholder, new shares of stock could be issued and sold, or a merger could take place. Also, unless warrants and options were issued before January 1, 1987, and exercised before January 1, 1989, the exercise of those items also constituted a shift in ownership under the new NOL provisions. Furthermore, changes in ownership are cumulative over the three-year testing period and may result from a series of unrelated transactions, none of which, if viewed separately, would necessarily have constituted more than a 50 percent change in ownership.

In the event that a "more than 50 percent change" in ownership occurs within the three-year testing period, the annual NOL carryover is limited to an amount equal to the value of the stock of the loss corporation (calculated just prior to the changeover) multiplied by the long-term, tax-exempt rate. The long-term, tax-exempt rate is not the municipal bond rate. Rather, it is defined as the yield on a diversified pool of prime, general obligation tax-exempt bonds with remaining periods to maturity of more than nine years.

If, for example, the value of a loss corporation is $10 million, and the long-term, tax-exempt rate is 6 percent, its future annual NOL carryovers would be limited to $600,000 per year. The rate was purposely set at a low value to discourage acquiring companies from purchasing targets solely because of the tax shield value of the targets' NOL.

Possible Effects of New Limitations on NOL Utilization

The new limitations on NOL utilization could have the effect of producing taxable income in a year where the corporation otherwise would not have had taxable income if the amount of NOL carryforward had not been limited. It could also have the effect of causing some of the NOL carryover to expire simply because it could not be used within the carryover period. Venture capital backed start-up companies, which often generate early losses, could well be hurt by the limitations on NOL carryforward. Valuations given venture capital-backed companies prior to an acquisition might be lower since the value of the start-up's accumulated NOL in offsetting future income is less under the 1986 law.

In addition to the above restrictions, under the revised law, NOL carryovers can offset no more than 90 percent of the Alternative Minimum Tax. Therefore, if a corporation has any taxable income for the year, it will pay some tax in that year irrespective of the fact that it has NOL carryforwards from prior years.

CHANGES IN THE CORPORATE TAX STRUCTURE

Corporate Tax Rates on Ordinary Income and Capital Gains Set Equal to 34 Percent

The corporate tax rate on ordinary income was reduced from a maximum rate of 46 to 34 percent. At the same time, the once preferential capital gains rate was increased to 34 percent. The transition to the 34 percent rate did not take place all at once. For example, corporations with a fiscal year-end paid a "blended rate" based on a weighted average of 46 percent for months prior to July 1, 1987 and 34 percent for months in the taxable year ending after July 1, 1987. The distinction between capital gains and ordinary income remain important, however, because capital losses can still be used only to offset capital gains, and cannot be deducted from ordinary income.

Comparative Tax Advantages of S-Corporations under the 1986 Law

Under an S corporation (as well as a limited partnership) there is no tax on the corporation's income. Instead, shareholders report the income of the S corporation against their personal tax returns, and it is then taxed at their individual tax rate for ordinary income. Since the corporate income tax is 34 percent and the personal income tax is 28 percent, individuals are taxed at a rate 6 percent lower than a corporation. Thus there is an absolute advantage to an S corporation. Even corporations that reinvest all earnings would prefer to have their income taxed to the shareholders at a 28 percent rate, and then distribute just enough money to enable shareholders to cover the taxes they paid. However, since income taxes for regular corporations are still graduated, prior to making the decision to convert to an S corporation one must be reasonably confident that the existing C corporation would generate enough after-tax income to put it into the 34 percent tax bracket. Otherwise there would be no comparative advantage to the S corporation's effective 28 percent tax rate.

An S-corporation structure can eliminate the problem of double taxation of ordinary corporate income, as well as tax on gains from the sale of assets if the company is sold, provided such gains were accrued (not just realized) after January 1, 1986. First we will focus on how the S corporation eliminates double taxation of ordinary income by comparing a regular corporation with an S corporation under the 1986 tax law.

Suppose the sole shareholder of a regular corporation nets $200,000 in profit, and has not drawn any salary. Assuming the new law was in full effect, at the corporate tax rate of 34 percent $68,000 would be paid in corporate taxes, leaving $132,000 available as a dividend payout. Applying the personal income tax rate of 28 percent will result in payment of another $36,960 in personal income taxes, leaving $95,040 for the investor after both corporate and personal income taxes have been subtracted from the $200,000 profit. The combined effective tax to the sole shareholder would be a whopping 52.48 percent.

In contrast to the preceding example, under an S corporation (as well as a limited partnership) there is no tax on the corporation's income. Instead, shareholders report the income of the S corporation against their personal tax returns, and it is then taxed at their individual tax rate for ordinary income.

Assuming the upper tier of 28 percent for our single shareholder, he would pay just $56,000 in taxes by converting to an S corporation, leaving himself $144,000 instead of $95,040, clearly a significant improvement.

In the case where our sole shareholder decided to sell his company, would he be taxed on the gains resulting from the sale of assets for an amount greater than book value? Closely held corporations which elected to become S corporations before January 1, 1987 did preserve the right to sell their companies in a tax-free transaction utilizing the benefits of the General Utilities doctrine. But a regular corporation that elected to become an S corporation after December 31, 1986 will remain subject to regular corporate tax on its "built-in gains" for a period of 10 years. However, since the assets are likely to continue to appreciate, there might be a possible future advantage in converting to an S corporation because the sale of gains which accrue above and beyond the built-in gains of the company prior to conversion to an S corporation would not be subject to tax at the corporate level. A final advantage under the new law for S corporations is that they are not subject to the new Alternative Minimum Tax.

Firms that think it might be advisable to change to an S structure must consider whether or not they can meet the restrictions governing the formation of S corporations, and if so, whether the costs imposed by those restrictions are worth the anticipated gain. The restrictions are significant and include:

- No more than 35 shareholders.
- No corporate shareholders. Must be an individual, an estate, or in rare circumstances a trust.
- Each shareholder must be either a resident or a citizen of the United States.
- One class of stock only. Different voting rights are, however, permitted for different shares of stock. All other rights must be the same; namely, dividend treatment, liquidation preferences, and so on.
- Owning 80 percent or more of the stock of a subsidiary is prohibited.

Businesses which cannot meet the technical requirements for an S corporation may consider putting some or all
of their assets into master limited partnerships (MLPs).
MLPs are taxed as partnerships with limited ownership
units that trade on securities exchanges such as corporate
shares. Like S corporations, MLPs are not subject to the
double tax that applies to corporate earnings distributed to
shareholders. And they will not be subject to the double tax
that will apply to corporations when the business is sold,
except for any built-in gains as noted above for S corporations
and closely held corporations.

Imposition of a Minimum Corporate Tax

The 1986 tax law requires corporations to pay the higher of
the 34 percent tax on regular taxable income or 20 percent of
Alternative Minimum Taxable Income (AMTI). The revised
tax is intended to raise additional revenue from the corporate
sector and, most importantly, to ensure that every profitable
company pays income taxes. The calculation of whether or
not a corporation will be subject to the Alternative Minimum
Tax (AMT), and if so, how much it might owe—is quite complex. For the purpose of simplification, the net effect of the
AMT is to create a separate parallel tax structure under
which many corporations will pay a tax approximately equal
to 20 percent of book income.

Elimination of the Investment Tax Credit

The Investment Tax Credit (ITC) was eliminated retroactively for any property placed in service after December 31,
1985, although there were exceptions for "transition property." Interestingly, in the revised law, special interests managed to include a number of exemptions of their property
from elimination of the ITC. For example, one such exception
is for "certain aircraft used in Alaska."
Under the 1986 law, investment credit carryovers cannot
offset more than 75 percent of tax liability compared to 85
percent under the old law. Foreign tax credits and investment

tax credits are the only credits allowable against the Alternative Minimum Tax, and combined they cannot reduce the liability by more than 90 percent of the Alternative Minimum Tax. However, because of interplay with the new Alternative Minimum Tax, ITC carryforwards can never reduce regular tax liability to less than 15 percent.

Residual Method Now Required for Allocating Purchase Price of Assets

Just prior to enactment of the Tax Reform Act of 1986 the Internal Revenue Service issued regulations requiring use of the "residual method" in allocating stock in a Section 338 election. The Tax Reform Act included the same rules for asset purchases, requiring the use of the residual method instead of the proportional method for allocating the purchase price to a targets assets.

Under the old proportional method of allocation, all assets, including goodwill, were separately valued. The purchase price was then allocated among the various assets, other than cash or cash equivalent assets, in proportion to their relative fair market values. Under the residual method, all assets other than goodwill are valued, and the excess of the purchase price (if any) over the calculated values is deemed to be goodwill. In general, the proportional method produces less goodwill than the residual method when the purchase price of a target stock (including liabilities assumed) exceeds the fair market value of the assets. Thus the Tax Reform Act of 1986 eliminates any tax recovery for paying a price higher than fair market value

Exclusion for Corporation Dividends Received Is Lowered

The "dividends received" exclusion was lowered from 85 to 80 percent. When combined with the lower tax rate, the effective tax rate on dividends received by a corporation is reduced from 6.9 to 6.8 percent. For example, a corporation receiving dividends of $100 now pays tax as follows: $(1 - .80) \times \$100 \times .34 = 6.8$ percent.

Greenmail No Longer Deductible

Payments made by a corporation in connection with the redemption of its stock are no longer deductible under the 1986 law. The law precludes "greenmail" payments made to stockholders to avert a hostile takeover. Also precluded are "standstill" payments in conjunction with stock redemptions. These rules became retroactively effective for payments made on or after March 1, 1986, irrespective of any contracts that may have been in force prior to that date.

TAX IMPACT ON LBO DEALS

Impact on Prices of Targets

For LBO deals that would have been heavily dependent on favorable tax treatment under the old law, there is little question that prices are dropping. Even if buyers were willing to pay the same prices, their bankers are not. The fundamental ability of buyers to finance an acquisition is the ultimate constraint on prices buyers are able to pay. The bankers providing the debt portion of the financing package are constrained by the postacquisition cash flow of the target. To the extent a particular deal's cash flow is less under tax reform, its price must drop.

LBO deals that have been hardest hit by tax reform are those whose assets are most undervalued, or else companies that rely very heavily on high depreciation to preserve cash flow. In the second category are lackluster manufacturing companies which may be suffering from obsolescence, foreign competition, and rising costs. Companies whose after-tax profits are vitally dependent on depreciation will find it most difficult to adjust to the post-tax reform environment and have benefited less than labor-intensive firms.

Smaller LBO deals involving the sale of family-owned businesses might also be subject to deep price cuts. First, family-owned businesses, such as retail stores, are likely to suffer most from double taxation since they have been owned for many years, and are apt to have a low book value relative to fair market value. Second, small business owners are often less well advised on tax issues, and are less likely to find the best approach to minimize the impact of tax reform on the valuation of their companies. Many small business owners don't give much thought to such considerations until they are actually trying to sell their companies, often under adverse circumstances, such as the death of a family member who played a major role in the business.

It appears that the Tax Reform Act will have the long-run impact on our economy that Congress hoped: to reward companies able to generate profit without an enormous amount of tax support, and to discourage companies that lack true economic vitality. Companies receiving the most "discouragement" have suffered the greatest drop in valuation by potential acquirers. Experts have estimated that prices of an "average" LBO have dropped from 10 to 25 percent. Yet it is important to remember that there really is no "average" LBO, and that any changes in LBO prices resulting from tax reform are highly specific cases.

Companies that are not heavily dependent on depreciation and investment tax credits, and which previously paid burdensome taxes, have benefited from the reduction in corporate income tax. Extra costs incurred by paying a premium for a company will be offset to some extent by the improvement in cash flow made possible from the drop in corporate taxes.

Impact on Deal Flow

Prior to enactment of the Tax Reform Act of 1986, it was widely publicized that several large billion-dollar deals that were heavily dependent on favorable tax treatment would not occur unless they could be completed before the beginning of 1987. Does that mean that such deals won't ever get done? While some marginal deals are less attractive, it doesn't mean that they now won't be done. Maybe they'll have a different structure and a different price. In fact, the change in the tax law will require companies to rethink much of their portfolio strategy. Tax reform over the next several years may actually generate an increase in divestments and acquisitions as companies align themselves to better match a post-tax reform competitive environment.

Over the long run the annual number of LBO deals completed before and after tax reform will probably not change very much unless other factors precipitate the change. Such factors as interest rates and the health of the stock market, probably have as much or more to do with the volume of LBO transactions as does LBO tax treatment. Most experts have predicted that the average drop in LBO target prices will bring LBO activity back into pretax reform equilibrium with respect to the volume of buying and selling. Perhaps, like the real estate market, it may take a short while for buyers and sellers to adjust to different tax treatment and the implications for the valuation of their specific deal. But after a brief adjustment period, the fundamental forces driving the LBO market—the need to divest, diversify, gain access to growth markets—should cause the volume of LBO transactions to resume.

While the number of LBO deals will likely remain about the same as the pretax reform steady state level, the type of deals that acquirers will prefer has changed. Obviously buyers are staying away from deals with punishingly high tax costs unless they receive a compensating price break. Buyers are looking more carefully for companies whose depreciable assets have a tax basis close to their market value. In general, buyers want companies that produce more cash and are not dependent on high depreciation to protect their cash flow.

Companies with high-growth rates will receive greater attention than ever before. The drop in the corporate tax rate, from 46 percent to about 40 percent in 1987, and 34 percent in 1988, means that these companies will get to keep more of their cash. Since service companies are less dependent on depreciation than manufacturing companies, tax reform may have reinforced the shift that the United States is making toward a service economy. The ideal post-tax reform acquisition might be a high-growth service company that spins-out a predictable amount of cash.

Impact on Sources of Financing for LBOs

A major feature of the tax reform bill was the negative impact on real estate tax shelters as an attractive investment vehicle. Some finance professionals have argued that because investment returns on LBO funds have been very attractive, such LBO funds are now financed in part with capital traditionally made available to real estate tax shelters syndications.

Another new source of financing is being funneled through employee stock ownership plans (ESOPs). Carefully nurtured by Senator Long, ESOPs emerged from tax reform as an even better tool for businesspeople as well as a way for workers to share in the fruits of the capitalist system. In particular, the provision enabling banks to exclude some of the interest on ESOP loans was extended to capital provided by mutual funds. This had the effect of strengthening the ability of ESOPs to be used as an LBO financing source.

Finally, for small, closely held companies, deferred payment of part of the purchase price paid by acquirers is becoming more popular. Since there is no longer any difference between ordinary income and capital gains tax, as long as buyers offer to adjust for the time value of money, some sellers prefer receiving partial payment for their share of the company in the form of deferred compensation. This could take the form of royalties, consulting services, or agreements not to compete, all of which would be tax deductible to the acquiring company. The rationale behind this idea is simple; the tax shield made available to the buyer via deferred compensation is quite valuable. Taking the tax shield into consideration, the buyer could even offer a small price premium to the seller while still spending less in present value terms than what the buyer would have spent without deferring part of the payment for the target.

Supply, Demand, and the Tax Law

Tax reform itself will spur the need for divestment and reconsolidation. New strategic requirements of potential acquirers may provide a great deal of motivation to acquire new companies despite potentially increased LBO tax consequences. Coupled with record high demand for acquisitions by foreign companies, competition for companies that fit post-tax reform specifications may become especially intense.

The final factor which makes the future of LBOs difficult to predict is the creativity and motivation of the players. Financial intermediaries, tax accounting, and legal professionals, as well as corporate management—are busy at work trying to invent new ways to achieve their goals while taking maximum advantage of every aspect of the existing law. If the existing law doesn't quite offer enough advantages, corporate America is welcome to try and change the law on their own behalf. Lobbyists are hard at work right now proposing reforms for the 1986 tax reform. In a few years it will be time to write another chapter on tax reform.

Pressures on Price, Deal Structure, and Financing Resulting from the Tax Reform Act of 1986

Old Law	New Law
1. Section 337 asset liquidation allowed companies whose assets had appreciated to avoid paying corporate tax on sale of assets made following a total liquidation of the company.	1. Assets sold in liquidation now subject to corporate tax of 34 percent.
2. Section 338 asset step-up elections allowed buyers to increase the basis of an acquired company's assets from its tax basis to its fair market value without a corporate gains tax on the step-up. Buyers did pay recapture taxes on the step-up.	2. Section 338 elections now trigger corporate gains tax of 34 percent in addition to recapture taxes.
3. The maximum effective personal capital gains tax was 20 percent. Corporate capital gains was 28 percent.	3. Personal capital gains tax increased to 28 percent. Corporate capital gains tax increased to 34 percent.
4. No minimum corporate income tax.	4. Imposition of a new minimum corporate income tax of 20 percent.

Pressures on Price, Deal Structure, and Financing Resulting from the Tax Reform Act of 1986 *(continued)*

Old Law	*New Law*
5. Net operating losses (NOLs) could be carried forward and utilized at a faster rate than under the new law.	5. New restrictions on NOL carryforward and lengthening of depreciation schedules for many classes of property.
6. Proportional method used for allocating assets to purchase price in an asset liquidation sale.	6. Residual method now required in an asset purchase (residual method had already been required for Section 338 stock acquisitions). Assets other than goodwill allocated on a basis equal to their fair market values; remaining purchase price allocated to goodwill.
7. Greenmail deductible.	7. Greenmail payments not deductible.
8. ESOP financing was an attractive method of helping to finance LBOs.	8. ESOP regulations made ESOPs more attractive as a financing tool. The deduction of principal as well as interest on ESOP loans now extend to mutual funds.
9. Overfunded pension plans an attractive source for LBO financing.	9. Any funds taken out of pension plans now subject to an extra 10 percent excise tax, bringing the total withdrawal tax to 44 percent (10 + 34).

Effects on Buyers	*Effects on Sellers*
1. Since additional tax on asset liquidation can't be avoided, tax-free stock-for-stock exchanges and poolings will be a less advantageous form of purchasing assets. In an asset liquidation there will be price pressure on buyers since the seller's tax bill is higher.	1. Sellers electing sale of assets through liquidation now subject to double taxation and will net less cash from the sale.
2. Buyers will no longer make Section 338 asset step-up elections. The present value of future tax shield savings from increased depreciation resulting from an asset step-up will almost never be as great as the immediate recapture tax cost of a Section 338 election.	2. Sellers will be pressured by buyers to reduce prices. Post-acquisition cash flow will be less without asset step-up, forcing acquirers to use more equity versus debt financing, unless they can pay a lower price.

Pressures on Price, Deal Structure, and Financing Resulting from the Tax Reform Act of 1986 *(concluded)*

Old Law	*New Law*
3. Buyers will be asked to pay more in an asset liquidation since sellers get to keep less of the gain. This will increase the incentive to use tax-free stock acquisition as a method of purchasing assets. Yet many sellers will still want to receive cash, rather than stock.	3. In addition to paying a corporate capital gains tax of 34 percent on the sale of assets in a Section 337 election, shareholders will pay a 28 percent personal capital gains tax on remaining after-tax gains distributed to them. Increases the effective net tax on this type transaction from 20 percent to 52.5 percent.
4. Minimum tax will decrease after-tax cash flow for some LBOs, thus requiring an increase in equity financing or a lower purchase price in order to decrease postacquisition interest debt burden.	4. Sellers will be pressured to lower price.
5. In general, NOL carryforward will be worth less to buyers.	5. Sellers will be pressured to lower price.
6. This change eliminates any tax recovery for paying an acquisition premium; that is, for paying a price in excess of fair market value.	6. Sellers will be pressured to keep prices in line with fair market valuations since buyers no longer get tax benefits for prices over fair market value.
7. Cost of unfriendly takeovers is increased.	7. Target is left with a higher cost due to greenmail.
8. Debt raised from the target's ESOP will be comparatively cheaper than currently more expensive debt raised from conventional outside lenders.	8. Companies that have future plans to sell out may adopt ESOPs as a way to facilitate financing for a future acquirer.
9. Use of overfunded pension plans as an LBO financed tool will be more expensive to buyers. Buyers will need to pay less or find additional financing to replace this source lost to taxes.	9. Sellers will be pressured to lower prices resulting from buyers' increased cost of financing.

CHAPTER 8

ESOPS: EMPLOYEES BUY CORPORATE AMERICA

Rarely in Corporate America will an opportunity go unexploited for long. Such is the case of the employee stock ownership plan (ESOP) which has become an attractive source of financing in everything from simple capital expansions to complete leveraged buyouts.

The four cases to be presented later in this chapter illustrate the application of ESOP financing to an LBO and some potential problems that can accompany this often controversial financing technique. Dan River desperately sought a means to fend off Carl Icahn's hostile takeover bid. The ESOP paved the way for management to maintain control while eliminating the possibility of future takeover attempts. Weirton Steel provides a good example of the extensive planning required for successful execution of a leveraged ESOP buyout. It also illustrates the use of an ESOP as an alternative to massive layoffs and plant shutdown. As leveraged ESOP buyouts (hereafter, LEBOs) have become more popular, involvement by the Department of Labor in these deals has increased. Scott & Fetzer was one of the first cases where Labor Department concerns of unfair equity distribution among management, investors, and employees prevented the completion of a LEBO. The Department of Labor was also

We appreciate the research, analysis, and writing done by Brian Gorman. Without his very significant contribution, the completion of this chapter would not have been possible.

actively involved in Blue Bell's ESOP and forced a reduction in management's share of the company.

These cases demonstrate the complexity of the use of an ESOP. A better understanding requires some further clarification.

IS THE ESOP A FABLE?
IF NOT WHAT IS IT?

The two types of ESOP most frequently used are the stock bonus ESOP and the combination stock bonus and money purchase ESOP (combination ESOP). A normal stock bonus plan is limited to a 10 percent holding of the employer's securities, may or may not tie the level of contribution to company profits and may not be leveraged. Dividend income on the securities held in a stock bonus plan may be distributed after a two-year holding period. This plan essentially becomes an ESOP if it is designed to invest primarily in employer securities and does not tie the level of contribution to company profits. The unlevered stock bonus ESOP may contribute varying amounts to the plan each year. These amounts may range from 0 to 15 percent of the total annual payroll of plan participants (covered payroll), as determined by the board of directors each year.

The stock bonus portion of the unlevered combination ESOP is identical to the unlevered stock bonus plan above. The money purchase portion of the unlevered combination ESOP is nothing more than a means for an additional, fixed contribution of up to 10 percent of covered payroll. This portion is fixed at the time the plan is initiated and may not change while the plan is in existence. The maximum allowable employer contribution to an unleveraged combination ESOP is thus 25 percent of covered payroll, 15 percent from the stock bonus portion and 10 percent from the money purchase portion.

If either the stock bonus ESOP or combination ESOP borrows money to purchase employer stock, it becomes a leveraged ESOP and the allowed employer contribution changes. Contribution to a leveraged ESOP is variable and can be up to 25 percent of covered payroll plus 100 percent of all interest charged on the loan. There is no limit on the amount of the interest portion. Either plan can borrow money to purchase employer stock as long as it conforms to the following rules:

1. The loan must be primarily for the benefit of the plan participants.
2. The lender must charge only a "reasonable" rate of interest.
3. If collateral for such a loan is required, it may be in the form of employer securities.

Obviously, these rules allow some degree of latitude. The Department of Labor is responsible for assuring that the ESOP is operated for the benefit of plan participants. Thus, it is because of the first requirement of an ESOP loan that the Labor Department has become involved in leveraged ESOPs, or LEBOs.

In summary, the three basic ESOP contributary arrangements are:

1. Unlevered stock bonus ESOP—variable contribution up to 15 percent of covered payroll.
2. Unlevered combination ESOP—variable contribution up to 15 percent plus fixed contribution up to 10 percent of covered payroll.
3. Leveraged ESOP—variable contribution up to 25 percent of covered payroll plus 100 percent of interest charged on loan.

CONTRIBUTION, ALLOCATION AND DISTRIBUTION: THE GUTS OF THE ESOP

Company contributions to the ESOP may be in the form of cash, Treasury stock, or newly issued stock. If stock is contributed, the value of the contribution is determined by the "fair value" of the stock. If the company's stock is publicly traded, this value is the market price of the stock. If the firm is privately held, this value is determined by professional appraisal. Such an appraisal is usually done once a year.

Plan assets are first allocated to the accounts of employee members based on their salaries. Employees have no claim to these allocated assets until they are vested. Vesting policy can differ across firms. The most common situation is a gradual vesting, increasing with years of employment up to 100 percent in 10 years. If an employee leaves the firm before total vesting, she or he forfeits the unvested portion of those assets allocated to her or his ESOP account. Such forfeitures are distributed to the other members of ESOP on the same basis as company contributions.

Forfeitures are treated as part of the total allowable company contribution in the case of a combination ESOP, but not with a stock bonus ESOP. This means that as long as there are forfeitures, the company with an unlevered combination ESOP will never be able to contribute the maximum 25 percent of covered payroll.

Vested assets are distributed to the employee upon retirement or departure from the company in the form of stock or the fair value of that stock in cash. The fair value is determined the same way for distribution to employees as for contributions to the plan. Distributions may be in one lump sum or in several annual payments. Assets allocated to ESOP members' accounts are not taxable to the employee until they are actually distributed, but the lump-sum amount may be averaged over a 10-year period for tax purposes.

According to the rules governing ESOPs, employees have the right to demand that distribution of their ESOP benefits be in the form of employer securities, unless such ownership is prohibited by the company's bylaws. If employees elect to take their benefits in stock, they may then sell it back to the ESOP; sell it in the market, if the stock is publicly traded; or keep it and sell it later.

Usually, if the employer is a privately held firm, the ESOP or employer has the right of first refusal to buy back the employee's stock. This is to guarantee that the stock will not fall into unfriendly hands. If the firm is public and its stock is not widely traded, the ESOP is required to buy back the distributed shares at fair market value because the employee may have trouble selling it elsewhere.

The issue of fair market value is extremely important as it is the basis for most legal action brought against firms which have employed ESOPs.

THE RIGHT TO VOTE: IS IT LOST?

Employees of a private company have the right to vote the ESOP stock allocated to their account only in matters requiring more than a majority of shareholder votes, such as sale of the company or a merger. The board of directors may elect to pass through additional voting rights on other matters requiring a simple majority vote, such as election of directors. About 15 percent of all closely held companies pass through full voting rights voluntarily.

Employees of a public company must be given full voting rights on all shares allocated to their ESOP accounts.

ADMINISTERING THE PLAN

ESOPs are administered by a trustee as required by law. The trustee acts as fiduciary to all employee participants and must operate the plan for the employee's exclusive benefit. The trustee, appointed by the board of directors, is usually a national bank or trust company, but it can be an officer of the employer company. A trustee can administer the plan independently or under the direction of a company-appointed ESOP administrative committee.

The trustee usually is empowered to vote those shares of stock not allocated to an employee account, including stock held as collateral for a bank loan. If the ESOP borrows from an outside lender to finance the purchase of employer stock, the purchased stock is usually held in a "suspense fund" as collateral for the loan and is allocated to employee accounts in proportion to the loan repayment.

There are no specific legal guidelines regarding the voting of unallocated shares held by an ESOP. The resulting flexibility is an extremely important advantage since it allows the directors to control the votes of large blocks of stock indirectly, through the ESOP administrative committee or the trustee. The extent of this control depends, of course, on the percentage of ESOP ownership. The average ESOP owns 28 percent of the employer's stock. When an ESOP is used in an LBO, that share is usually in the range of 60 to 80 percent.

It should be noted that the trustee need not always vote ESOP stock in accordance with the wishes of management. For example, in 1982 Martin Marietta attempted an un-friendly takeover of Bendix Corp. The trustee for Bendix's ESOP, Citibank, tendered 4.5 million shares to Martin Marietta, citing fiduciary responsibility to Bendix employees.

LEGISLATING ESOP BENEFITS

The Deficit Reduction Act of 1984 has provided the largest incentives for employee ownership of any legislation to date. The act contains four major provisions:

1. One half of the interest income a lender receives from a loan to an ESOP is tax exempt. The bank can pass some of this tax saving to the ESOP in the form of lower interest rates. This could prove a significant advantage in an LBO, since a lender typically charges two to three points above the prime rate for LBO financing to compensate for the greater risk associated with higher debt levels.

2. Employers are allowed to deduct all dividend pay-ments passed through the ESOP and distributed to plan participants. This removes the effect of double taxation associated with normal dividend payments and provides an immediate reward to plan partici-pants. The latter is presumed to add to the motiva-tional effects of the ESOP. The dividend payment to the employee is treated as normal income and is excluded from the usual dividend exclusion.

3. In an ESOP purchase resulting in employee ownership of at least 30 percent of the outstanding employer stock of a company, the act provided that the seller need not recognize the capital gain for tax purposes. One qualification is that the proceeds of the sale must be reinvested in "replacement securities" within a 15-month period, beginning 3 months before the sale and ending one year later. Presumably the "replacement" securities purchased in the three-month period before the sale could have been bought in anticipation of the sale. A qualified replacement security is any stock, bond, warrant, option, and so on, issued by a domestic company that does not receive more than 25 percent of its gross revenue in the form of passive investment income (i.e., dividends, interest, and so on).

4. The estate of a plan member may transfer the tax liability (the equivalent amount of stock) to the ESOP. The ESOP may then pay the tax over a 15-year period at favorable interest rates.

The brightest spot in the Tax Reform Act of 1986 relative to LBO financing can be found in the treatment of ESOPs. The following is an overview of the key ESOP amendments.

1. The corporate deduction for ESOP dividends paid out to employees and beneficiaries was extended to include dividends used to repay ESOP loans. The extension of deductions on dividends lowered the effective cost of ESOP borrowing due to the increase in tax savings.

2. An exclusion from an estate is now permitted for 50 percent of the proceeds realized on an estate's sale of stock to an ESOP. The effect of the exclusion will certainly increase the use of ESOPs in closely held corporations. A common use of ESOPs is to help facilitate the purchase of a closely held company by a friendly buyer. Sale of stock to an ESOP can provide an owner with badly needed liquidity while simultaneously ensuring the perpetuation of the business. In the event of an owner's death, the need to find a friendly buyer with cash is even more important. While the owner's

estate may consist of mostly closely held stock, the
government requires its estate taxes paid in cash. By
selling the estate's stock in a leveraged transaction to
an ESOP trust, the estate can meet the cash requirements of the government while rewarding the employees who helped build the company with stock.

There is already some indication that the Internal
Revenue Service will act decisively to limit potential
abuses of the new estate tax exclusion. Such abuses
could occur if stock were purchased after a person's
death, or if the ESOP resells the stock that it purchases from the estate. Prevention of such abuses
would keep ESOPs from becoming a tax shelter mill
which bought stock from estates at a discount and
then resold the stock.

3. The partial exclusion from tax on interest earned on
   ESOP loans was extended to loans matched by contributions of stock to an ESOP if the stock is allocated
   within one year. The exclusion was extended to loans
   held by mutual funds and the tax benefit may flow
   through to mutual fund investors. The entry of mutual
   funds provides a new source of financing for ESOP
   debt.
4. The new law imposes a 10 percent tax on pension
   reversions (i.e., pulling money out of an overfunded
   pension fund and giving it back to the company)
   unless the money is given to an ESOP. This will
   increase the cost of using overfunded pension plans to
   finance acquisitions unless the funds are contributed
   to an ESOP.

CASH FLOW ADVANTAGES

Establishment of an employee stock ownership plan (ESOP)
can be a source of cash if it replaces an overfunded defined
benefit pension plan. When a company terminates such a
plan, it usually buys an annuity to cover the pension liability
and can use any of the remaining assets.

The ESOP is a source of new equity if the company makes contributions in the form of newly issued stock or money to purchase new stock. The company can issue new equity to the ESOP and satisfy its defined contribution liability to the plan without any immediate cash outflow.

The issuance of new stock to the ESOP can also be viewed as a means to reinvest pretax dollars for capital expansion. Normally, reinvestment of profits would come from that portion of after-tax net income that is not distributed as dividends.

The above-mentioned benefits are available to any ESOP, leveraged or unleveraged, stock bonus or combination. The only cash flow difference between these types of ESOP arises from the different contribution level allowed with each.

The most powerful use of an ESOP as a vehicle of corporate finance comes when it is used to borrow money for the purchase of stock. The advantages of a leveraged ESOP provide the greatest attraction for ESOP participation in an LBO.

The power of this method is best illustrated through a simplified example. Suppose that a company has earnings before interest and taxes of $1,000, interest expense of $100 and pays 40 percent of gross income to the government in taxes. Normally, pretax income would be $900, taxes would be $360, and net income would be $540. Repayment of the loan's principal would have to come from the net profit, as would dividends and reinvestment.

When the leveraged ESOP is used, any amount of the $900 pretax income (up to 25 percent of covered payroll) can be contributed to principal repayment. The ESOP would borrow money to purchase newly issued or Treasury stock from the company. The company would use its ESOP contribution to repay principal plus the $100 in interest. In the extreme case, the company could contribute all $900 to principal repayment and would pay no taxes. Although this is an unlikely scenario, it illustrates that cash flow to retire a loan can be dramatically increased and taxes similarly decreased through a leveraged ESOP.

In practice, any time that an ESOP borrows directly from a third-party lender, the company is required by the lender to

Simple Leveraged ESOP

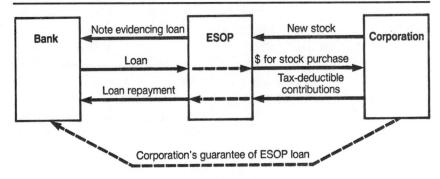

guarantee the ESOP's debt. The reason for this stems from the requirement that the only collateral that may be used to secure a loan to an ESOP is employer stock. With no other collateral for a loan than stock, the bank effectively loses the benefit of the seniority of debt over equity. With the company's guarantee, the bank gains a claim on the company's assets, similar to the claim it would have with secured debt.

The above exhibit depicts this simple leveraged ESOP. The dotted lines show that this is essentially a loan to the corporation that has been routed through the ESOP.

TAKING ON DEBT: THE LEVERAGED ESOP BUYOUT

As the popularity of leveraged buyouts has been rapidly increasing in the past few years, so too has the interest in using ESOPs to help finance them. The leveraged ESOP buyout offers tax and cash flow advantages which make it attractive to management, sellers, and lenders. Additionally, there is good reason to believe that ESOPs have a positive motivational effect on employees. Probably the most publicized use of the LEBO is as an antitakeover measure. However, there are a few other good reasons for considering a LEBO. Here, three uses of a LEBO are considered.

THWARTING A HOSTILE TAKEOVER

There are certain characteristics of an attractive target for an unfriendly takeover attempt. These include good liquidity, low debt, a relatively stable earnings record, and large asset base. Combined with these, the typical takeover target often is experiencing some short-term difficulties which have driven the stock price below its fundamental value.

If management thinks that its company is a potential target, it might undertake a LEBO in order to avoid a hostile bid. An example of this is Parsons Corporation which found itself with a lot of cash and little debt, strong earnings growth and a large backlog of future work. Its management made it clear that avoiding an unfriendly takeover was a primary concern in the decision to go private.

Another engineering and construction company, Raymond International, went private via a LEBO. Raymond's stock was depressed and, similarly, management feared the company might be a target.

Once a hostile takeover is in progress, a LEBO can provide a means for management to deprive a raider of the shares needed to gain control. Usually a hostile bid is followed by a race with time as management tries to come up with a defense before too many shares have been tendered to the raider.

The LEBO offers management some distinct advantages over a conventional LBO when used as an antitakeover measure. The most significant of these are the cash flow advantages. Indeed, quite often the ESOP loan can be obtained at a reduced rate due to the tax treatment of interest income to lenders. This is an important feature, given the fact that a lender typically will require a 3 or 4 point premium over the prime rate to compensate for the high financial risk associated with an LBO. Management may be able to outbid the raider if it can obtain funds more cheaply.

Another big advantage of the LEBO as a defense comes from the control of voting stock. Normally, if a company tries to buy up stock in order to avoid a takeover, that stock becomes nonvoting Treasury stock. When the stock is purchased by the ESOP, it retains its voting rights and is almost certain to be voted in favor of management. Obviously, the directors will influence the vote because they appointed the ESOP committee or the trustee. If the employees have voting rights, in the words of one merger and acquisition attorney, they tend "to vote with the devil they know rather than the devil they don't."

Nevertheless, because the formation of an ESOP is very time consuming and expensive, a LEBO is not always appropriate as a takeover defense. Adoption of an ESOP can require that the interests of several parties be satisfied. Done properly, a LEBO requires an in-depth feasibility study by experienced professionals.

Next to the ability of the firm to support buyout debt repayment, the most important issue is the buyout price. Consider the Parsons LEBO. Four investment bankers, including Kelso, the father of ESOPs, and at least five law firms were involved in the Parsons deal. Separate committees were set up to determine the fairness of the proposed purchase price from the standpoint of the public shareholders and that of the ESOP. Three investment bankers gave written opinions of fairness, representing each side in the buyout.

Parsons was not under the immediate pressure of an unfriendly takeover and the LEBO took more than six months to complete, from the formal proposal in July 1984 to completion in January 1985. The actual structuring of the LEBO took almost three months, which was relatively quick for an ESOP.

Scott & Fetzer tried to use an ESOP to fend off a takeover bid. Although it initially tried a conventional LBO, the lesson Scott & Fetzer learned applies well to a LEBO. If a company decides to undertake an LBO, whether or not it uses an ESOP, it will draw the sharks' attention and may well be "put in play." If the company had not been a target for other bidders prior to the proposed LBO, it is likely that the LBO announcement will draw in other bidders. Given the amount of time needed to organize a LEBO, the company is especially vulnerable to a takeover attempt during the planning stage. Scott & Fetzer made the mistake of bidding too low for its own stock. Ivan Boesky quickly offered his appraisal of the company in a counteroffer. The result was a costly struggle for control of the company, a waste of both management time and other company resources.

Fees for a LEBO vary quite a bit, depending on the particular deal. They typically increase with the size of the deal and represent a smaller percentage of the total cost in larger buyouts. The Dan River and Scott & Fetzer buyouts, both involving hostile takeover attempts, were relatively expensive. The $140 million Dan River deal generated fees of $4.3 million or about 3 percent. Scott & Fetzer, unable to complete the LEBO, still paid out fees of $20 million. For the proposed buyout of $574 million, that also came to about 3 percent.

In several cases, disgruntled employees and shareholders have sued the company over the handling of a LEBO. Often, minority shareholders feel that they are forced to accept too little for their stock and employees feel that they have been "used" by management. The latter complaint results from the idea that the defensive ESOP is often viewed as a means for incompetent managers to preserve their jobs.

This complaint has introduced another member to the family of ESOP jargon: the MESOP or management entrenchment stock ownership plan. It is useful to look at the underlying implications of complaints featuring the MESOP jargon.

Entrenchment of poor management is actually less likely with a LEBO or conventional leveraged buyout because the competency of management is a key factor in securing bank and other investor financing. In any LBO management comes under considerable scrutiny from these investor groups. It is highly unlikely that "bad" management would pass the test of investor scrutiny simply to secure their jobs through a MESOP.

Recently, the U.S. Department of Labor has become increasingly critical of LEBOs, especially those used as a defensive measure. Department of Labor objections to the equity distribution among the ESOP, management, and investors, prevented the Scott & Fetzer deal from going through.

It is important to note that no matter how well an ESOP is structured, some dissension is inevitable. The chances of problems occurring increase dramatically if the LEBO is not properly structured and well communicated to employees. The complex nature of a LEBO and the importance of setting it up equitably suggest that a hasty solution to save the company from a takeover might lead to more headaches for management down the road.

SELLING A DIVISION OR SUBSIDIARY

A LEBO offers an attractive way for a company to spin off a division or to get out of a business without having to shut it down or sell it at a depressed price. The most publicized example of this use of a LEBO was the purchase of the Weirton Steel Division of the National Steel Corporation by an ESOP. In March 1982, as will be described in the Weirton ESOP drama, National announced that it would be winding down the Weirton operations. During that year, Weirton had produced $60 million in losses for National. However, the plant was the major employer in the Weirton area and a shutdown would have meant the loss of several jobs and dealt a severe blow to the local economy.

By adopting the ESOP alternative, the employees were more willing to take wage cuts to help keep Weirton alive. The LEBO offered National a way to get rid of the plant without the hardship caused by a shutdown.

Although, it may be well argued that the LEBO can provide a means to keep a business alive, as in the Weirton case, a great deal of controversy surrounds this use of an ESOP. The argument against this use holds that the government is providing an incentive to keep noncompetitive businesses alive through ESOP tax subsidies.

SELLING A CLOSELY HELD COMPANY

A LEBO offers the majority owner of a closely held public corporation the opportunity to liquidate a significant portion of his stock without having to make a public offering. In effect, this preserves the closely held character of the firm and allows the seller to maintain significant control. In addition, tax treatment of such a sale enables the seller to avoid tax on the sale if it is converted to "replacement securities" within a 15-month period.

A colorful example of this involves the Mott family, heirs to the General Motors fortune and the U.S. Sugar Corporation. The Motts were 72 percent owners of U.S. Sugar, and they wanted to diversify some of their holdings without surrendering control of the company. Through a first-time-ever joint tender offer by U.S. Sugar and an ESOP, the Motts were able to sell two thirds of their stock for $150 million and still retain 53 percent of the company. The Motts started out with 72 percent, they sold two thirds of that or about 48 percent, that leaves 24 percent. Right? Wrong—that leaves 53 percent and this is how.

Through the joint offer, the company bought 55 percent of the shares outstanding and the ESOP bought 21 percent. That left the Motts with 24 percent, the ESOP with 21 percent, and the company with 55 percent. The company then retired its 55 percent, leaving only 45 percent of the original shares outstanding. The combined shares of the Mott family and the ESOP made up the entire amount remaining. The Mott's 24 percent of the original stock became 53 percent of the new amount. The ESOP's ownership share became 47 percent.

The joint tender offer was for $68 a share, $18 over the $50 market price. Ironically, some minority shareholders sued on the grounds that they had been forced to accept too little for their stock.

THE TYPICAL LEBO

Any leveraged buyout is a fairly complicated transaction. Various tax treatments and individual financing requirements can result in a myriad of different financing structures and can involve the use of several types of securities. When an ESOP is added to the equation, the basic structure is much the same but some specific options become available which need explanation. Before discussing some of the unique treatments of the LEBO, let's look at a hypothetical example step by step.

Although several investment bankers and commercial banks are now actively involved in this use of ESOPs, the structure of this deal will follow closely a typical Kelso deal. To avoid some complexity, the several legal advisers and other investment bankers that would be required will be left out. The numbers are purely fictitious, but fairly typical for a LEBO.

This deal will be structured as a tender offer and cash merger through a two-tier, holding company structure. The merger subsidiary will tender for the outstanding shares of the target company, convert those shares to the right to receive cash, and then merge into the target. The surviving, wholly owned subsidiary will be referred to as the "operating subsidiary" to distinguish it from the merger sub.

ABC COMPANY: AN EXAMPLE

The management of Old ABC Company wants to do an LBO to take the company private—there's been talk in the boardroom that Old ABC could be a takeover target. The chairman of ABC has contemplated the use of a LEBO, so he calls Kelso for some advice. He is delighted to hear of the juicy tax benefits that he might be able to obtain. After careful analysis of expected future cash flows and identification of enough sources of financing, the decision is made to go ahead with the LEBO.

ABC hires Kelso to set up the LEBO and Kelso recruits some investors who might be interested in financing part of the deal. After these outside investors are brought in, and Old ABC has received a tentative offer from the bank to finance a major portion of the buyout, work begins on formulation of the actual mechanics of the LEBO. A realistic time frame for organizing financing and deciding on the proper structure is probably four to six months.

The total buyout will require $100 million. Management

first forms a holding company, ABC Holdings, and a wholly owned subsidiary (merger sub) to act as the merger vehicle.

After careful planning and several informational meetings with employees to educate them about the ESOP, and what it means for them and for the company, management sets up an ESOP.

Realizing that, due to the high-debt levels, cash flow is going to be very important in the few years after the LEBO, management terminates an existing defined benefit pension plan which had been overfunded. The pension liability of the terminated plan is satisfied by the purchase of an annuity. This takes care of payments to employees for pension benefits that they have already earned. The net cash generated from termination of the past plan is $6 million.

An additional $10 million short-term bank loan is obtained to be repaid from working capital and the sale of unprofitable assets after the LEBO has taken place.

The outside investors, which include Kelso, agree to provide $1.5 million for a guarantee of a certain percentage of equity participation.

Management is asked to participate in the investment to give confidence to the bank and other investors that management will remain with ABC Holdings until the loan is repaid. The financial contribution of management is $2.5 million.

The total investment of Kelso, the other outside investors, and management is thus $4 million. These three will be referred to as the investment group.

The bank loan is made to the merger sub in the amount of $80 million with a scheduled five-year repayment. This amount will be reloaned to the ESOP in exchange for a note. The ESOP will use the loan to purchase stock of ABC Holdings.

The merger sub makes a tender offer for the outstanding shares of the target company. Funds for the buyout will come from the investor group, termination of a past pension plan, a short-term working capital loan, sale of unprofitable assets, and the bank loan which has been routed through the ESOP.

In as close to a chronological explanation as is possible, the merger sub borrows from the bank and reloans to the ESOP, through ABC Holdings. The ESOP then buys stock of

ABC Holdings. The merger sub goes ahead with the tender offer for Old ABC. The offer is financed by ABC Holdings from the proceeds of the stock sale to the ESOP. It is perhaps easiest to think of these transactions all occurring at the same instant. The loan to the ESOP is in effect only a paper transaction to gain the cash flow advantages associated with the leveraged ESOP.

Within a month, enough shares have been tendered so that the company can go ahead with the cash merger of the merger sub into Old ABC. Upon completion of the merger, all shares of Old ABC that are still outstanding are converted into the right to receive a certain amount of cash, and Old ABC becomes the subsidiary of ABC Holdings (operating subsidiary). The operating subsidiary assumes the debt of the merger sub and the note from the ESOP.

The loan will be repaid with funds generated from the operations of the operating subsidiary. Payments are made from the company to the ESOP as tax-deductible contributions. The ESOP then repays the subsidiary an amount representing principal and interest payments on the loan.

The ESOP and the investor group will own all of the equity of ABC Holdings after the LEBO has been completed. Ownership will be represented by two newly issued classes of stock, A and B.

With cash provided by the loan from the merger sub, the ESOP will purchase 100 percent of the class A at, for example, $10 a share. This represents an investment of $80 million and a total of 8 million shares. The investor group will receive a total of 2 million shares of class B for $2 per share. This equals their combined investment of $4 million.

The class B stock will be subordinate to class A in liquidation rights. Furthermore, B stock will have one tenth the voting rights and one tenth the dividend of class A. A fixed differential of $8 will be maintained between the A and B stock for the repayment period of the bank loan. When this loan has been retired, the B stock is convertible to A stock on a one-to-one basis.

The A stock, owned by the ESOP will be held in a special fund as collateral for the loan. This stock will be allocated to the ESOP members' accounts as the bank loan is paid down.

While the loan is outstanding, the appraised value of the class A stock may be significantly less than the $10 purchase price due to the high level of debt. During this period, ESOP members who are entitled to distributions from their accounts are guaranteed at least $10 per share.

THE ESOP: DOES IT IMPROVE COMPANY PERFORMANCE?

Many have called employee ownership America's answer to the Japanese concepts of "corporate family" and guaranteed lifetime employment. While it is unlikely that employee ownership alone will narrow the gap between American and Japanese productivity, there is some evidence that ESOPs have a positive effect on company performance. A Senate Finance Committee study found that the performance of 72 ESOP companies was dramatically better than the average for all U.S. corporations.

In addition, a study, published in the *Journal of Corporation Law,* found that 129 ESOP companies had an average annual productivity growth rate 1.52 percent higher than the average non-ESOP company. However, results of this study should be taken with a grain of salt. The researchers surveyed 1,400 ESOP firms and only 129 of them offered data on labor productivity. It seems highly likely that this survey suffers from a "response-bias." A firm which has experienced increasing productivity might be more apt to publicize it than a firm which had experienced a decline in productivity.

Unfortunately, ESOPs have only been popular for about a decade and there are too few reliable studies to draw a firm conclusion. The studies above show aggregate figures and thus cover up any individual examples where an ESOP hasn't led to better results. Clearly these examples exist and it seems that the reason for failure of these plans to boost productivity or morale is the result of poor structuring or implementation of the plan.

The number one problem is effective communication to the employees of exactly what the ESOP is and what they can hope to gain from participation in the plan. The *Journal of Corporation Law* survey found that 43 percent of the ESOP firms surveyed did not publish a handbook explaining the ESOP to employees, even though this is required by law.

The leading misconception concerning the establishment of an ESOP is the issue of control. As mentioned, relatively few closely held firms with ESOPs pass through full voting to employees. It is understandable that there will be cynicism if an employee is told that he or she is a part owner but has absolutely no control. Employees questioned by the National Center for Employee Ownership have indicated that they don't seek control of the day-to-day management decisions. The common theme was that they want more control of their individual job or of workplace policy decisions which affect them.

Another factor that is important to the success of an ESOP is the amount of employee ownership. A University of Michigan study found that performance is directly related to the amount of stock an employee owns. Most researchers agree that an ESOP must own more than 20 percent of the employer's stock for any motivational effects to be felt.

It is unlikely that an ESOP is going to have a positive effect if the employees can't see their stock growing. Companies in industries that are struggling may have a very difficult time showing such growth. The harsh reality is that no amount of employee ownership can provide a market for products or an easing of competition.

The perfect example of the problems that can arise in such a circumstance is the case of Dan River. As will be described later, Dan River instituted an ESOP during a period when the textile industry faced slack demand and stiff foreign competition. When business conditions caused the closing of some plants and the layoff of workers, the employees felt betrayed and cheated by management. Since the ESOP wasn't helping the business, it was seen as a management scheme to gain at the expense of the employees.

Do ESOPs improve company productivity? Does giving employees "a piece of the action" help moral and motivation? It's still up for debate. The most likely answer is—yes, if the employees can be made to feel that they are indeed owners.

Congress has certainly been convinced that ESOPs are for the better. Obviously, it has answered yes to the above questions. Since 1974 it approved 13 pieces of legislation which encourage employee ownership.

ARE ESOPs FOR YOU?

Using an ESOP to finance an LBO is not for everybody. There aren't many situations where it is as critical to be able to learn from the mistakes of others as with business failures. After a look at a few examples of situations where failure has occurred following a LEBO, the resounding conclusion is that a LEBO is no substitute for economic strength.

A good example is that of Iowa-based Rath Packing Company. In trying to avoid bankruptcy, the company formed an ESOP which purchased 60 percent of the outstanding stock. Along with the formation of an ESOP, the employees agreed to wage concessions. At the time, Rath was already heavily loaded with debt, in an industry characterized by cutthroat competition. Within a year and a half, Rath had filed for Chapter XI bankruptcy.

Another example is the case of Superior Switchboard, a company formed when a division of a large electronics company was spun off via a LEBO. Bruce Miller, a former executive with Superior, noted that after his company went private, both the attitude of the employees and their productivity improved dramatically.

Superior was the leading supplier of electric meters, like the one that is read every month by the meter reader. The sale of meters was dependent on the level of new home construction. Of course, the level of housing starts was very closely tied to the availability and cost of new home loans. At the time Superior spun off, the prime rate stood near 21 percent. Housing starts nose-dived and within a year, Superior could no longer service its debt. The company was rescued in a friendly buyout and the ESOP was terminated.

Bruce Miller emphasized that an ESOP can be a risky move for a small company "if there aren't enough assets to maneuver with." Superior was a relatively small company with annual sales of about $12 million. The ESOP purchased Superior for $4.5 million. Miller suggested that corporate managers are often far too optimistic about prospects for future growth and earnings. He advocates using pessimistic assumptions when the uncertainty about these prospects is high, warning, "even a little optimism can kill you."

These examples illustrate the need for sound business fundamentals for an ESOP-LBO to be successful. Kelso and Company offers this list of points to look for in a good LEBO candidate:

- Strong market position.
- Expected growth.
- A history of predictable earnings and cash flow.
- Proven management.
- Proprietary products or services.
- Valuable franchises.
- Sufficiently high ROA—to support high-debt levels.
- Moderate working capital/liquidity requirements.
- The potential for meaningful equity appreciation.

Although implied in the list above, company size deserves additional mention. The high costs associated with organization of the LEBO may keep the very small company out of the game entirely. Furthermore, a business which is highly capital intensive may not have enough employees to assure that 25 percent of covered payroll will be sufficient to cover debt repayment.

CONFLICTS OF INTEREST: WHERE DO THEY ARISE

The potential for conflicts of interest is particularly great in the case of a LEBO. Because management has ultimate control over the ESOP whether it be through an ESOP committee or a trustee, it can always be deemed to have fiduciary responsibility. When members of an ESOP committee are also officers of the sponsor company, this responsibility is even more directly tied to management. Corporate management usually engineers the LEBO; moreover, it often receives a premium on its investment in the buyout. This conflict is magnified when the investment of the ESOP in the buyout is large and there is a significant disparity between the return on investment received by the ESOP and that received by management or investors.

When the ESOP is formed in response to a hostile takeover, the conflict of interest takes on an additional dimension. It certainly will appear to employees and the Department of Labor that the primary motivation for establishing the ESOP is to retain corporate autonomy or entrench management. The Department of Labor has made it clear that when an ESOP is used as a defensive measure, management and trustees will have the burden of proving that defeating the takeover is truly in the best interest of the plan participants. Usual management arguments stress that the benefits of corporate autonomy, facilitation of employee ownership, and the actual employment of plan members might be threatened by an unfriendly takeover.

THE HEART OF THE DEAL: VALUING THE ESOP

The terms *reasonable amount* and *adequate consideration* are often referenced in literature concerning how much an ESOP should pay or receive for employer stock that is bought or sold. When the stock is publicly traded, the accepted valuation for both is generally the market price. When no broad market for the stock exists or in the case of a new issue, there is a great deal more ambiguity involved and even professional appraisals vary widely.

The focus here is on the price paid by the ESOP for employer stock, as this has become the most important issue in recent Labor Department action on LEBOs.

The Department of Labor follows a somewhat subjective standard of valuation which states that "...the plan not pay more or receive less than that which a third party dealing at arms' length would pay or receive under comparable circumstances." Yet, in the case of a LEBO, management's responsibility to the shareholders and to the ESOP participants (as fiduciary) clearly seem at odds.

On the one hand, management must strive to maximize the value of the company's stock for the benefit of its shareholders. In a LEBO, this could only mean securing as high a buyout price as possible. On the other hand, that buyout price must be fair to the ESOP as defined by the arms' length criterion. Naturally, both viewpoints are seldom fully satisfied. It is for this reason that almost every LEBO draws protests from both sides.

It is interesting to note that often the Labor Department is called in to review proposed LEBOs by the Securities and Exchange Commission. The SEC of course is concerned about management's responsibility to shareholders and the fairness of such deals from that perspective.

Because LEBOs have really only gained visibility in the past five or six years, no definite rules have been issued by the Labor Department regarding these issues. Since Labor Department involvement was relatively inconsequential until three or four years ago, the only way to get a flavor for the attitude of that agency is to take a look at some cases of Labor Department involvement.

In October 1981, a Grumman Corporation ESOP purchased about 9 percent of the Grumman shares outstanding to help turn away an unfriendly takeover bid by LTV Corporation. As is usually the case, the tender offer drove the price of Grumman stock up and the ESOP's purchase was made when the price was high. LTV eventually backed down due to fears of antitrust objections. When the battle ended, the stock price fell and the value of the ESOP's holding dropped by $58 million.

Grumman's chief executive officer and two other high-ranking corporate officials served as trustees for the Grumman ESOP. Claiming that they had breached fiduciary responsibility to act prudently, the Labor Department took the three to court. The department's contention was that the fiduciaries had failed to impartially evaluate the interests of plan participants and paid a price that was highly inflated by the tender offer. The department also felt that the three should be personally liable for the ESOP's loss.

The Labor Department's views were well summarized by a representative of that agency in a quote which appeared in *The Wall Street Journal,* "Basically, it's illegal for a company to use pension funds defensively or offensively to serve its own corporate purposes."

In February 1984, when the case finally went to trial, the price of Grumman stock had gone up considerably and the ESOP had sold its shares at a profit. The court ruled that although the three officers had indeed breached their fiduciary responsibility, the profit to the ESOP on the sale of the stock negated any potential losses from the breach.

Although this case ultimately was dismissed, it is important to note that the three corporate officers were found to have breached fiduciary responsibility. If the stock price hadn't recovered, they could have been required to make up the ESOP's losses. Since a tender offer will often inflate the stock price, this is a serious risk to any fiduciary who decides to use plan assets as a defensive measure.

In late 1983 and again, a year later, the Department of Labor became involved with the proposed buyouts of Raymond International and Blue Bell. These cases are significant because they are the first where the Labor Department's protests altered the proposed structure of a major buyout. They also illustrate the type of procedural requirements that the department is likely to favor in future deals.

The Raymond buyout was a true LEBO, much like our ABC example. The Keslo-structured deal used two classes of stock, with the price of A set at $10.00 and the price of B, $1.09. As the value of the stock increased, there was to be a fixed price differential between the two classes.

In a letter written in September 1983, the Labor Department protested that a conflict of interest existed due to the fact that the ESOP committee which bore fiduciary responsibility was made up of Raymond directors. The department went on to say that as a result of this conflict, the necessary fiduciary considerations (prudence) had not been adequately attended and that the ESOP had not received sufficient consideration for its investment.

The Labor Department held that management would receive too large a share of the potential gain if the stock value increased. For instance, if Raymond prospered and the price of A rose to $20.00 and the price of B to $10.00, the ESOP's investment would have appreciated 100 percent but management's equity would have increased over 800 percent. As a result of this disproportionate growth, the greater the increase in the value of the company, the greater share of ownership would be represented by management's stock.

The result of the Department of Labor's complaint was a cap on management's ultimate ownership share of the company at 20 percent. In fact, this cap could have been reached only if the company experienced capital appreciation of almost 300 percent, a highly unlikely event by all estimates at the time.

The year 1985 brought more indication that the Labor Department would not look favorably on the use of an ESOP as an antitakeover measure. In early 1985, Phillips Petroleum attempted to use an ESOP to help kill Carl Icahn's hostile takeover bid for the company. The Labor Department responded with a letter stating that it objected to the pass-through of voting rights of unallocated ESOP stock in response to any tender offer, friendly or unfriendly. Phillips consequently settled with Icahn without using the ESOP.

It is very important to note that the loss of voting rights on unallocated shares takes away a significant advantage of the ESOP as a takeover defense.

The most notable Labor Department's involvement in a LEBO to date has been its intervention in the proposed Scott & Fetzer buyout. Again, the ESOP was set up to aid in defense of hostile takeover bid, this time by Ivan Boesky.

Like Raymond International, the Scott & Fetzer deal was organized by Kelso with a two-stock structure. The equity distribution in this deal would have given investors about 9 percent for $6 million; management, 20 percent for $9 million; the ESOP, 41 percent for $182 million from a loan from the General Electric Credit Corporation (GECC); and GECC, the remaining 30 percent (in warrants).

Once again, the Department of Labor protested because

of the disproportionate opportunity for gain that was to be afforded management in the deal. Only this time, their protest had more serious effects.

GECC had stipulated that it would pull out of the deal if the Department of Labor threatened action to stop the LEBO. Furthermore, the deadline for making the 1985 ESOP contribution was August 15, about a week after the Department of Labor protest.

This made it virtually impossible for Scott & Fetzer to restructure the deal to the liking of the Labor Department in time to meet the contribution deadline.

The Department of Labor issued a no action letter and offered not to oppose the buyout if the ESOP equity share were increased to 50.1 percent and management's share reduced to significantly less than the original proposal of 20 percent. Unfortunately for Scott & Fetzer, this didn't come until August 15; too little, too late.

Failure of the Scott & Fetzer deal brought down the wrath of Louis Kelso on the Labor Department. In his opinion, "Such high-handed, legally unauthorized regulatory interventions chill the financial world away from ESOP-leveraged buyouts."

In the current atmosphere it seems that there are certain actions that might be taken to reduce the likelihood of unfavorable Labor Department involvement:

1. Secure independent, professional evaluation of the fairness of the deal from the standpoint of the ESOP and the shareholders.
2. Appoint a completely independent trustee to bear fiduciary responsibility to the plan. The trustee should not have affiliation with the company or with a lending institution involved in the proposed LEBO.
3. Ensure that management's share isn't grossly out of proportion to the share of the ESOP. This is certainly a judgment call.
4. Bear in mind that use of an ESOP formed during a takeover defense is likely to be viewed unfavorably. Use of an existing ESOP stands a better chance of avoiding MESOP claims.

Gambling for Jobs: The Wierton Steel ESOP Leveraged Buyout

Wierton Steel was one of three major steel divisions of the National Steel Corporation. Standing alone, it would be a Fortune 300 company with sales of $1 billion. As such, the Wierton ESOP leveraged buyout represented one of the largest employee buyouts in history. Wierton's major products were tinplate for the food and beverage container industry and sheet steel for automobiles and appliances. Unfortunately, the tinplate market was coming under heavy pressure from aluminum cans and plastic packaging materials. Wierton workers were not members of United Steelworkers of America (USWA), but instead had their own union, The Independent Steelworkers (ISU). The town of Wierton, population 28,000, was located in the northern finger of West Virginia along the Ohio River. It's one of the largest company towns in America. The local economy was totally dependent on Wierton Steel for its survival.

On February 27, 1982, in his letter to stockholders in National Steel's annual report, Howard M. Love, National's chairman, stated that National had embarked on a program of "downsizing" its steelmaking facilities to "whatever size is required to meet market demand and earn a return for its stockholders." It did not take long for Love to back this ominous message with action. Just a few days later, on March 2, National Steel issued an ultimatum to the employees of its Wierton mill. Either they would have to buy the entire facility and operate it themselves or National would gradually shut it down.

To many who know the company, the decision came as no surprise. The signs were evident long before the announcement was made. First, there was the state of the economy. The long and deep recession of the early 1980s was taking a

---

We appreciate the research, analysis, and writing done by Dan Herbert. Without his very significant contribution, the completion of the Weirton Steel case would not have been possible.

devastating toll on the industry. Growing world capacity, plummeting demand, and the low-price dumping by foreign competition were producing conditions in the steel industry described as "worse than any seen since the Great Depression." Over 4,000 white-collar workers and considerably more blue-collar workers had been laid off. Many were being advised to seek employment in other industries. Steelmakers were operating at just 60 percent of capacity, a disastrous situation in a high fixed cost industry. Foreign steelmakers were selling steel at as much as $100 per ton below the already discounted U.S. prices.

National's intentions became clear as they attempted to diversify out of the troubled steel industry. As a result, Wierton suffered increasing neglect. In its diversification program, National acquired United Financial, a large savings and loan, and also expanded into insurance and real estate.

At the same time no new investment was made in the Wierton mill. Older equipment such as the coke plant was being allowed to deteriorate beyond repair. Orders usually slated for Wierton were being funneled to other National mills, and a steady stream of layoffs reduced the work force from 11,500 in 1980 to just 7,500 by the time of the announcement. This neglect was deeply resented by Wierton employees and would later fuel their desire to prove that Wierton had no need for National.

Ironically, Wierton was one of the few profitable steel mills in the industry, eking out a 1 percent profit in 1982, while National's recent acquisitions lost money. The problem was that National was now determined to make a 20 percent return on new investment. So when they ascertained that Wierton needed $1 billion in new investments just to remain competitive, it became clear that Wierton didn't figure in National's future.

But National didn't have an easy way out. Wierton was almost more expensive to close than it was to keep open. The existing union contract contained generous layoff, severance, and pension provisions which would result in shutdown costs of $800 million. National had only $350 million in reserves to cover these shutdown costs. It also wouldn't get any tax write-off from the closing since it wasn't paying any taxes. In fact, National already had $264 million in unused tax credits. Finally, National did not want the bad publicity and blame for devastating the economy of an entire region just 35 miles west of its corporate headquarters in Pittsburgh.

Although the projected purchase price was termed *amazingly cheap* by a Paine Webber steel analyst, who else would want to buy an aging steel mill given the state of the industry? Thus, selling the plant to the workers through an ESOP leverage buyout seemed the only way out. Knowledge of National's predicament probably assisted Wierton in driving a hard bargain.

Interestingly, it was Wierton's management, not the local union (The Independent Steelworkers Union, ISU), which took the first step. They established the Joint Study Commission (JSC). The JSC was a corporation formed as a cooperative effort by some 20 management and union representatives of the Wierton Division. Their purpose was to determine if an independent Wierton could survive, and explore National's offer to negotiate a sale.

Their first step was to select a consulting firm for the feasibility study. After considering many offers, they finally chose the prestigious and expensive McKinsey and Company. In May 1982, with preliminary findings from McKinsey, the JSC lined up the legal and financial help to negotiate the sale. Again, the JSC went with prestigious firms. They selected the New York law firm of Wilkie, Farr and Gallagher, a prominent name in mergers and acquisitions, and the investment bank of Lazard Frères.

The JSC had two good reasons for going with such expensive established firms. First, to finance the acquisition, Wierton would have to borrow heavily. Given industry conditions and banks' cautious attitude toward employee-owned companies, the JSC felt they would have to market themselves to the financial community. Their feeling was that the approval and support of such highly regarded firms would help legitimize their efforts.

The JSC was also trying to distance itself from National. In April 1982, Allen Lowenstein, a lawyer who had helped negotiate the Hyatt Clark deal, was hired by the JSC. He was promptly let go in May when the JSC hired Wilkie Farr. He was criticized for trying to move too quickly in a complex situation. In addition, there was no love lost between Wierton and National. Wierton workers were angered by the indignity with which they had been treated by National over the past few years.

The McKinsey report concluded that even under their worst case economic scenario, an independent Wierton could be profitable, meet its financial obligations, and eventually restore part of the required compensation reductions through profit sharing. However, the report also concluded that sweeping changes were needed in order to make the new Wierton a viable economic enterprise.

The toughest of these changes was the need for a 32 percent reduction in overall compensation. Through management's effort to keep out the United Steelworkers of America and avoid strikes, Wierton workers were the highest paid in the industry. The average ISU member received over $24.50 per hour in total compensation while the industry average was around $21.50.

Staughton Lynd, an Ohio attorney who filed suit on behalf of 25 workers, said he failed to see why a 32 percent reduction was necessary when wages were only slightly above the industry average. He was obviously missing some major points. An independent Wierton had to do more than break even and cover production costs; it had to generate sufficient cash flow to support a substantial amount of debt and make significant new capital investment. McKinsey estimated that about $1 billion would be needed over the next 10 years. Wierton also needed to build an equity base of about $200 million in order to attract lenders and reduce risk. Without the wage cuts, Wierton would face a cash shortfall of up to $1.7 billion over the next 10 years.

Other concessions were also necessary. Wierton workers were used to five weeks of paid vacation per year. This would have to be reduced. Overtime meal allowances, payment for casual sick days, vacation bonuses, pyramiding of overtime and other luxuries would have to be eliminated.

Since National had agreed to remain liable for pension, health and life insurance obligations for certain retirees, and since salaried workers had recently taken a 10 percent wage cut, the actual wage reductions required to meet the 32 percent total labor cost reduction were significantly less. ISU hourly workers would take a 19.5 percent cut of $4.875 per hour. About 12 percent of the total 32 percent reduction could be transformed into employee-owned stock. Over the first three years, each employee would invest up to $18,000. If the company did well, it was estimated that this stock could be worth $90,000 by the end of the decade. So what at first appeared like a tremendous sacrifice could actually turn out to be a pretty good deal for the workers.

Pension liability was a hotter issue than the wage reductions. The significance of pensions to Wierton employees could not be understated, especially to those who had put most of their adult life into the mill. The division's unfunded pension liability of $102 million could be settled in the negotiations, but other problems were not as simple. The issue which really had the potential to divide Wierton workers was the Rule of 65. This rule would enable certain groups of older workers to retire with full benefits plus an extra $400 per month if the plant was ever permanently shut down. The younger workers had little immediate concern for pensions; they needed the mill for their livelihood. But the older workers had significant pension interest on which they could retire comfortably if the mill were closed. National had agreed to be liable for these shutdown benefits if the mill failed in the first five years; after that, Wierton was on its own.

But except for a few minor lawsuits, the issue never amounted to much. "When the issue was brought up," said Skip Spadafora, a member of the Joint Study Commission, "I would just ask them what they would do with their house if the mill closed?" This question was inevitably met with silence. Also many potential retirees had to be concerned with their sons, brothers, and nephews whose future was dependent on the mill.

The rest of the pension issue was pretty routine. National

would continue to be responsible for all pension liabilities and other employee benefits incurred while Wierton was still a National division. All related assets would be transferred to a separate pension trust to be used for the pensions of former and present division employees. Except for some minor cutbacks, Wierton employees would continue to receive pension, insurance, health and other benefits similar to those received under National.

The town of Wierton is one of the largest and oldest company towns in America. The Wierton mill is also the state's largest employer. What happened in Wierton was a truly unique event in the history of company towns and corporate community relations. The *New York Times* likened it to Frank Capra's "It's a Wonderful Life" in which a town is threatened with calamity and the citizens band together to save it.

Failure of the Wierton ESOP would have meant economic disaster for the entire region. Just about everyone in Wierton either works for the mill or is dependent on the mill's paycheck for his/her livelihood. Residents paid no local taxes. The company provided street repair, sewage disposal, and a fire and police department.

Support for the ESOP plan could be seen and felt almost everywhere. There was a huge Fourth of July parade dedicated to saving the mill. Green ribbons and bows representing spring and rebirth could be found everywhere. Billboards around town proclaimed "Life goes on with ESOP."

Donations to fund the cost of the lawyers and consultants were coming in from everywhere. Local merchants contributed $500 to $1,000, with Michael Starvaggi, a local millionaire, donating $20,000. Even West Virginia's Governor Jay Rockefeller put up $125,000. The group which gave the least turned out to be the employees themselves. But the workers were already taking big pay cuts and had given $500,000 from their unused strike fund.

In late September 1983, District Judge Robert Maxwell rejected the final lawsuit and cleared the way for the vote. The suit had been filed by dissident workers who demanded that all material used by McKinsey in making its 32 percent wage reduction recommendation be made public. The judge concurred with McKinsey that disclosure of its proprietary analytical models and estimates of Wierton's costs could seriously jeopardize Wierton's competitive position. Richard Arango, the recently dismissed president of the ISU, filed a complaint with the NLRB, claiming the study commission had engaged in illegal bargaining practices, but this was also dismissed.

When the vote finally came, it wasn't even close. The plan was approved by a better than 5 to 1 margin.

In the words of National's Chairman Howard Love, the Joint Committee's $225 per-hour lawyers had succeeded in driving a hard bargain. Wierton would pay $193.9 million for the assets of the division. Of this, just $71.5 million, or a mere 22 percent of the book value, was paid for the mill itself. While this may seem incredibly cheap, the market value for steel assets was generally far less than their book value given the depressed state of the industry. Wierton would also assume $192.3 million in current and long-term liabilities, bringing the total value of the deal to $386.2 million.

The payment schedule was generous. Wierton would pay $74.7 million up front in cash, $47.2 million more by 1993, and the last $72 million by 1998.

Financing consisted of a $120 million line of revolving credit that Lazard Frères secured from a consortium of banks headed by Citibank for just 1.5 percent above prime.

After the acquisition, 6.65 million shares in the new company were placed in an ESOP trust. Workers were to be allocated shares in the trust each year based on their wage level. Distribution of shares from the trust would not begin for five years. And no wage increases, strikes, or lockouts would be allowed for six years.

Who were the winners and losers in this deal? The workers received an ownership share based on their salary. The town of Wierton and surrounding communities certainly won. The workers won. Although they had to take a pay cut, they saved their jobs, the value of their houses, and avoided the trauma which would have accompanied a shutdown.

Unlike many ESOP leveraged buyouts, management did not get a disproportionate share of the company.

National was a winner too. While they sold Wierton for a highly discounted price, they did get rid of it, and avoided $800 million in shutdown costs. The consultants, bankers, and lawyers were also big winners. Their fees totaled over $5 million. McKinsey received $515,000, Lazard Frères $2.3 million, and Wilkie, Farr and Gallagher $2.1 million.

Sadly one of the few losers was Jack Redline, president of the Wierton Division under National; he was replaced by Robert Laughhead, the former head of Copperweld Steel in Ohio.

The JSC had felt that Redline did not have broad enough executive experience to run the new company. This decision left some bitter feelings since Redline had campaigned hard for the ESOP buyout.

During their first nine months of operation, the new Wierton earned $48.3 million on $845 million in sales. This is in an environment where many steel companies were losing money. It looks like the ESOP worked. So far, Wierton has lived up to its grand expectations.

The Dan River ESOP: A Product of Carl Icahn's "Scare 'Em Strategy"

Investor Carl Icahn's "scare'em strategy" had been very profitable. Prior to his purchase of TWA in 1985, his strategy had been to purchase shares in a vulnerable company and then, by creating a "fear of Carl Icahn," forcing the management into one of two decisions. One was to throw itself on the mercy of another buyer. The other was to buy back Icahn's

We appreciate the research, analysis, and writing done by Judy Kirshner. Without her very significant contribution, the completion of the Dan River case would not have been possible.

shares. In either case Icahn won, walking away with a substantial profit.

In August 1982, Carl Icahn was actively greenmailing Corporate America. He sold back stock to American Can, Anchor Hocking Corp., and Owens-Illinois, in each case receiving a hefty premium over the market price. Though the month of August was busy, no one expected Icahn to rest. On September 16, 1982, he announced his newest target, Dan River, Inc. As usual, it all started with the acquisition of a stake in the company. This time he bought 6.9 percent followed by his traditional threat to seek control.

ICAHN ON THE PROWL

In the next few weeks, Icahn strengthened his stock position, increasing it to 15 percent, at which time he arranged for a September 30, 1982 meeting with the board. At this confrontation, Icahn stated his intent to purchase, either from Dan River or through a tender offer, additional shares at $16 to $17 a share. His stated goal was to control an additional 40 to 50 percent of the outstanding stock so as to merge the textile company with his Icahn Capital Corp. In the second step of the transaction all remaining shareholders would receive debt securities valued somewhat less than the amount paid for shares acquired the first step of the offer. Icahn also said that he would offer employment contracts to certain Dan River officers and that he "was willing to explore the possibility that the second step [of the] merger include agreements with Dan River's management to sell some or all of the newly merged corporation to them and that the sale might be made via a leveraged buyout technique."

FIGHTING IN THEIR BLOOD

Dan River is one of the nation's major textile manufacturers. Its products consist of two types: materials for apparel and other uses, and finished products for the home and other interiors. The combination of a weak economy, high interest rates, and record imports of textiles were responsible for depressed 1982 sales, a 22 percent decline from 1981. In addition, Dan River reported a net loss of $8.73 million compared with net earnings of $14.54 million in 1981. This was in part a result of write-downs of unprofitable assets, six plant closings, and other nonrecurring charges. At that time, Dan River was continuing its long-term commitment to modernize plant and equipment. In addition, it was undergoing a major reorganization, including the concentration of top management in one location which was expected to produce an annual pretax cash savings of $5 million. Certainly, the appearance of Carl Icahn was not planned as part of the reorganization. However, the fact that profits were declining set the stage for some potentially unhappy shareholders. With the quarterly dividend cut from $0.28 to $0.14 a share and with the stock selling at half its book value, Dan River became a prime takeover target for Icahn.

Icahn's takeover threat was not the first time that Dan River was under siege. In 1979, two Hong Kong-controlled companies, Unitex Ltd. and its subsidiary Mannip Ltd., purchased 461,500 shares which amounted to 8.6 percent of Dan River's outstanding common stock. Dan River took them to court, and on June 5, 1981, an agreement was reached in which Unitex and Mannip were limited to aggregate holdings of 12 percent of Dan River's outstanding securities through December 1, 1984. Under this agreement, Dan River was provided with Unitex's expertise in Hong Kong textiles and Unitex's managing director became a member of Dan River's board. Icahn should have known that having fought this battle as hard as they did, Dan River's management wasn't going to relinquish control to him without a fight.

Interestingly, several other astute investors had also become aware of Dan River's asset value relative to its stock price. They also managed to profit handsomely. In 1981, David H. Murdock bought 5.6 percent of the company's common stock. To avoid a takeover attempt from Murdock, at the end of January, 1982, Dan River made a greenmail payment of $5.6 million to buy back 327,400 shares of its common stock. Maybe Icahn was hoping for the same fate.

THE BATTLE BEGINS

Four days after Icahn's meeting with Dan River's board, the board responded with the statement so often made, that the "Icahn proposal was not in the best interest of the company and its stockholders." At this meeting, the decision was made to take the first move in the legal battle.

Even though Carl Icahn had a successful greenmailing history against targets such as Marshall Field, Saxon Industries, Tappan, and Hammermill Paper, Dan River management was determined to fight back, ignoring the expense of a bitter battle and its need for capital resources to be spent on operations.

Dan River's defense started with a lawsuit in the Federal District Court for the Western District of Virginia to prevent Icahn from acquiring more stock. More importantly, on October 5, Dan River issued a new series of convertible preferred stock to a benefit plan for its nonexempt employees. The stock would be held in a trust for five years and converted at a rate of four preferred to one share of common. When these shares were converted to common, they would represent 22 percent of the company. With the issue of this stock came a clause requiring that any acquisition attempt would need ratification by more than 66 percent of this new class of stock. The intentions were clear—fending off the unwanted raider.

In response, Carl Icahn immediately rescinded his tender offer and countersued Dan River in an attempt to reverse the new stock issue. He claimed that the issue was a violation of New York Stock Exchange regulations. Dan River quickly amended its original lawsuit, and in mid-October charged Icahn with racketeering, a charge normally associated with organized crime. A pattern of racketeering is defined under the Federal Racketeer Influenced and Corrupt Organization (RICO) Act of 1970 as any two violations of a number of different laws during a 10-year period. The New York law firm of Paul, Weiss, Rifkind, Wharton & Garrison represented Dan River in this action. Dan River's complaint stated that Icahn bought Dan River stock with "proceeds derived through prior acts of extortion, mail fraud, and securities fraud." The suit focused on the Securities and Exchange Commission charges that Icahn failed to disclose tactics to exert influence on Saxon Industries and Hammermill Paper.

Before the legal warfare between Dan River and the Icahn group was over, Dan River added more complaints to its suit. They charged that Icahn's attempt at greenmail was deceptive and manipulative under the Securities Act of 1934. Icahn also faced complaints that his disclosures regarding the takeover were insufficient under both Virginia and federal laws, and finally that he operated with the intention "to loot Dan River," a violation of Virginia corporate law.

Icahn tried to move the case from Virginia to the federal court in New York, but on November 1 this request was denied.

THE TENDER OFFER

Dan River's hostile resistance may have been an unexpected response to Icahn. One reporter mentioned that "maybe this time Mr. Icahn reached farther than he intended." Regardless, the fight had begun and Icahn was not about to throw in the towel. In response to the Dan River resistance, Icahn filed counterclaims aimed at Dan River's stock bonus plan, charging that the establishment and issuance of the plan violated several New York Stock Exchange rules. Icahn also filed an amendment to his filing with the SEC, announcing a two-alternative plan: an $18 per share tender offer for 3.1 million shares, or 54 percent of the company, if the company would drop its suit against Icahn. Alternatively, if Dan River would not accept these terms, Icahn was prepared with a lower offer of $15 a share for 700,000 shares which amounted to 12 percent of Dan River shares. This acquisition was expected to bring Icahn's total holdings in Dan River to 27 percent. According to the tender offer materials, the Icahn Group intended to call a stockholders' meeting to elect replacements for the majority of Dan River's board. In order to put more pressure on Dan River's shareholders, the Icahn Group also indicated that a two-step merger would be considered in which each share of common stock would be traded for a debenture of less value than the original tender offer. On October 22, 1982, the last business day prior to the Icahn Group public announcement, Dan River common stock closed at 14⅜, 3⅝ below that of the Icahn proposal. In light of this, Paul Carrother, a vice president at Dan River, said that although he hadn't heard of the $18 offer, he felt "Icahn would probably get it if he made the offer."

NOTHING'S CHANGED

In reviewing the tender offer, Dan River's board considered the following information:

- The recommendation of Kidder, Peabody & Co., which had been retained to review the Icahn offer. They determined that "the offer was not fair from a financial point of view."
- Dan River's business including past performance, future prospects, current financial position, and replacement cost of Dan River assets.
- Icahn's lack of experience in operating a textile manufacturer.

Based upon these factors the Icahn offer was subsequently rejected.

At this point, the board requested Kidder, Peabody to explore the options that were available to protect Dan River and its stockholders from the potentially adverse consequences of a tender offer such as Icahn's, which was perceived to be unfair. Specifically, Dan River said it instructed Kidder, Peabody to develop opportunities and proposals with other buyers. Amazingly, this led to discussions with 34 prospective acquirers.

A BRIEF SIGH OF RELIEF FOR DAN RIVER

On November 3, 1982, Icahn raised the offer to $16.50 a share for as many as 2 million shares. This represented a 34 percent stake in Dan River. The group also left open the offer of a higher price if Dan River would agree to a friendly transaction. In contrast to the earlier offer that was made, the group stated that it would not drop the offer because of any Dan River legal action against it. Moreover, this offer was extended until midnight, November 12, 1982. An Icahn statement noted that although the Dan River board rejected the terms of the previous tender offer, it was "free to change its intent" before November 12 to obtain the $18 a share price.

Next, Dan River won a round in the courtroom. On Monday, November 15, the federal court in Virginia announced a preliminary injunction against Icahn, which barred him from voting his shares and set a trial date for February 7, 1983. In the same order, the court stated that Dan River was to conduct business as usual. However, it could not sell any assets, pay any special dividends, or issue new stock. Upon learning of the court's decision, Icahn issued a statement which noted that the court order did not prevent him from buying stock, only from voting them. One day after the court's ruling, Dan River rejected the latest Icahn offer, using again the statement so often made by targets "that the offer was unfair and not in the best interest of the stockholders" of Dan River.

But the Dan River victory was short lived. A week after the federal court decision, Icahn's luck on the legal battlefield changed. On November 22, 1982, the Fourth District of the U.S. Court of Appeals dissolved the preliminary injunction against Icahn. On the day of this decision, Dan River's stock jumped $2.25, to $17, suggesting that "some traders [were] willing to bet that a higher rescuing bid is in the works."

ANNOUNCEMENT OF A NEW
DEFENSE TACTIC

Nevertheless, no one expected Dan River's board to sit idly on their seats. Responding quickly, on November 23, 1982, it announced that it was talking with a possible white knight. In addition, it announced that it planned to spend up to $15 million to buy 900,000 of its own shares. Wall Street observers felt that both moves were aimed at driving up the stock price and fending off the Icahn takeover offer. The purchase was to include either shares purchased on the open market or those privately negotiated. No price was set, allowing for flexibility on the part of Dan River to beat any higher tender offer Icahn might make. In response to this latest development, one Dan River follower said:

> This is the first defensive measure they've taken. The others were stopgap measures. . . . The way I see it is that this doesn't necessarily mean another company is going to buy out Dan River. The Dan River release tells me that they'd like to keep the company intact.

The purchase of the 900,000 shares, 15.5 percent of the common outstanding, was to be financed through short-term borrowing on existing credit lines. The shares reportedly would be held in the Dan River treasury to be used "for any proper corporate purpose including possible sale to one or more parties." Dan River confirmed that "stock purchases would be for the purpose of aiding the company's efforts to oppose the Icahn offer. . .and to reduce the number of shares that may be available for purchase by the Icahn group."

The day before, on the New York Stock Exchange, Dan River closed at $18 a share. Although Wall Street believed that the price wasn't high enough to foil the Icahn offer of $16.50 a share, the announcement was seen as a promise to Dan River shareholders that Dan River would pay more than that offered by Icahn. It was also felt that speculators who had tendered to Icahn's $16.50 a share offer were at an increased risk of missing out on any additional premium if Dan River were to agree to a takeover at a higher price.

Outraged by this latest development, the Icahn group amended its pending court case against Dan River, charging that Dan River's management was working on a "scheme" and that its buying blitz constituted an illegal tender offer under federal law. This anger was compounded by the fact that by midnight, November 22, the day of the Dan River announcement and the expiration date of the Icahn offer, the number of shares tendered to Icahn had decreased. At this point, the Icahn group extended its $16.50 offer by one week. Between November 24, 1982 and December 16, 1982, Dan River purchased approximately 7.7 million of its own shares at an average price of $18.01 per share.

CARL ICAHN GETS A NOTE FROM HOME

"STAY OUT" read a message sent to Icahn from the Danville, Virginia, community where Dan River is located. The conservative town was in full support of Dan River fighting off the Icahn group tender offer. Twenty local businesspeople devised a strategy with the theme "Keep Dan River in Danville, buy Dan River stock." The strategy was a success in that it lured many new investors into the market for the first time. Many of the calls received were reported to be preceded by "I've never bought stock before, but I have this much money to spend. . . ." One of the businesspeople remarked "We hope enough people buy to keep the price over his offering." Indeed, as of Monday, December 6 only 181,424 shares had accepted the Icahn tender offer. Perhaps feeling frustrated by these kinds of tactics is what prompted Icahn and his associates into boosting their bid to $18 a share. This new offer was extended to midnight, December 26, 1982, and was contingent on the Icahn group receiving at least 2 million shares.

THE BRITISH COME TO THE RESCUE

On December 14, it seemed Dan River had cause to be hopeful again. Kidder, Peabody brought in McDonough Co., a subsidiary of a British textile manufacturer, as a buyer of 8 percent of Dan River stock. McDonough previously had bought a position in Avondale Mills, unaware that it would get involved in a takeover battle. It switched its sights to Dan River because Dan River was now in a position to look favorably at a white knight. Dan River announced that McDonough bought 5.8

million shares of Treasury stock at $18.50 per share. The $8.8 million in proceeds from the sale would supplement the Dan River war chest to buy back more stock. McDonough's price was $0.50 higher than Icahn's most recent offer, and $1.75 above the market close on December 13.

The agreement between Dan River and McDonough implied that the two would work together on exploring the possibility of McDonough acquiring the remainder of Dan River's outstanding shares. However, according to a Dan River statement, there was no assurance that McDonough would acquire Dan River, and as a result, it planned to continue to develop other offers.

Carl Icahn's response to the McDonough deal was a new offer at $21 per share for all of Dan River's outstanding shares. Playing it safe, the offer was conditioned on his obtaining the needed financing within 30 days and Dan River releasing to him certain financial information.

It appears that the very information that Icahn wanted was what prevented McDonough from considering Dan River as a possible mate for very long. In its amended filing with the SEC, McDonough revealed confidential information on Dan River which Kidder, Peabody had forwarded to them. This information included the following Dan River projections: net income would be $7.1 million in 1982, $19.6 million in 1983, $30.9 million in 1984, but slipping to $28.8 million in 1985. Capital spending was also scheduled at levels above $30 million for the following three years. Dan River planned to achieve these results by restructuring some of its operations, including closing its mill in Burlington, North Carolina, and its plant in Chickamuaga, Georgia, as well as by benefiting from an improved economic climate and a general recovery for the textile industry as a whole. Along with these projections, McDonough disclosed it "believes that Dan River's management presently intends to make fewer [asset] dispositions than those contemplated in the report which Dan River forwarded to McDonough via Kidder. The result would be expected to show higher sales, a lower reduction of total debt and lower net income than set forth in the projections."

A NEW WEAPON TO FEND OFF ICAHN

On December 29, 1982, in an attempt to put a permanent end to the continuing battle between Dan River and the Icahn group, Dan River announced a plan for its employees to buy the company for $22.50 a share. The proposal involved creating a holding company in which an employee stock ownership plan (ESOP) would be the largest shareholder. However, the merger was subject to the approval of the board and two thirds of all voting securities. On January 5, 1983, Dan River's board approved in principal the proposed ESOP buyout. The board also announced that it had appointed a committee of outside directors to review the fairness of the proposal and to negotiate the details of the proposed merger. The board emphasized that the plans for the merger could be terminated if a more favorable offer was received before the merger was completed.

By January 13, 1983, the Icahn group, following the 10th extension of its tender offer deadline, held 836,030 shares, a 30 percent stake in Dan River. One reporter noted that "the series of extensions relates to a waiting game Mr. Icahn is believed to be playing while Dan River proceeds with [the arrangements for the financing of the ESOP]." In an attempt to settle all litigation between Dan River and Icahn, the two parties agreed, subject to court approval, to a truce until September 15, 1983. This agreement barred Icahn from buying or selling Dan River shares except under the provisions that were set forth in the agreement. In addition, the Icahn group could not "solicit proxies or seek representation on Dan River's board," and would not "assist any other party from doing anything that it is prohibited from doing." Dan River, on the other hand, agreed that "it would not buy any of its own shares, and would not authorize or issue any new class of equity securities." It was reported that the standstill agreement would not affect the company's plans to go private in the meantime "if the directors and the shareholders decided to go that route."

THE ESOP

In early December 1982, representatives of Kelso & Co., approached Dan River with the possibility of a leveraged buyout using an ESOP as the financing vehicle. At Dan River's request, Kelso conducted a study and determined that a price of $22.50 per share of series A common stock, $3.25 per share of series B common stock, and $1.10 per share of preferred was feasible as well as fair to stockholders. It was noted that the price on the series A shares was almost 50 percent higher than the 15½ per share at which it was trading on September 16, 1982, the last day prior to Icahn's SEC filing and was higher than the $18 a share offered by the Icahn Group. The price determined by Kelso was also based on the fact that Dan River had recently closed at its all-time high of 22⅛ per share.

The buyout plan was structured so that Dan River, Inc., would become a subsidiary of a new holding company, the Dan River Holding Company. Ownership of the Holding Company would be divided among the ESOP (71 percent), a management group consisting of certain directors (25 percent), and Kelso & Co. (4 percent).

The scheme called for the ESOP to borrow the majority of the funds needed for the share purchase, with Dan River guaranteeing the loan using the stock as collateral. As the loan is repaid from funds contributed by Dan River to the ESOP, shares would be released to the participants' individual accounts. At the completion of the merger, the ESOP was planned to replace all existing pension plans. Employees of Dan River would become eligible for participation in the ESOP after one year of service, conditioned on at least 1,000 hours of work. Present employees' past service would be counted for eligibility and vesting, and each individual account would be vested at a rate of 10 percent a year. At retirement, death, total disability, or termination, each member's account would be paid in full. The plan stipulated that each employee be given the option to sell the stock back to the ESOP at the fair market price.

FINANCING OF THE ESOP

Of the total $153.9 million that was required to pay the present stockholders, $148.89 million was expected to be obtained through a term loan from Chemical Bank to the holding company. The remaining $5 million would be raised through the issuance of equity securities to the Kelso firm and the management group. The term loan would bear interest at the higher of Chemical Bank's prime rate plus 1

Structure of the Deal

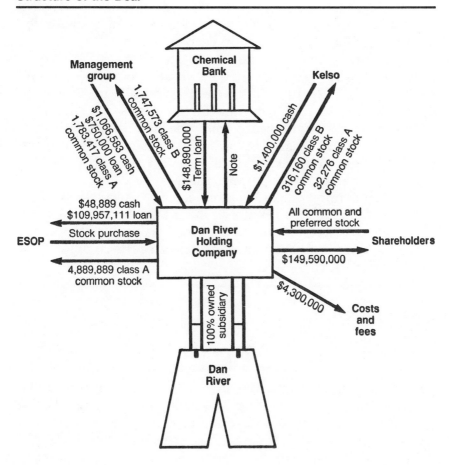

percent or its certificate of deposit rate. Repayment of $49 million of the term loan was required by September 30, 1983, and funds for this were expected to be obtained through:

- The issuance of 10.5 million in preferred stock to the profit sharing plan, and 2.5 million to the Dan River's tax reduction act stock ownership plan (TRASOP).
- A federal income tax refund of $20 million.
- The recapture of approximately $16 million in excess assets from terminated pension plans.

The plan called for the ESOP to purchase 4.89 million shares of class A stock at a price of $22.50 a share. Financing for this would be through a 15-year 9 percent note for $109.95 million and $48,889 in cash.

The management group would purchase 1.74 million shares of class B stock for $2.06 a share. Financing for this would be with $1 million in cash, $750,000 in 10-year 9 percent notes, and $1.8 million in common stock valued at $22.50 a share. Eight years from the date of its issuance, each share of this class B stock would be convertible into one share of class A stock. This device is frequently used to encourage management performance.

The remaining 33,276 shares of class A stock and the 316,160 shares of class B stock would then be purchased by Kelso & Co. at $22.50 and $2.06, respectively. The Structure of the Deal diagram on page 343 illustrates the complexity of the transaction.

THE DECISION

On May 25, 1983, the fate of Dan River was at last decided. Holders of about 5.4 million shares, or 70.23 percent of the voting shares, approved the buyout proposal, allowing the company to be purchased by its employees. Although Icahn controlled 22 percent of the voting shares, he abstained from voting on the merger proposal "because of the possible application of federal securities laws." Specifically, in question was the rule that requires large stockholders to forfeit profits on sales of shares held less than six months. By abstaining from voting, this provision was rendered inapplicable. Two days later, the Virginia State Corporate Commission issued the Certificate of Merger of Dan River into the employee-owned Dan River Holding Company.

WHO WINS? WHO LOSES?

Dan River proxy material stated the following:

> It is expected that by providing the Holding Company ESOP with a substantial equity interest, employees' productivity and morale will be improved since the employees will have direct financial interest in Dan River and their retirement and similar benefits will depend primarily upon the performance of Dan River...the merger would also assure that Dan River will remain intact as an ongoing business enterprise.

It seemed like Dan River's story exemplified the American dream. Not exactly so. Nearly two years after the merger, *Business Week* interviewed dozens of salaried employees at Dan River and found that "there is a near unanimous feeling that the majority ownership has not produced even token democracy in the workplace." They also noted that it had failed to strengthen job security. Dan River's work force in 1985 was reduced to 8,000 from the 12,000 that it employed in 1983. Ironically, it was Dan River's management that convinced the employees that an Icahn takeover would eliminate many of their jobs. It also appears that many of the workers could not figure out specifically what the ESOP provided them in terms of their pensions, and in general many of them felt that "they just got took."

As often happens, the dealmakers did not lose. As illustrated by the Paychecks of the Dealmakers table, the estimated costs and fees for the ESOP totaled $4.3 million.

Kelso & Co. received $900,000 for its services and Kidder, Peabody & Co. received over $1.2 million. Another party who walked away from the ESOP buyout smiling was Carl Icahn. He made an estimated $8 million profit from the shares he

DAN RIVER
The Paychecks of the Dealmakers*

Goldman Sachs	$ 350,000
Kidder, Peabody	1,296,000
Kelso	900,000
Legal fees	700,000
Accounting fees	25,000
Proxy solicitation fees	25,000
Printing and mailing	300,000
Disbursing agent fees	125,000
Bank transaction fees	375,000
Miscellaneous	204,000
Total	$4,300,000

*Estimated fees and other transaction costs.

sold back to Dan River. Dan River's management may have maintained control of its company, but it sure looked as though Icahn had won again!

The Sharks and the Blue Bell ESOP: Playing in the Big Leagues with the Bass Brothers and the Belzbergs

WRANGLING THROUGH THE DEMOGRAPHICS

By 1983, Blue Bell was a company in a difficult position. The blue jean maker, best known for its Wrangler, Jansen, Rustler, and Red Cap labels, was in an industry that had peaked. The 1970s were a period of explosive growth in the jeans

We appreciate the research, analysis, and writing done by Mary Ellen Eagan and Janet Kracke. Without their very significant contribution, the completion of the Blue Bell case would not have been possible.

business. It was a time when anyone over 30 remembers jeans as the only pants he owned. The industry continued to grow through 1981, when a movie called "Urban Cowboy" spurred the nation's highest ever sales of blue jeans. Jeans makers thought the boom would never end and responded to the anticipated demand by increasing production. However, the boom did end. Jeans sales dropped dramatically. From peak sales of 588.8 million pairs in 1981, up 8.1 percent from 1980, sales declined 4.8 percent in 1982 and remained level in 1983. Analysts at the time predicted that demand was likely to remain flat.

This forecast can be attributed in part to demographics. The baby boomers had grown up, got married, moved to the suburbs, and put on "slacks." They once wore jeans to school but they weren't wearing them to work. There was also a decline in the youth population, the group most likely to wear jeans. In fact, by 1995, the 18- to 24-year-old group was expected to drop by 23 percent.

Another major contributing factor was the shift from basic blue jeans to designer fashions. While the introduction of high fashion into the jeans industry made the situation unstable, analysts said fashion jeans represented the industry's best chance for growth. As a result of these factors, the jeans industry has gone from a stable and secure business to one that is significantly riskier and more competitive.

Faced with flat sales, jeans makers tried to create new growth by cutting themselves a larger piece of the existing pie through aggressive marketing and fierce competition.

For Blue Bell, which together with Levi Strauss and Lee represented about 42.5 percent of unit sales in the United States, it meant that although earnings were up, sales had fallen and Blue Bell was replaced by Lee as the number 2 jeans maker. Their respective market shares were Levi with 21 percent, Lee with 12 percent, and Blue Bell with 9.5 percent.

In 1983, Blue Bell's sales were the lowest in four years. Although profits were up from the previous two years, they remained well below peak levels. Its stock price ranged roughly in the neighborhood of Blue Bell's $35.44 book value at the end of 1983, and \$33.75 at the end of 1982. Still, Blue Bell was a fairly liquid firm. From 1981 to 1983, it reduced its debt as a percentage of shareholders' equity from 40 to 22 percent. At the end of 1983, it had \$111 million in unused lines of credit, and its liquidity did not go unnoticed.

AN UNINVITED GUEST

Not surprisingly, the Bass Brothers took an interest in the company. By the latter part of 1983, they had acquired about 24 percent of Blue Bell's outstanding stock. Although in their filing with the Securities and Exchange Commission they claimed that the purchase was for investment purposes, their presence made management extremely nervous. In response, management attempted to remedy the situation.

In November 1983, Blue Bell worked a greenmail deal with the Bass Brothers. It bought back 1.9 million shares of its common stock for about \$90.1 million, or \$47.50 per share. In addition, Blue Bell was granted an option to purchase additional shares. On March 30, 1984, as a result of the option, Blue Bell announced it had acquired another 1.1 million shares or 9.9 percent of the shares outstanding from the Bass Brothers at a 40 percent premium over the \$36.25 market price.

The Bass Brothers' group average cost was about \$32.00 per share, giving them a profit of close to \$50 million. In justifying the ransom paid to the greenmailers, Blue Bell said it acted out of concern "about anyone having that kind of ownership with a different business philosophy than we have." It stated that the Fort Worth-based Bass Brothers' group was made up of "financial people. They don't know anything about running a manufacturing business. . . "

MORE VISITORS

No sooner had Blue Bell breathed a sigh of relief when the new sharks appeared. The Belzberg brothers, Canadian financiers, began to acquire the stock through First City

Financial Corp., a corporation the Belzbergs controlled and often use in their raids.

This caused Edward Bauman, chairman of Blue Bell, to consider taking the firm private. Bauman contacted Kelso & Co., a New York-based investment firm whose specialty is buyouts financed through employee stock ownership plans (ESOP). In May 1984, Blue Bell announced that it was considering a $494.1 million leveraged buyout, at $50.00 a share, using an ESOP. The proposal would involve Blue Bell's acquisition by a newly formed company that would be owned by the Blue Bell employees through an ESOP, by members of the management and by Kelso & Co. The market liked the news. Following the announcement, Blue Bell stock closed up 8⅛ at $49.75.

Immediately afterward, the Belzbergs announced that they had increased their holdings in Blue Bell to 9.2 percent. In a filing with the SEC, First City Financial said it had several conversations with Kelso representatives and lawyers representing certain Blue Bell managers. These discussions involved the possibility that the Belzberg group might be interested in providing financing or participating as an investor in the buyout. However, it was also stated that "no understanding had been reached." Blue Bell for its part understood perfectly. They did not want the Belzbergs any more than they wanted the Bass Brothers. First City Financial said the Blue Bell shares were acquired as an investment. In addition, it filed with the SEC for government antitrust clearance to buy as much as 40 percent of the company. This move was clearly designed to put pressure on Blue Bell to invite the Belzbergs to take part in the buyout. However, Ed Bauman said the Belzbergs' assistance would come at "a terrible price. I think government regulators should do something about greenmail. The average little stockholders are getting ripped off."

In July, Kenneth E. Tutterow, Blue Bell's vice president for finance said the firm had agreed in principal to go private for $469.9 million or $47.50 a share. The price was reduced from $50.00 a share to $47.50 because of potential difficulties in obtaining financing at the higher price. There was concern among potential creditors. The financial concern evolved around the debt level, and the operating concern focused on the softness of the jeans market. The agreement was authorized by the special committee of independent directors, organized specifically for this purpose. However, as often is the case, the agreement was conditioned on definitive financing and other procedural arrangements. The total cost of the proposal would be $650 million, of which a significant portion would be debt. This cost included refinancing Blue Bell's debt. At the time, Blue Bell carried long-term debt of $72 million.

Following the announcement of the $47.50 offer, it didn't take long for two separate lawsuits to appear. Naturally, they charged that the price was too low. In August, Blue Bell agreed to raise the price by 15 cents to $47.65, pending court approval. The suits were subsequently dropped.

At a special shareholder meeting in late October, the $47.65 offer to take the company private was approved. In November 1984, the firm went private and the Belzbergs sold their 9.2 percent stake back to Blue Bell for $43.2 million or $47.65 a share. Interestingly, since they bought their last block of 50,000 shares at approximately $50 a share, they sold it at a loss.

Essentially, Blue Bell was acquired by 53 members of management, the Kelso group and the ESOP. Management was to receive 24.7 percent of the company, or a total of 900,000 shares of common. They were to pay $10 a share, of which $1.1 million was paid in cash and $3.3 million was financed by a loan from the company at the below market rate of 9 percent. The rest was payable through paper transactions involving the surrender of Blue Bell common stock and stock options from the employee incentive plan previously held by management. With the proceeds of a loan, the ESOP bought $67 million worth of stock. This included the purchase of 100 percent of the preferred and 32.8 percent of the common.

However, the golden path for going private was not yet cleared. The Department of Labor objected on the grounds that the ESOP's stock ownership was determined by the company, rather than by arms' length bargaining with the ESOP, management, and the investors. It claimed that the managers were being unduly enriched at the ESOP's expense. As a result, Blue Bell changed the ownership percentages. In the final analysis management received 21 percent and the ESOP walked away with 37 percent. The Kelso group also received 140,000 shares, or 3.8 percent. When the dollars and percentages were added up, management received their 21 percent ownership of the common stock for $9 million, the Kelso group received 3.8 percent ownership for $1.4 million, and the ESOP received its 37 percent of the common and 100 percent of the preferred for a whopping $67 million.

Interestingly, under the new organization, the directors remained in control. Certain members of the board were appointed to the ESOP's Administrative Committee which was to direct the trustee as to how to vote the ESOP shares of stock. This effectively placed the directors in a position to control the firm until a better deal came along.

EPILOGUE

In 1986, that better deal did come along. Blue Bell, which had previously spurned offers from the Bass Brothers and the Belzbergs, agreed to be acquired by VF, the manufacturer of Lee Jeans. The acquisition set the stage for a shootout between Levi with a 24 percent share of the $6 billion jeans market and the combined Wrangler, Rustler, and Lee brands with an identical combined share. After all their battles against unwanted suitors, Blue Bell must have felt this $775 million deal was too snug a fit to reject.

The Labor Department versus Management: The Case of the Scott & Fetzer ESOP

Scott & Fetzer's chief executive officer, Ralph Schey, could finally relax. The company had finally been acquired in a friendly takeover by Berkshire Hathaway, a Chicago-based insurance holding company. The acquisition ended a year-and-a-half saga of attempted takeovers of the cash rich conglomerate by an in-house management group, then by Ivan Boesky, and then most painfully through a leveraged buyout involving a company employee stock ownership plan (ESOP) that was halted by the Department of Labor. This was one of the first cases in which the Labor Department stepped in to stop an ESOP leveraged buyout. Their argument was that the ESOP was not receiving its fair share of the company's equity. Scott & Fetzer learned just how expensive the use of an ESOP can be.

A LOOK AT THE TAKEOVER BIDS

Scott & Fetzer was a conglomerate that grew through acquisition. It appeared to be a good candidate for a leveraged buyout. As of February 29, 1984, it had a strong balance sheet, which included $97 million in cash and short-term investments. In addition, a low debt-equity ratio gave the company borrowing power. Moreover, some subsidiary businesses such as World Book were strong cash producers, since only modest investment was required to support its sales and profits.

On April 14, 1984, Scott & Fetzer's board received a leveraged buyout proposal from Savannah Inc. for $50 per share or $350 million. Savannah was organized by a Scott &

We appreciate the research, analysis, and writing done by Tom Murphy. Without his very significant contribution, the completion of the Scott & Fetzer case would not have been possible.

Fetzer management group led by Ralph Schey. The group had retained Manufacturers Hanover as their adviser and expected to finance the purchase mostly through loans from a group of banks and insurance companies. The proposal involved the merging of a wholly owned subsidiary of Savannah into Scott & Fetzer. Scott & Fetzer (S&F) retained First Boston as its financial adviser to evaluate the proposal.

AN UNEXPECTED PLAYER

On April 26, 1984, Ivan F. Boesky, then operator of one of Wall Street's best-known and most profitable risk arbitrage firms, filed a Schedule 13D with the SEC. Before revelation of the insider trading scandal, *The Wall Street Journal* described Mr. Boesky as, "a 43-year-old lawyer, amateur theologian and educator who has become Wall Street's most successful takeover speculator." He had been called the "king of the New York takeover stock speculators or risk arbitrage, and had run up the capital of the limited investment partnership managed by Ivan F. Boesky & Co. from $700,000 in 1974 to a rumored $100 million at the end of 1980." His SEC filing disclosed that the Boesky Group had purchased a 5.4 percent stake in S&F, which totaled 357,100 common shares. The filing also revealed that Boesky was "considering the possibility and desirability of acquiring" the company. It was indicated that Boesky had verbally informed First Boston of his interest in making a proposal to acquire S&F in a leveraged buyout transaction for $60 per share, making the total offer more than $400 million.

On the same day, Savannah withdrew its proposal citing that its lenders were unwilling to provide additional debt financing to fund an offer higher than $60 per share. The lenders felt that this additional cost would increase the post-transaction debt burden beyond acceptable limits.

On April 26, the Boesky Group sent a letter to S&F, formally proposing acquisition of the outstanding common shares for $60 a piece. The proposal was subject to the following conditions:

- The Boesky Group's ability to obtain sufficient financing to consummate the transaction.
- S&F's granting the Boesky Group an additional stock purchase option.
- S&F agreeing to pay the Boesky Group a cancellation fee of $4 million if the transaction were terminated as a result of S&F's acceptance of another offer to purchase all or a substantial part of its assets. This implied that the S&F should not solicit or encourage other proposals.
- Current S&F management be offered the opportunity to acquire 15 percent of the equity in the new company.

Two weeks went by before S&F's board met with First Boston and the company's legal advisers to discuss the Boesky proposal. The directors unanimously rejected the proposal, citing "significant uncertainties and conditions relating to the proposal." The primary uncertainty involved Boesky's ability to secure commitments for the required financing. Other unacceptable conditions were the cancellation fee and Boesky's request for options to purchase additional common stock.

A week later the Boesky Group responded by modifying its original proposal, eliminating the stock purchase option and the cancellation fee. Boesky proposed that negotiations begin, conceding that S&F would be free to solicit other offers during the negotiations. Once the Boesky Group had firm financing commitments, S&F would be expected to stop encouraging other offers.

The board then met again with First Boston and the company's legal advisers to consider the revised Boesky proposal. Once again, the proposal was rejected. This time the rejection was based on First Boston's opinion that the Boesky Group lacked the ability to secure the necessary financing. The board concluded that "the Boesky proposal as presently constituted doesn't have sufficient financial credibility." *The Wall Street Journal* speculated that "Mr. Schey [CEO of S&F] shunted Mr. Boesky's offer in hopes of reviving his own bid." The board did authorize First Boston to begin an inquiry among qualified prospective purchasers for a more credible offer of $60 or more per share.

BOESKY GROUP OUT, BUT CONTINUES
TO SPECULATE

Apparently unable to secure the required financing, Boesky gave up his takeover bid. While much happened in the intervening period, on October 15, the Boesky Group filed an amended Schedule 13D with the SEC, disclosing that it had decreased its shareholdings to 227,100 common shares, amounting to 3.4 percent of the then outstanding shares. Continuing the speculation game, on February 24, 1985, the group filed a new Schedule 13D, indicating that it beneficially owned an aggregate of 366,800 common shares or 5.5 percent of the outstanding common shares. However, in both filings the Boesky Group indicated that such common shares were "not held for the present purpose of acquiring control" of S&F.

COMPANY CONTINUES ITS SEARCH
FOR A SUITOR

Since the revised Boesky proposal was rejected, First Boston continued to seek potential buyers for S&F. In early July 1984, the company sent out publicly available company information to approximately 30 companies. Some were solicited by First Boston, while others such as the Boesky Group were independent inquiries. Sixteen of the potential suitors requested additional information. Upon completing a confidentiality agreement, 12 of the companies were provided with unpublished business and financial data. The company held discussions with several prospective buyers. However, it became apparent that only those who could take advantage of tax benefits from losses (to offset S&F's earnings) would be able to justify the acquisition price of $60 cash per share. In the fall of 1984, two companies remained in serious acquisition discussions with S&F. Management felt that both companies would be able to shield taxable income by utilizing substantial net operating losses carried forward. The companies involved were Triangle Industries, a manufacturer and distributor of vending machines, wires and cables, and Itel

Corp., a firm engaged in equipment leasing. Although several discussions were held, no definite agreements were ever reached.

While management was preoccupied with the prospective buyers, several stockholders' representatives were starting to express their concern about the company's search for a purchaser. Some suggested that the best way for the stockholders to realize the value of their investment was to break up the company and sell the assets and subsidiaries separately. In September 1984, the board considered the breakup alternative, as well as the possibility of a complete liquidation. It determined that "the potentially adverse tax consequences of the sale of assets and businesses of the company might significantly reduce the net proceeds that could be distributed to shareholders and therefore it did not seem to be an attractive alternative." The adverse tax consequences involved corporate income taxes, which would be paid if individual assets were sold. These taxes would be avoided in an LBO.

ANOTHER ALTERNATIVE—THE USE OF AN EMPLOYEE STOCK OWNERSHIP PLAN (ESOP)

Back in June 1984, Kelso & Company, a leading investment bank specializing in ESOP-financed LBOs, appeared on the stage. It approached First Boston with a proposal that S&F enter into an exclusive agreement with Kelso to structure a leveraged buyout of the company utilizing an ESOP. Management was interested. They met with Kelso to explore the concept, but rejected the notion of an exclusive agreement so they could also explore other alternatives.

Since management expressed continued interest in the ESOP concept, Kelso approached General Electric Credit Corporation (GECC) proposing that it arrange the required debt financing. On September 27, 1984 management retained Kelso for $250,000. Their charter was to study the feasibility of structuring an ESOP-financed leveraged buyout which would meet the minimum $60 stock price requirement set by the board. Kelso then retained GECC to develop a proposal to finance such a transaction.

On November 1, 1984, Kelso proposed a plan to S&F in which a corporation set up by Kelso, employing ESOP financing, would acquire all outstanding common stock at a price of $61 each, or a total of $435 million. Kelso also presented a proposal from GECC to provide the debt financing required to complete the deal. Kelso's proposal was considered to be friendly and intended to invite management to participate in the transaction. It was also contingent on obtaining an agreement in principle by November 8. Concurrently, Itel had verbally informed the company that it was exploring the possible acquisition of the company at a price of $63 per share. S&F's board met to review the proposals. In a press release, the company stated that it was reviewing various proposals and "given the serious nature of these proposals it would not be in the best interests of S&F shareholders not to make a determination about the Kelso proposal at this time." Though the company continued discussions with Itel, a definite proposal was never made. After a meeting with the board on November 27, Itel announced it was no longer interested in the acquisition. Speculation in the market was growing, with one arbitrager quoted as saying "S&F's board can't afford not to let somebody buy the company at this point." He reasoned that if the company blows three bids, the board and management could face litigation and possibly a proxy fight. Another individual close to the situation asked "what would they do at their annual meeting next year if they haven't got a deal by then?"

On December 6, management further retained Kelso to assist S&F in structuring a buyout using the company's ESOP, in which the shareholders would receive at least $62 per share. Kelso was also to obtain debt financing similar to their original proposal, as well as to provide the equity financing. Kelso's retainer was $500,000 with an additional $100,000 for retaining GECC. The agreement also specified that certain members of management would be offered equity interests. However, there were no required levels of management participation. Since management saw no other prospective buyers, they signed an exclusive agreement with Kelso which included a $2.5 million penalty fee if other arrangements were actively pursued by the company.

Continuous negotiations were carried out between the company, Kelso, and GECC. On February 13, 1985, the board met to review a financing plan, written and verbally presented by Kelso representatives. The plan included GECC's commitment to provide up to $500 million in debt. The financing was needed for completing the transaction, retiring existing debt, and providing working capital required in the post-buyout period. It also included Kelso's commitment to finance or arrange financing of 100 percent of the equity required by GECC. At this board meeting First Boston verbally expressed its opinion that the consideration received by the stockholder in this proposed merger was fair from a financial point of view. After private discussions among the nonmanagement members, the full board of directors unanimously approved the proposal, with some further details to be arranged.

Negotiations were then continued in order to resolve and finalize the remaining issues which included the structure of the ESOP, other equity participants in the merger, and the terms and financing of the debt. The Citizens and Southern National Bank was chosen by the board to be the trustee for the company's ESOP. Houlihan, Lokey, Howard and Zukin Inc. was named as the independent valuation consultant and financial consultant for the ESOP. The final agreement was approved by the stockholders and on July 5, 1985 it was unanimously approved by the board.

THE DEPARTMENT OF LABOR STEPS IN

In late July, the Department of Labor informed the company that it was reviewing the buyout plan and had some concerns about the terms of the ESOP's participation in the transaction. Although the Labor Department's approval was not required for an LBO, it was required for the set-up and use of an employee stock ownership plan. Under the Employee

Retirement Income Security Act (ERISA), the Labor Department was empowered to ensure that ESOPs were set up as Congress stated, "primarily for the benefit of plan partici pants and beneficiaries." GECC's financing plan required the absence of litigation or threat of litigation by the Labor Department. Basically, the Labor Department argued that the ESOP was getting too small an equity share, considering its investment. A *Barron's* article described the situation as follows: "Under the terms, investors brought into the deal by Kelso were to get an 8.5 percent equity position for $6 million; management would get 20 percent for $9 million, and General Electric Credit Corp., the lender for the transaction, would take 30 percent for $407 million, leaving the ESOP 41 percent for $182 million raised via a tax-sheltered loan. At least on paper, that meant that the investors were to get slightly more than one fifth as much equity as the ESOP, while paying less than one thirtieth as much, and managers were to get about half as much equity as the ESOP, while putting up one twentieth as much."

Richard Bensinger, who was an employee union representative, also objected to the high fees paid to organize the buyout, and to the employees' inability to control the stock plan by selecting the trustee. The company also faced a tax filing deadline of August 15, relating to the company's ESOP contribution. In response to the Labor Department's concern, Kelso worked out a new structure which would give the ESOP 50.1 percent, Kelso 14.8 percent, management 1.1 percent with the option for an additional 4 percent depending on the company's performance, and GECC would still have warrants to buy 30 percent. Although the new terms were acceptable to the Labor Department, they had to be approved by stockholders. The company also had to complete all requirements of the GECC financing arrangement before it could be secured. There was little time to complete all requirements prior to the August 15 tax filing deadline relating to the company's contribution to the employee stock plan. Management decided that it would not make the $25 million contribution unless the financing had been secured. This essentially allowed the deal to die in its tracks. *Barron's* stated that "it was the first time, after two years of threats and bickering in prior ESOP buyouts, that the agency's [Labor Department's] stand had scotched a deal."

Then on October 29, 1985, the board agreed to be acquired by Berkshire Hathaway for $60 per share, or $402 million. Berkshire Hathaway is headed by the well-known, 55-year-old billionaire investor, Warren Buffett. Buffett's investment strategy is primarily "asset-based investment, buying cheap by exploiting the difference between the share price and the higher asset values of a business." Buffett offered to pay all the fees that were involved in the attempted ESOP-LBO, including Kelso's bill of $2.7 million.

Before the deal was concluded, Scott & Fetzer was sued by a holder seeking to block the proposed sale. The suit sought to prevent certain officers from receiving "grossly excessive, outrageous and illegal" golden parachutes and to recover "substantial" sums of corporate funds "wasted by the improper activities" of the company. But a week after the suit, Scott & Felzer shareholders approved the deal. Buffett slightly upped the ante and shareholders walked away with $60.77 a share.

INDEX

A

Acquisition agreement
  asset lockups, 241
  contingent clauses in, 238–39
  defined, 238
  expenses and fees in, 240
  fiduciary-out termination, 240
  litigation-out provision, 241
  no-shopping clause, 163–64,
    239–40
  security fund provision in, 230
  stock lockups, 240
Adjusted book value method,
  42–43, 65–66, 85–86
Adler and Shaykin, 160–61, 167
Advance rates, 184
Alliance Capital Management
  Corporation, 136
American Home Products, 160–61,
  167
Antidilution protection, 258
ARA Services, 9–13
Arcanum 1 Partners, 98, 101–3
Armstrong, Richard, 79, 83, 95
Ash, Mary Kay, 115–17
Asset valuation method, 43–44

B

Bankers Trust, 16, 31, 74
Bank of New York, 36

Barclays American Business
  Credit, Inc., 27–28
Bauer, John, 134, 145
Beatrice Foods, 45, 51, 54, 245, 247
Bendix Forest Products, 39
Bennett, Robert, 5
Bergerac, Michel C., 52, 147, 150,
  154, 160, 162, 168
Berkshire Hathaway, 260, 352
Beta factor
  defined, 49
  in leveraged buyout targets,
    221–22
  relevering, 49–50
  unlevering, 49–50
Blue Bell, 298, 321, 346–51
Boesky, Ivan F., 95, 143, 352–55
Boot
  defined, 262
  in Type A merger, 265
  in Type B merger, 272
  in Type C merger, 274
Bootstrap financing, 2; see also
  Leveraged buyouts
Booz Allen & Hamilton Inc., 115
Boston Ventures Management, 5–6,
  40
Brazell, Carl, Jr., 8–9
Brentano's, Inc., 34–37, 55
Brentwood Associates, 192
Buchsbaum, Michael, 43, 53–54,
  97–108, 113–14

Buffett, Warren, 191, 360
Bunker, John, 101
Bushnell, John, 101, 114

C

Capital Asset Pricing Model
   (CAPM), 49, 122
Cash flow generation analysis,
   216–20
Cash flow valuation method, 86–89
   and asset value, 47, 50
   base case determination, 67–70
   and cost of capital, 48–49, 72–73
   cost of debt, 70–71
   and cost of equity, 48–49, 71–72
   defined, 46
   discount rate determination,
      70–73
   growth formula, 47–48
   and net income, 46
Castle & Cooke, 84, 88, 90–93
Chambers, Ray, 25–30
Chase Manhattan Bank, 31, 74
Chemical Bank, 12, 152, 343
Citibank, 63, 330
Citicorp Venture Capital, 91
Cizik, Robert, 591–92
Clayton Dubilier, 42
Clements, W. W., 52, 76-79, 82–83,
   92–93
Comcast Inc., 142–46
Conair Corporation, 259–61
Coniston Partners, 133–39, 141
Cooke, Jack Kent, 5
Cooney, Thomas M., 26, 30
Cross-collateralized loans, 184

D

Dan River, 297, 309, 316, 331–46
Dart & Kraft, 30–34
Data Probe Acquisition v. *Datatab*,
   241
Davis, Marvin, 5, 8
Davis, Robert, 55
Dean, Tom, 104–5

Dean Witter, 172
Debt-to-equity ratios
   analysis, 204–5
   range of, 2 39–40
Deficit Reduction Act of 1984,
   302-3
Denny's Inc., 171–74, 180–81
Depreciation, 217
Dillon, Read & Co., 138, 143–44
Divisional spin-offs, 171, 173–74,
   219, 310
Dominick & Dominick, 30–34, 40
Donaldson, Lufkin and Jenrette,
   136
Doyle, Joseph J., 78
DPCC Acquisition Corp., 51, 76,
   83–84, 86, 88, 90–94
Drexel Burnham Lambert, 7–8,
   14–16, 40, 84, 91, 152, 177–78,
   245
Dr Pepper Company
   leveraged buyout of, 51–52,
      75–96, 188, 191, 240
   valuing of
      adjusted book value, 85–86
      cash flow, 86–89
      sensitivity analysis, 88, 90
Due diligence
   and fraudulent conveyance, 233
   and Going Private Rule, 242
   questions, 174–77
Duncan, George, 5
DuPont formula, 211–12

E

Earnings valuation method, 66–67
Edgecomb Metals Corporation,
   267–68
Employee stock ownership plans
   (ESOPs)
   administration of, 301–2
   appraisals for, 300
   cash flow advantages in, 304–5
   in closely held companies, 310–11
   combination, 298

Employee stock ownership plans
(ESOPs)—*(continued)*
and company performance,
315–17
conflicts of interest in, 318–19
distributions in, 299–301
fees involved, 309
financial incentives for, 302–5
good candidates for, 318
and hostile takeovers, 307–9, 319,
323
Labor Department involvement
in, 319–23, 358–60
leveraged, 298–99, 305–12
as leveraged buyout financing
source, 293, 297, 310–11, 317
management entrenchment, 309,
323
risks in, 317–18
stock bonus, 298
tax considerations, 303–4
valuing, 319–20
vesting policies, 300
voting rights in, 301–2
Equitable Life Assurance Society,
63, 136, 187
Equitable subordination, 226–28,
257
Equity investors
advantages for, 188–89
attractive targets for, 193–94, 197
deal structures for, 195
need for, 192
pooled leveraged buyout funds,
191–94
return for, 189–90, 192
venture capitalists, 192–93
Equity kicker, 187
Evan, Edward, 35

F

Fairness
burden of proof of, 237
and financing, 235
procedures for, 234, 237
of stock prices, 235–38

Federal Bankruptcy Code, 256
Federal regulations
Going Private Rule (13e-3),
242–43
Regulation T, 241–42
Ferguson, Ken, 36
Financing considerations
advance rates, 184
cash sources, 6–8, 16, 27–28,
63–64, 180
collateral ratios, 246
equity financing, 188–92, 247
fairness issues in, 235
fees, 183
interest rates, 39–40, 183, 185,
187, 245
loan duration, 3, 183, 185, 187
mezzanine financing, 3, 187–88
negative pledges, 185
revolving credit, 184
senior debt, 183–86, 246
strip financing, 180–82, 246
subordinate debt, 186–88, 247
and tax reform bill, 293
traditional, 180
Finkelstein, Edward S., 56–57, 60,
75
First Boston Corporation, 3, 16, 40,
189, 354–55, 358
First City Financial Corporation,
348–49
First National Bank of Boston, 268
Forstmann, Theodore J., 90, 93–94,
96, 165
Forstmann Little and Co., 41–42,
82–84, 86, 88, 90–96, 159–68,
188–89, 240
Fraudulent conveyances, 230–33,
256
Fraiden, Stephen, 52
Friese, George R., 14

G

General Electric Credit
Corporation, 27–28, 55, 63–64,
75, 105–6, 187, 322–23, 356–59

Gibson Greeting Cards, 2, 23–30, 248
Gillette, 223
Gleacher, Eric, 191–92
Goldberger, Herbert H., 14–15, 17
Goldberger, Stephen A., 14–15
Goldman, Emanuel, 82, 90
Goldman, Sachs & Co., 12, 40, 54, 57, 64
Goldring, Stanley, 106
Gollust & Tierney, 133–34, 136–37
Greenberg, William H., 31–32
Grumman Corporation, 320–21
Guilford Industries, 195–97

H

Haas, Robert B., 96
Haas, Robert H., 18–22
Hall, Nancy, 159
Handler, Mark S., 56
Hellman and Friedman, 21, 40
Hicks, Thomas O., 96
Hicks & Haas, 96
Hillibore, Inc., 35
Hollander, Carl, 36
Hollander, Monica, 35–36
Holly Sugar Corporation
  leveraged buyout of, 97–114
  valuing of, 50, 53
    adjusted book value, 107–10
    asset valuation, 43
    discounted cash flow, 46, 110–13
Hostile takeovers, 307–9, 319, 323
Houlihan, Lokey, Howard and Zukin, 358
Hughes, Joe K., 95
Hunnewell, Francis Oaker, 36–37
Hurwitz, Charles, 93, 104
Hutton, E. F., 52, 54, 177

I

Icahn, Carl, 297, 322, 331–42
Indemnification, 228–30, 256
Interest rates, 39–40, 245

Interest rates—*(continued)*
  on senior secured debt, 183
  on senior unsecured debt, 185
  on subordinate debt, 187
  usury laws regarding, 257
Investment advisers
  appraisals by, 234
  buyer's, 178
  choice of, 177–78
  as equity investors, 190–92
  fees of, 16, 177
  list of leading, 178
  role of, 40, 172–78, 182, 188–92, 233, 238
  seller's, 177–78

J

Jacobs, Irwin L., 29
Jarvie, Chuck, 77, 79
Junk bonds
  avoidance of, 189
  use of, 7–8, 245
JWK Acquisition Corporation, 5–6

K

Kelso and Company, 308, 318, 321–23, 342–46, 349, 356–60
Kidder, Peabody & Co., 336, 339–40, 345–46
Klein, Gene, 5
Klein, William, II, 52
Kluge, John W., 4–9
Kohlberg Kravis Roberts, 3, 39, 41, 51, 54–55, 139–47, 182, 190, 245, 20
Kozloff, Joseph, 161

L

Lansdowne Financial Service, 36, 40
Lazard Frères & Co., 44, 82–83, 91–93, 163, 166–67, 191, 326, 330–31
Leasing arrangements, 28

Lee, Terry, 128
Lee, Thomas H., & Co., 14–18,
    195–96
Lenders; *see also* Equity investors
  equitable subordination, 226–28
  information sources for, 185, 187
  secured, 183–84
  senior, 183–86
  subordinate, 186–88
  syndicated, 186
  unsecured, 184–86
Leverage analysis
  debt-equity ratio, 204–5
  debt to total capitalization, 204–6
  importance of, 103–4
  information sources for, 204
  times interest earned ratio, 206–8
  total debt to total assets, 205–6
Leveraged buyouts
  advantages of, 3, 21, 42, 170–71
  cash conservation strategies in,
    34, 253
  defined, 244
  disadvantages of, 3, 42
  failures of, 30, 33–34
  fairness issues in, 233–38
  federal rules regarding, 241–43
  financial structures, 245–77; *see*
    also Financing considerations
  information necessary to, 174–77,
    185, 187, 200–224, 234
  legal issues in, 225–43
  mechanics of, 42, 171–73, 179,
    244–47, 251–54, 259–61
  nepotism in, 17
  security fund provisions in, 230
  stock fluctuations during, 12,
    106–7
  targets for; *see also* Valuing
    methods
  cash flow generation of, 216–19;
    see also Cash flow valuation
    method
  characteristics, 193–94, 197,
    199, 307
  leverage analysis, 203–8
  liquidity analysis, 200–203

Leveraged buyouts—*(continued)*
  liquidity analysis—*(continued)*
    profitability analysis, 208–16
    risk analysis of, 219–24
  tax considerations in, 247–48
  timing of, 38–39
  types of, 171, 173–74, 297
    asset-based, 247–55
    early, 1–2, 8
    stock-based, 248, 255–63
    taxable, 248, 262
    tax-free, 248, 261–77
    Type A, 263–70
      forward triangular, 263,
        265–68
      reverse triangular, 265,
        268–70
    Type B, 270–73
    Type C, 274–77
Levi Strauss & Co., 18–23, 276
Levitz Furniture Co., 177–78
Lewis v. *Oppenheimer & Company,*
    235
Liability
  in asset-based transactions, 251
  insurance, 229
  in stock-based transactions,
    256–58
Lincoln Capital Management
    Company, 17
Lipton, Martin, 191
Liquidity analysis
  using acid test ratio, 201
  using current ratio, 200–201
  using quick ratio, 201
  using working capital to sales
    ratio, 201–3
Loan durations, 3
  on senior secured debt, 183
  on senior unsecured debt, 185
  on subordinate debt, 187
Lowenstein, Allen, 326

M

MacAndrews and Forbes Holding
    Inc., 101, 150–51, 153

McCombs, B. J., 9
McDonough Co., 339–40
McKinsey and Company, 326–31
Macmillan, Inc., 35–36
Macy, R. H. & Co., Inc.
   leveraged buyout of, 56–65,
      74–75, 223
   valuation analysis of
      using book value, 65–66
      using cash flow, 45–46, 67–74
      using earnings, 66–67
Management
   and company valuation,
      52–54
   conflict of interest of, 52–53
   entrenchment, 309, 323
   importance of leadership in,
      37–38
   leveraged buyout participation,
      12–14
Manufacturers Hanover Trust, 5,
   16, 31, 63, 181, 353
Marshall and Stevens, 121
Mary Kay Cosmetics
   leveraged buyout of, 115–28
   valuing of, 50
      adjusted book value, 120–21
      discounted cash flow, 121–26
      sensitivity analysis, 126–27
Master limited partnerships, 288
Meade, Daniel H., 154, 156
Meadors, Dean, 115
Merrill Lynch, Pierce, Fenner &
   Smith, Inc., 142, 171–73, 178,
   180
Metromedia Inc., 4–9
Meyers, Jesse, 81, 96
Mezzanine financiers, 3, 187–88
Milken, Michael, 7
Moore, Ed, 107–10
Morgan Guaranty Trust Co., 12,
   74, 181, 186
Morgan Stanley, 8, 40, 191
Murdock, David H., 333
Murdock, Rupert, 5, 8

N–O

National Bank of North Carolina,
   31
Negative pledges, 185
Neubauer, Joseph, 9–10, 12–13
New England Mutual Life
   Insurance Company, 63
No-shopping clause, 163–64,
   239–40
Ohran, Paul, 35–36
Oppenheimer & Co., 45–46

P

Pantry Pride, 147, 150–69
Parsons Corporation, 307–8
Paul, Weiss, Rifkind, Wharton &
   Garrison, 334
Perelman, Ronald O., 151–52, 156,
   164, 166, 169
Perenchio, Jerry, 5
Picower, Jeffery, 103–4
Poison pills, 145, 152–53
Profitability analysis
   activity ratio in, 210–11
   return on assets, 211–13
   return on equity, 212–16
   sales-based, 208–10
   total asset turnover, 210–11
Proxy statements, 239
PruCapital, 182, 196
Prudential Insurance, 6, 63, 187

R

Radaker, Byron, 53
Rath Packing Company, 317
Raymond International, 321–22
Recapture costs, 280–81
Republic Bank of Dallas, 105
Revlon Inc., 45, 52, 147–69
Revolving loans, 184
Risk analysis
   importance of, 219

Risk analysis—*(continued)*
  information sources for, 219, 221
  volatility in, 221–24
Rogers, Richard, 115
Rublin, Lauren R., 43

S

Salomon Brothers, 21–22, 40
Savannah Inc., 352–53
Schiff, Herbert H., 14
Scoa Industries, Inc., 14–18
S corporations, 285–88
Scott & Fetzer, 297, 308–9,
  322–23, 352–57, 360
Sensitivity analysis, 88, 90,
  185–86
Shearson Lehman Brothers, 15–16,
  40, 96
Shell companies
  accounting treatment of, 252–53
  and liability, 251–52, 267
Siegel, William M., 9–10
Simon, William E., 23–27, 29–30,
  248
Simonson, Bob, 53
Skadden, Arps, Slate, Meagher, &
  Flom, 101
Slater, Peter, 35
Stanwood Corporation, 43
Steinberg, Saul, 29
Stock swaps, 29
Storer, Peter, 128, 137
Storer Communications Inc.,
  128–47, 270–71
Strip financing, 180–82
Subotnick, Stuart, 5
Superior Switchboard, 317–18

T

Tax considerations; *see also* Tax
  Reform Act of 1986
  asset step-up, 280–81, 294

Tax considerations—*(continued)*
  in employee stock ownership
    plans, 303–4
  in leveraged buyout structuring,
    247–48, 290–96
  taxable mergers, 248, 262
  tax-free mergers, 248, 261, 271
    Type A, 263–70
    Type B, 270–73
    Type C, 274–77
Tax Reform Act of 1986
  Alternative Minimum Tax, 285,
    287–89
  asset step-up under, 281–82, 294
  capital gains tax under, 285
  and closely held corporations,
    282, 293
  corporate tax rates under, 285
  dividends received deduction,
    289
  effect on buyers, 295–96
  effect on leveraged buyouts, 3,
    42, 255, 264, 290–96
  effect on sellers, 295–96
  employee stock ownership plans
    under, 303–4
  and the General Utilities
    doctrine, 279–81, 287
  greenmail payments under, 290
  and the Investment Tax Credit,
    288–89
  and leveraged buyout financing
    sources, 293
  liquidation under, 281–82, 294
  master limited partnerships, 288
  and net operating loss
    carryforwards, 282–85
  real estate tax shelters under,
    293
  residual method of asset
    allocation, 289
  S corporations under, 285–88
  standstill payments under, 290
Teachers Insurance and Annuity,
  63

Thatcher Glass Manufacturing
Company, 30–34, 55
Thomas, Charles, 10

U–V

Uniform Fraudulent Conveyances
Act, 231–32
U.S. Sugar Corporation, 311
Valuing methods
accuracy in, 55–56
adjusted book value, 42–43,
65–66, 85–86
asset valuation, 43–44
break-up value, 44–45
cash flow, 45–51, 67–74
earnings valuation, 66–67
in employee stock ownership
plans, 319–20
expected dividends, 50–51
fairness issues in, 235–38
financing constraints in, 54–55

Venture capitalists, 192–93
Vitule, Alan, 187
Vockar, Larry, 14
Voidable preferences, 257

W–Z

Walt Disney Productions,
29–30
Wasserstein, Bruce, 165, 191
Weinberger v. *UOP, Inc.,* 236–38
Wells Fargo, 21–22
Wesray Corporation, 24–30
Whiteman, Charles, 32
Wierton Steel, 297, 310, 324–31
Wilkie, Farr and Gallagher,
326–27, 331
Wilson, Ian R., 84, 93
Wometco, 55, 147
Young, Brian, 2
Zero coupon bonds, 6–7